Portfolio

by: Art Ketchum

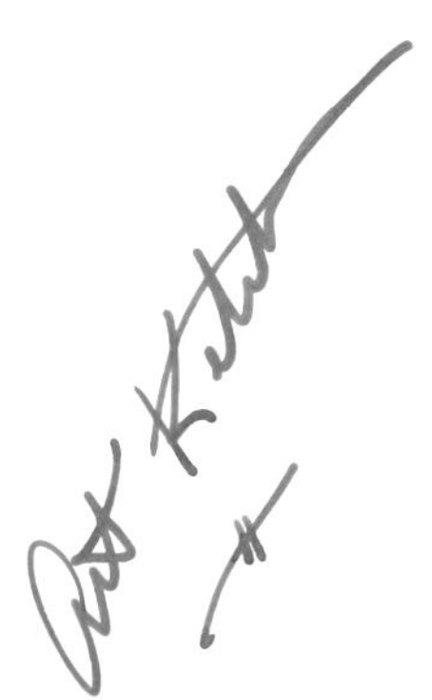

Web Site : http://www.artketchum.com

Portfolio © 2001 ISBN: 0-9714916-0-7

This book is dedicated to the greatest man I ever knew, as I had the pleasure to be his son.

Leslie Ketchum

Special Thanks

To Shannon Smith (my soulmate) for her endearing love, patience and help in editing and proof reading with her great english skills. David J. Lee, my assistant, for his great insight and drawing the lighting diagrams in this book. Duane Wooters for his time and patience in teaching me Photoshop. My three daughters Laura, Karen, and Heidi, along with my two great sons-in-law, Sanjay and John, and for their support for all the years they have put up with me and my idiocyncrocies and having the confidence in me to help push me to higher levels.My mom for being there for me. And my 7 grandchildren for all the joy they have brought me.

To all my very special friends: Jim & Sophia Abenante, Ron Anthony, Glenn Baruck, Chris Busse, Bill Barnard, John Bitterman, Clay Davis, Lisa & Clay Purifoy, Bob Cortier, Spencer Colquhoun Jr, Mark Diamond, Andy Douglas, Ross Fasano, Vince Fasano, Mike and Rose Guinta, Gary Giesel, Michael Harvey Jimi Iannizzotto, John James, Paul Harris, Allen Harris, Ed Harris, Marvin & Ginet Kesselman, Melissa Koczur, Betsy LaCasse, Bill Lemon, Dan Locke, Tracey Walker-Kincade, Tony Montes, Doug Meade, Stan Malinowski, Bill Netzel, John Olszewski, Linda & Mike Pauly, Gino Pascazio, Gary Regester, Rich & Monica Rubel, Art & Lucia Rubel, Paul Radomski, Matt Shaver, Martin Smith, Walt & Jean Steinmetz, Joy & Jim Schroeder, Gary & Delrose Scott, Ron Smith, Paula Siebert, Nick Sinadinos, August Tye, Dick Towle, Ruth Vasecky, Bob & Sharon Weides, Ken Williams, Bill Winton, and Rick & Kathy Wooton.

Thank you, Karen, for all the great advice and your and Sanjay's invaluable computer skills in completing this book. You mean the world to me.

Sponsor Appreciation
to:
Backdrop Outlet
800/466-1755
White Lightning Co.
800/443-5542
Call for a FREE Catalog

Thank you for your continued support in sponsoring my Photographic Workshops

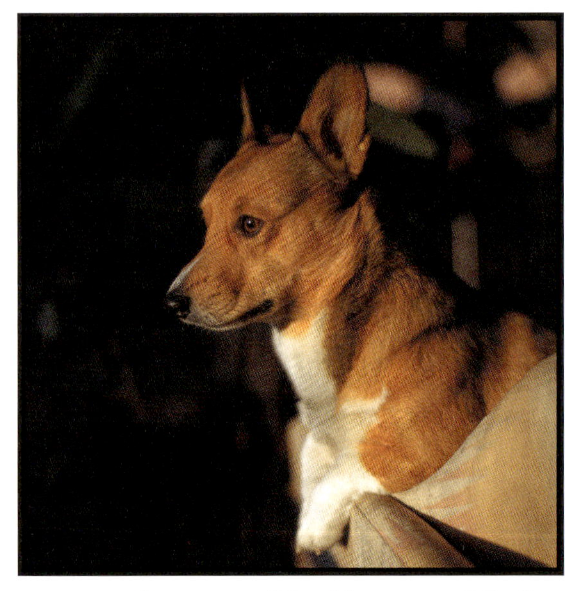

To my good buddy, my sidekick, and my constant companion. Shorty.

Portfolio

Introduction

For most of us who take our photography seriously, we drive ourselves to produce better images. This book is dedicated to all of my students and to those whom have never met me but have that same inner driving force to produce dynamic images.

Close to an eon ago(or so it seems) when I was9 years old, the Chicago Tribune sponsored a giveaway of a Herco Imperial 620 box camera for selling a subscription to the Tribune. For days I knocked on doors; by the third day I sold a subscription; within a couple of weeks I received my camera. From that day on, I was hooked on photography!

For many years I was a salesman in photographic-related industries, from selling cameras to photofinishing for major photo-processing companies. While I had achieved gratification from my sales management career, I was never totally fulfilled because I did not have the creative outlet I so longed for. Only photography could do that for me. My creative desires were pressuring me to change careers.

In 1978 I decided to quit my job as marketing manager for the largest photofinishing firm in the United States and open a photo studio. I was so naive as to think that upon opening my studio, the world would beat a path to my door recognizing my fantastic photography. Looking back on that time in my life, if I knew what I know today, I might never have made the move. But reminiscing upon two decades of owning my own studio and the many rough financial times during those years, I still would not change my decision. The rewards of being my own boss and the opportunity to soar to creative heights have been well worth it.

Portfolio

About the Author

Art Ketchum, author/photographer, started his career at the age of 8 years old when his father taught him how to make black and white prints in a home darkroom. Art has taught at Winona school of photography and published over 40 articles in photo related publications all over North America and Europe. Art has over 20 cover shots to his credit, has won numerous awards for his photography and has published two books entitled, "Profitable Model Photography" and "$100- An-Hour Photographing Models".

Art has given programs on lighting and posing to thousands of photographers in major cities across North America. His two-day workshops have been highly acclaimed by professional photographers and amateurs alike. Art has presented programs to many professional photographers in trade shows, Professional Photographers of America state organizations, and other regional photo-related groups.

Art has built a successful commercial photo career with his clients in Chicago, including some of the largest corporations in the United States. His 2400 square foot studio is located one mile south of downtown Chicago

Art's Arsenal of Shooting Equipment

Consists of the following:

35mm

Leica M-6 (my favorite) with lenses from 15mm to 135mm
(This is the one they will pry from my cold dead hands.)
Pentax PZ-1, 2-Pentax LX's , lenses from 20mm to 300mm.

Medium Format

Hasselblad 201F and Hasselblad Super-Wide, Lenses include; 30mm,38mm, 50mm, 80mm, 110mm F:2 (my favorite), 150mm, 220mm with the 2X tele-extender.

The Classics:

Two Nikon SP rangefinder cameras with lenses from 28 to 135mm
Leica M-2, IIIG and IIIF with lenses from 15mm to 135mm.
Contax IIA with lenses from 21mm to 135mm.

Digital:

Olympus Camedia E-10 w/35mm to 140mm
Olympus Camedia 4040 w/35mm to 105mm.

Lighting:

15 White Lightning flash units and various accessories.
Balcar spot lighting unit with Calumet 3000 w/s power pack.

Accessories:

Gitzo Carbon Fiber and one Bogen tripod with Gitzo ball heads.
Two Sekonic L-308 light meters, (the best compact meter made).
Filters for every possible situation.

Do I need all of this equipment? NO! But it comforts me........

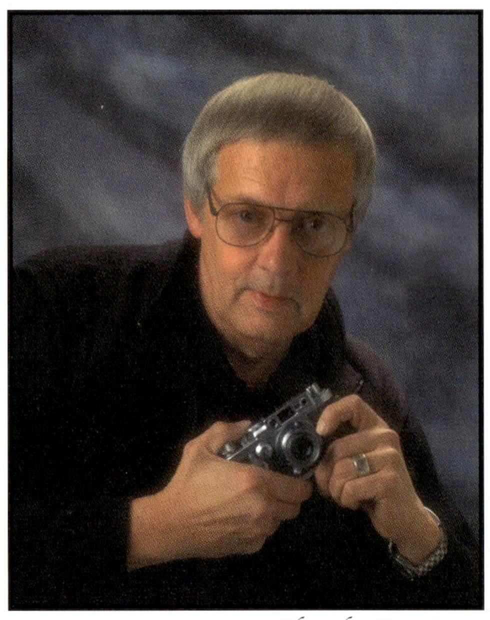

Photo by Gary Scott

Portfolio

The *Art* of Lighting

In the pages of this book you will see first-hand how and why each image was created. I invite you to copy my lighting techniques, try my posing ideas, and imitate the promotional concepts that have worked for me.

I am often asked if I have a favorite image in my portfolio. My only answer to this question is this: my favorite image is still in my head and not on film yet! Once the image is executed and I have created the idea that was in my mind, I must move on to the next project or look for a concept that will top the last creative venture. This is what drives me on.

For a number of years I operated my studio with my good friend, Mike Guinta as studio manager along with employees. We produced product photography for large retail corporations like Ace Hardware, Sears, Dayton Hudson Co., Shell Oil and others. All the images we created for these companies were created with 4x5 or 8x10 cameras using sheet film and polaroid film for testing lighting and image placement.

We as photographers have been operating with large format cameras much as Matthew Brady did in the 1860's, using film holders, viewing images upside down and contending with a black cloth to cover the rear of the camera. Those of us involved with medium format or 35mm photography do not have the drawbacks of the large format shooter.

Now we stand on the threshold of a new photographic phenomonom. The digital age. I can see the handwriting on the wall. Over the coming decade we will see the demise of our beloved film photography. I always thought that my Leica and Hasselblad would have to be pried from my cold dead hands. I thought that I would never consider replacing film with electronic imaging.

However, late in 2000 I had the opportunity to shoot digital images professionally and am now a convert to this new medium. The camera is nothing more than a tool, like all cameras, allowing you, the creative photographer, the ability to create images that start out in your head. Any film camera or digital camera will allow you to create outstanding images. This book will be a valuable tool to assist you in achieving your photographic goals.

Glossary of Lighting Terms

This page is designed to help you find lighting methods, create exciting new effects, and understand the purpose of each type of lighting technique used.

Fill-Flash: The most basic lighting technique and most misunderstood lighting method. Fill-Flash is using the auxiliary flash on your camera to supplement the natural light (ie., sunlight, street lights, interior room lighting). For more examples of Fill-Flash, see pages; 26,27,

Flat Lighting: When lighting a subject with one, two, or more lights from the front and set to produce the same F:stop. This type of lighting creates flat lighting with no modeling of the subject. This type of lighting is used extensively in fashion and model photography, group portraits, and children's photography. For more examples of Flat lighting, see pages; 8,9,44,45,92,127.

Ratio Lighting: When two lights are set up to light the subject and one is brighter than the other, you create Ratio lighting. Used extensively in fine portraiture and when you are trying to slenderize your subject or create a more three dimensional effect in your photography. This same technique can be achieved with one light and a large fill reflector. Ratio Lighting is sometimes referred to as Short Lighting, Broad Lighting and Rembrandt Lighting, which are variations on ratio lighting. For more examples of Ratio lighting, see pages; 12,13,20,21,24,25,49,73,81,109,113.

Rim Lighting: Sometimes referred to as a kicker light. Designed to create more separation between subject and background. Rim Lighting creates the same effect indoors as fill-flash does outdoors. Sometimes eliminates the need for a separate hair light. For more examples of Rim Lighting, see pages; 12,13,24,25,39,59,73,121.

High Key Lighting: The lighting effect that is most associated with an all white background and light colored subject or costume. Highly effective for women and children, designed to create the effect of an endless white background behind the subject (no shadows). This effect can also be created with pastel colors. For more examples of High-Key lighting, see pages; 29,55,87,95,117.

Low-Key Lighting: The opposite of High-Key lighting, used to create dramatic images with everything in the photo being on the dark side. Best used for fine portraiture and very common with men's portraits, can also be used with women and groups. For more examples of low key lighting, see pages; 16,17,59,119.

Spot Lighting: True spot lighting can only be created with an optical spot projector and an electronic flash or with optical spot tungsten light source. The optical spot attachment is designed to allow the user to focus the light on the subject or background. One of the advantages with the optical spot is the ability to use cookies, small metal cut-outs creating a pattern of light. (A very useful creative lighting tool) The cost of an optical spot attachment is $300 to over $1000. For more examples of spot lighting, see pages; 11,23,51,57,67,71,81,89,113.

More Glossary of Lighting Terms

Soft-Spot Lighting: While the words *soft spot lighting* is really an oxymoron, I use this technique to create certain effects in facial lighting and highlighting an important area within the image. Soft spot lighting is created with a standard 7" reflector and a honeycomb grid. For more examples of Soft-Spot lighting, see pages; 37,59,111.

Grid Lighting: For use in brightening one select area of the photograph. By using a reflector and a honeycomb grid, available in varying degrees from 10 to 40 degrees and also available in a very fine 3 degree grid. This lighting technique is used for highlighting a background or creating rim lighting that is more selective in size, also works for creating a hair light. For more examples of using grid lighting, see pages 14,15,16,17,20,21,23,37,71,109.

Hard Lighting: In certain conditions, hard lighting is a desirable effect as it builds contrast in the subject matter and background. Normally, soft lighting is preferred with most color imaging. But on occasion, especially with black & white photography,. Hard lighting with metal reflectors creates more contrast, if that effect is desired. When creating hard shadows is desirable in your image, hard lighting is best for strong shadows and more contrasty lighting. For more examples of hard lighting, see pages; 12,13,14,15

Hair Lighting: One of the most impressive and useful lights is the hair light. The hair light in my studio is a Balcar PRL-50 mini soft box with a 40 degree grid attached to keep light from lighting the face or traveling back to the background. This light measures 24"long X14" wide and about 4" deep. This is what I consider to be the ideal hair light mounted on an adjustable boom arm. The thin configuration allows this light to be used in almost all room conditions, even rooms with low ceiling heights. The 24" width allows my subject to move and still retain the hair light and its fantastic lighting effectiveness. For more examples of hair lighting, see pages 8,9,12,13,24,25,39,71,81,113,119.

Soft Lighting: This light can be created with soft boxes, umbrellas or by shooting through light control panels. All of these attachments do basically the same thing. The umbrella, if large enough, will create the same soft light conditions as a soft box but with a little less control when feathering the light. The least expensive soft light is the light control panel, but with less control. The fastest to set up when traveling or using in different locations is the umbrella. All of these light sources are excellent for color and B&W imaging. For more examples of soft lighting, see pages 8,9,14,15,16,17,33.

Gel Lighting: One of the effects for producing dramatic images is the use of colored gels (Acetate colored filters) over a light source to create different backgrounds and add dramatic highlight to a specific part of the background or subject. For more examples of gel lighting, see pages; 8,9,11,13,23,39,41,71,73.

Window Lighting: One of the most beautiful lighting techniques is to use light coming through a window. Or create the same effect with an optical spot projector. When shooting with natural light, it may be necessary to use a tripod for best results. Also, the use of a reflector will create a more pleasing result. When using an optical spot projector to create a window light effect, it may be necessary to have a second light to light the subject and cut the high contrast effect created by using the optical spot by itself. For more examples of window lighting, see pages; 19,85.

The Antique Camera

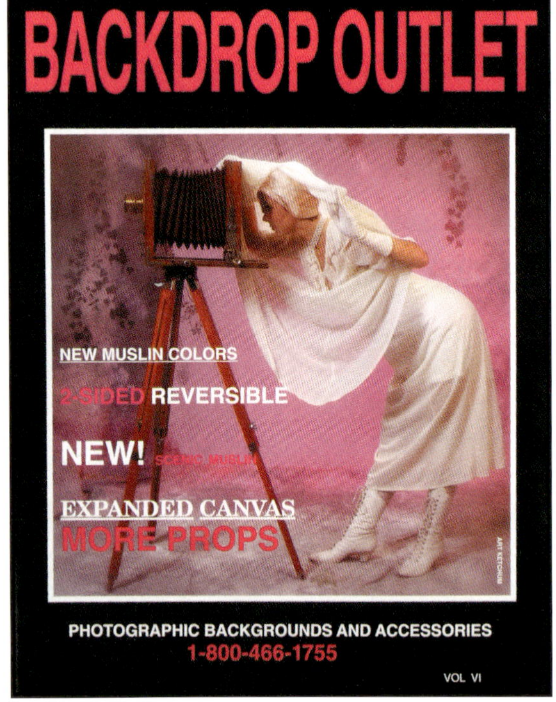

Backdrop Outlet decided to use this version of the Antique Camera photo for their cover image as it would be less controversial to their clients.

They received many calls from customers who felt the image was too risque. I guess these same customers never picked up any of the current fashion magazines.

Variations of this image of Heather with the old camera have appeared in Shutterbug Magazine and other photo publications.

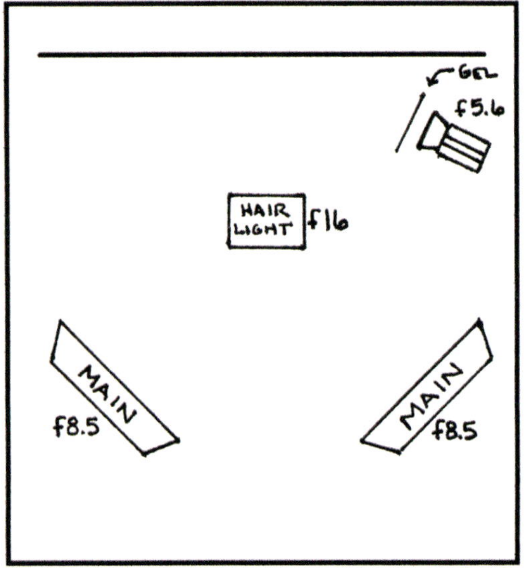

In 1994 I traveled to Germany, Switzerland and India with my daughter, Karen, and my son-in-law, Sanjay. While I was in Germany, I shopped many of the camera stores looking for interesting cameras. When I came across the old turn of the century 8x10 camera, I knew I wanted it for a conversation piece in my home or studio, but more importantly, for an image that had been floating around in my brain for years. Once I purchased the camera, I needed a model to make the shot work.

I started telling a few of the professional models that I knew about my idea to use the models dress to create the dark cloth. When I suggested the idea to Heather, she told me about her collection of old fashioned clothing. Heather worked part time for a resale shop and was always on the lookout for interesting old costumes. I planned the shooting during one of my Chicago hands-on photo workshops. In this way I could accomplish my image idea while my students would benefit by seeing first hand how the execution of a promo piece image was created for Art Ketchum Studios.

Heather was one of those rare models who always came to a shoot prepared and with as much enthusiasm as me for creating a dynamic image. When I saw Heather's outfit, I chose the one shown in the image illustrated and ordered a backdrop from Backdrop Outlet. The background had to convey an old fashioned quality. Backdrop outlet was quick to respond and now offers a whole line of similar backdrops to their customers.

Lighting: This was a 4 light set-up using White Lightning ultra 600's. I always try to use a hair light, In this case, I was using a Balcar Prisma light soft box that is very low profile, allowing me to create a wide pattern hair light with a soft box that is only 4 inches deep. As all balcar accessories fit the White Lightning lights, this allows me to create some spectacular images with my lights and wonderful accessories
The image was lit with two Plume wafer soft boxes (54"x36") using flat lighting to create an F:11 f-stop and a hair light set one and a half stops brighter at F:16 and a half. The fourth light was aimed at the background using a magenta gel over the light to provide the pink color.
The background light was set for F:8 The camera was set for F:11 and all lights were metered with my Sekonic L-308 meter. This image was created using a Hasselblad and 110mm lens.

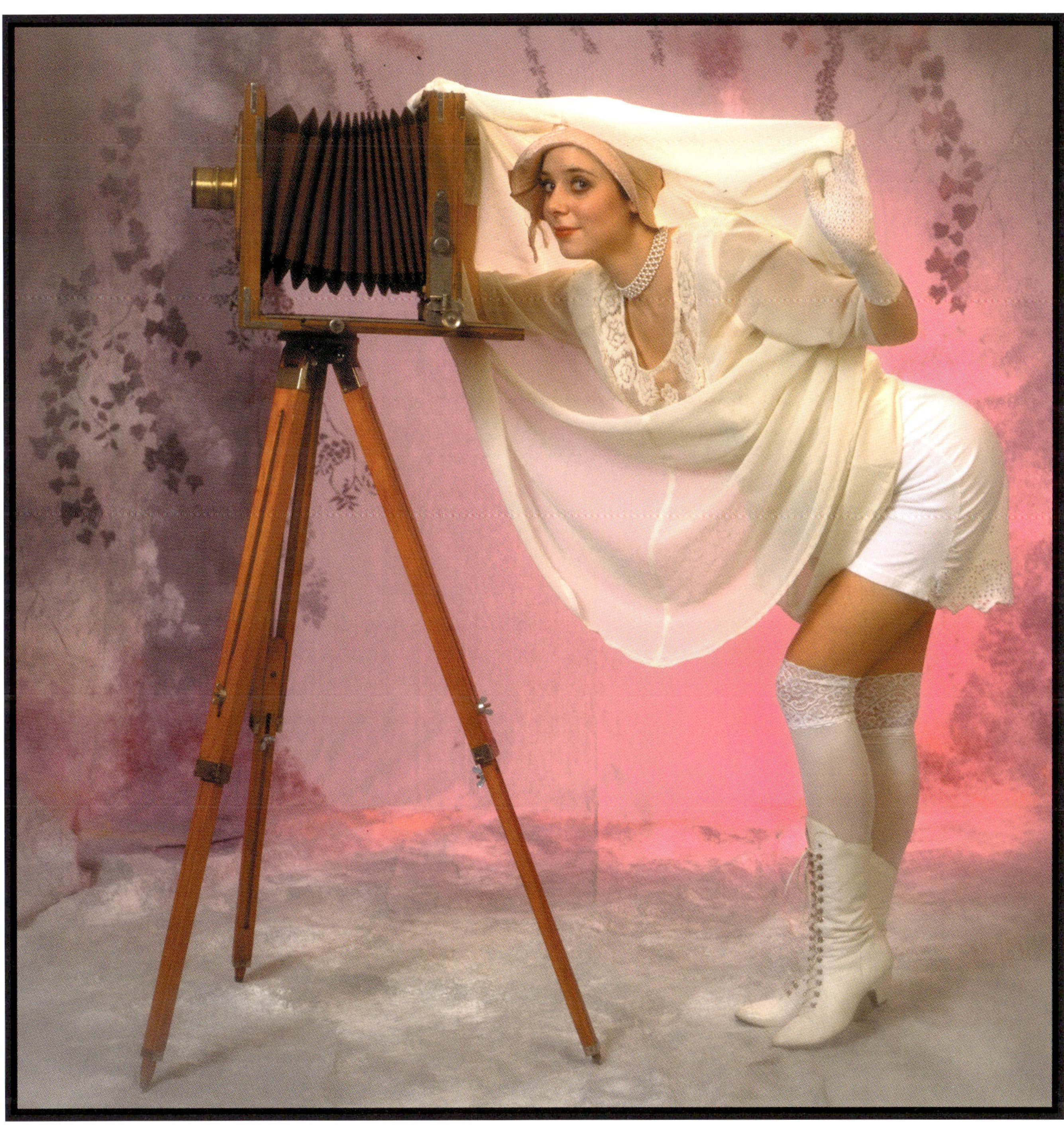

The Face and the Hand

One of the unrivaled advantages of being a commercial photographer specializing in people photography is the beautiful models, make-up artists, and stylists I have had the pleasure to work with. When this image was created, it was done for my portfolio and the make-up artists portfolio. Phillipe is a very talented artist who formulated the idea for the makeup; our attractive model provided the outfit.

When I meet a new model to see how she is made up and what she plans on wearing, I always try to organize props, backgrounds and lighting that will give my creation a unique place in my portfolio. I also strive to provide the model with an image that is different than anything she currently has in her portfolio.

In this case, dramatic lighting is an optical spot projector mounted an X2400 White Lightning flash unit and projecting a triangle of light on the face to create the hard line or light fall-off on the cheek. The use of an optical spot projector is useful because it creates a hard line of light. No other lighting tool will allow you to create a hard line shadow. Bear in mind that this type of lighting is to be used on a model who has excellent features and perfect make-up, not the typical high school girl who may walk into your studio for senior portraits. The background is rather large; a 6'x6' window frame with some chiffon or sheer fabric draped over the frame giving a flowing effect. I lighted the fabric at very acute angles to create strong shadows. (Light head was about one foot in front of the fabric, and off to the sides of the fabric). Two background lights were aimed down with a cyan gel on one and a magenta gel on the other to give the multiple lighting effects on the background. The use of gels on a background is a favorite technique of mine.

Posing your subject is as important as all the other aspects of creating a dynamic image. In this case, I was looking for a pose that shows diagonal lines with the model's arms and body parts. The upturned head angle, the extended arm, the pointed fingers all lend themselves to creating the lines I was looking for. The diagonal draping of the background fabric and the model's hat pin and gold brocade shoulder trim all add to the diagonals I was trying to fabricate.

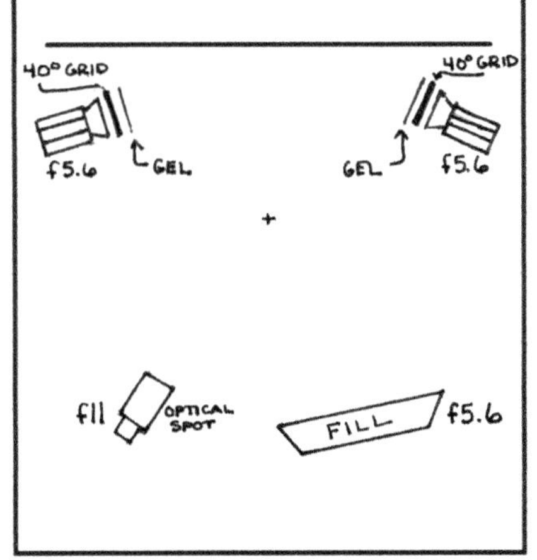

Remember, ***diagonals are dynamic.*** I always test my basic idea with a polaroid back on my Hasselblad or use a separate polaroid camera to see if my lighting, model and pose are close to coming together. If my polaroid turns out well, it then becomes a matter of fine tuning the pose. I prefer the Polaroid #679 Pro-100 or the #689 Pro-Vivid film for testing, as it will best match your final film. With the advent of digital photography, you will now be able to test with an instant image. Either polaroid or digital testing will tell you if your idea and model are working together the way you desire. The ability to see the image immediately is your insurance policy guaranteeing you the best possible image every time.

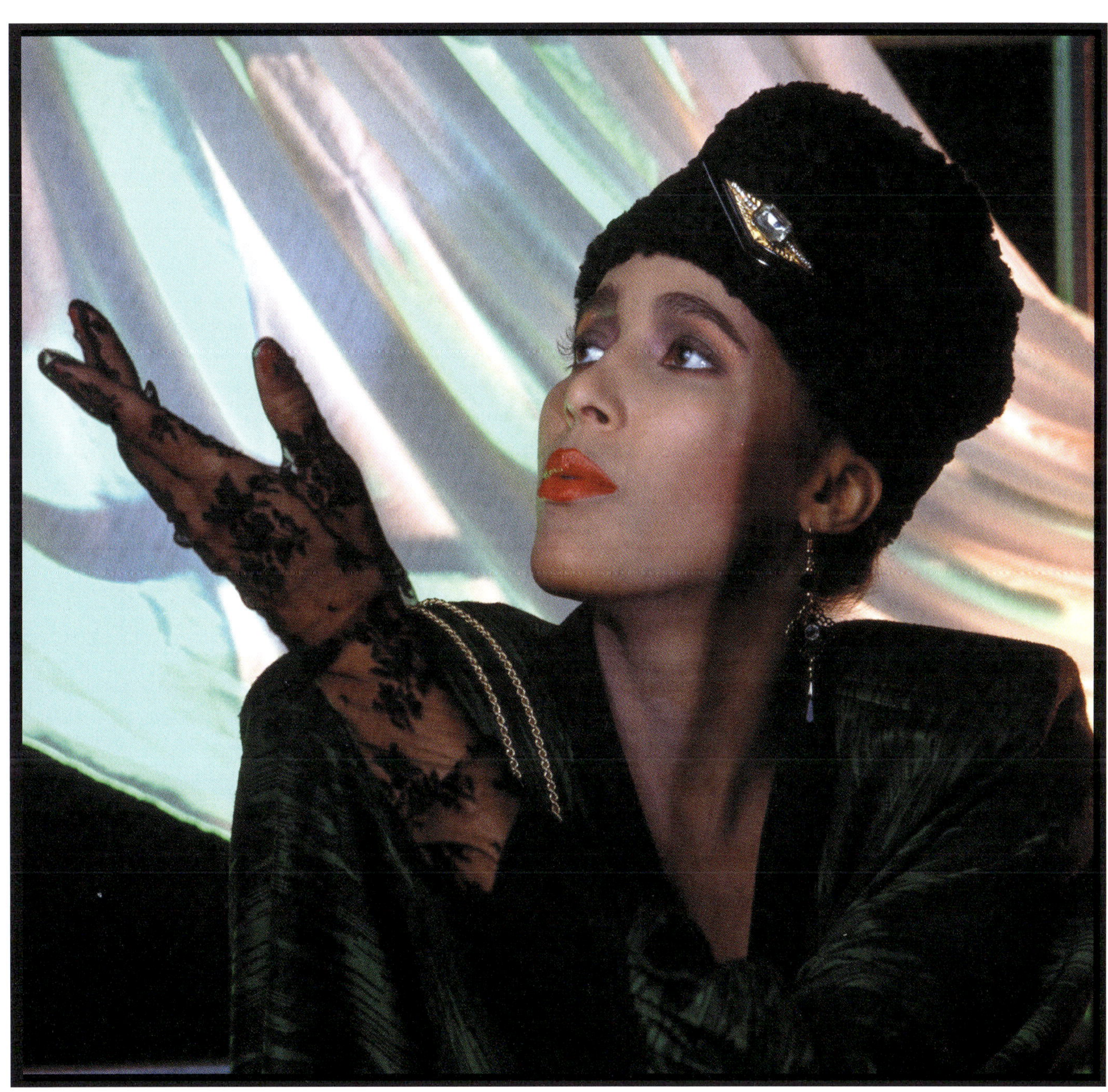

The Seven Year Itch

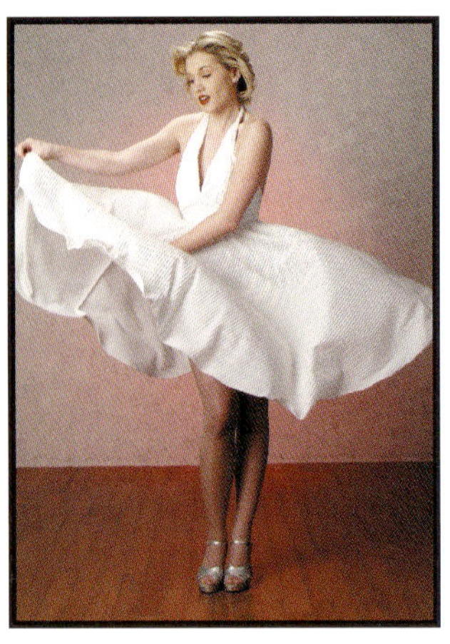

All models, young and old, wish to present a sensual image in their photos. Maybe it is my love of the opposite sex that brings sensuality to my photography. I don't mean that I ever get personally involved with the model I am shooting. But while that person is in front of my camera, I try to create a love affair with the subject to feel comfortable with me and with my camera. At that moment, that model is the most important person on earth!

Recently, one of my students suggested that I shoot a model he had worked with. I normally don't put much stock in requests like this because I have found that what some photographers consider beautiful does not always work in a classroom situation. However, I decided to have Ben bring the model to the next workshop.

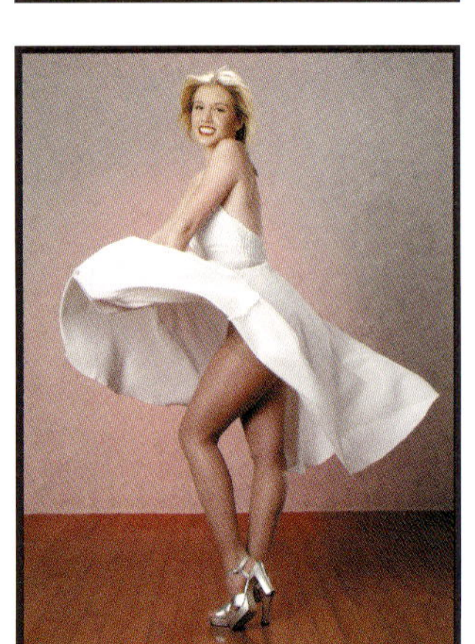

My student, was right. The model was exceptional! My feeling when shooting her for the first time was that she had that elusive Marilyn Monroe quality that flows into the photograph. <u>That is a love affair with the camera!</u> Camille is very photogenic and deserved more than this one little workshop could provide in terms of photo opportunities.

I suggested to Camille that she come back to another workshop with a dress like Marilyn Monroe wore in the movie, "The Seven Year Itch". Everyone remembers the street scene with Marilyn talking to Tom Ewell as the air from the subway grate blows her dress up. This was a very risque image for the 50's.

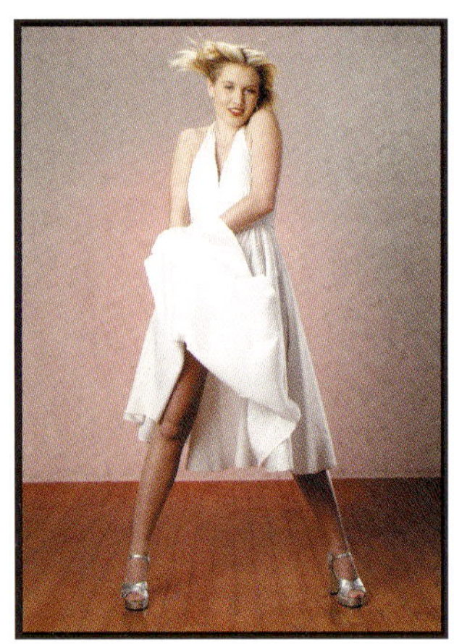

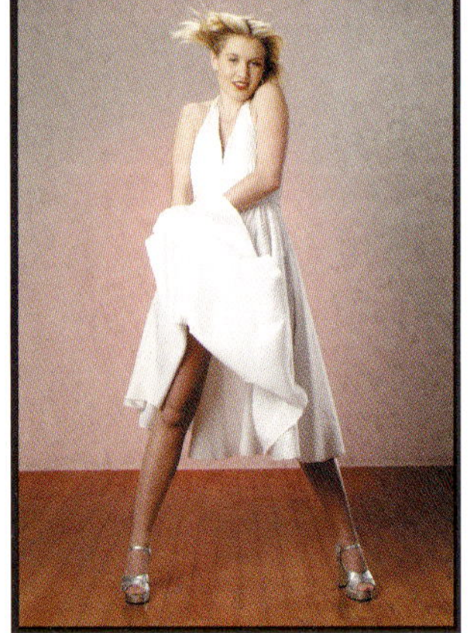

When Camille came to the next workshop, she had the dress. She had rented it from a costume store. I knew this was a model who took my suggestions seriously and wanted to make a career for herself in modeling. Through the years I have found that very few models take the time, money and trouble to make an image spectacular. They expect the photographer will have everything to create the shot. In reality, it is a <u>joint</u> effort between model, photographer, and make-up artist to create a fabulous picture.

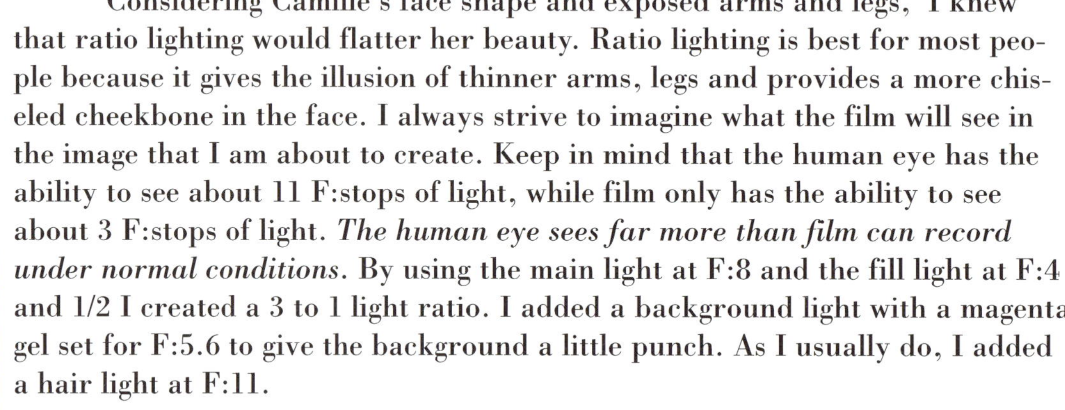

Considering Camille's face shape and exposed arms and legs, I knew that ratio lighting would flatter her beauty. Ratio lighting is best for most people because it gives the illusion of thinner arms, legs and provides a more chiseled cheekbone in the face. I always strive to imagine what the film will see in the image that I am about to create. Keep in mind that the human eye has the ability to see about 11 F:stops of light, while film only has the ability to see about 3 F:stops of light. *The human eye sees far more than film can record under normal conditions*. By using the main light at F:8 and the fill light at F:4 and 1/2 I created a 3 to 1 light ratio. I added a background light with a magenta gel set for F:5.6 to give the background a little punch. As I usually do, I added a hair light at F:11.

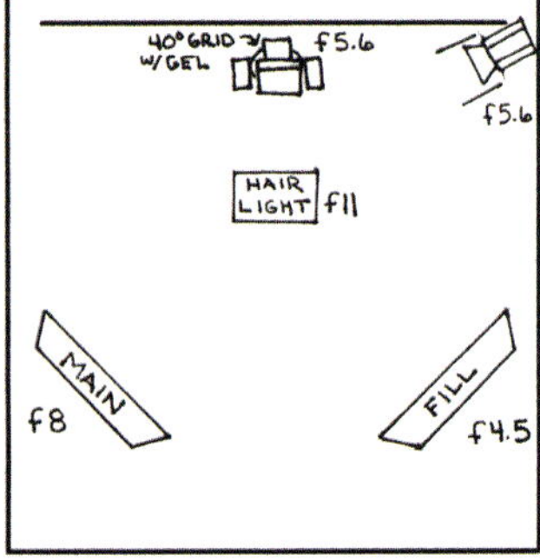

The air bouncing off the floor in front of Camille was created with a Bowens wind machine. Many images had to be taken because of hair getting messed up, eyes being closed and dress not being in positions that were billowy-looking for the shot.

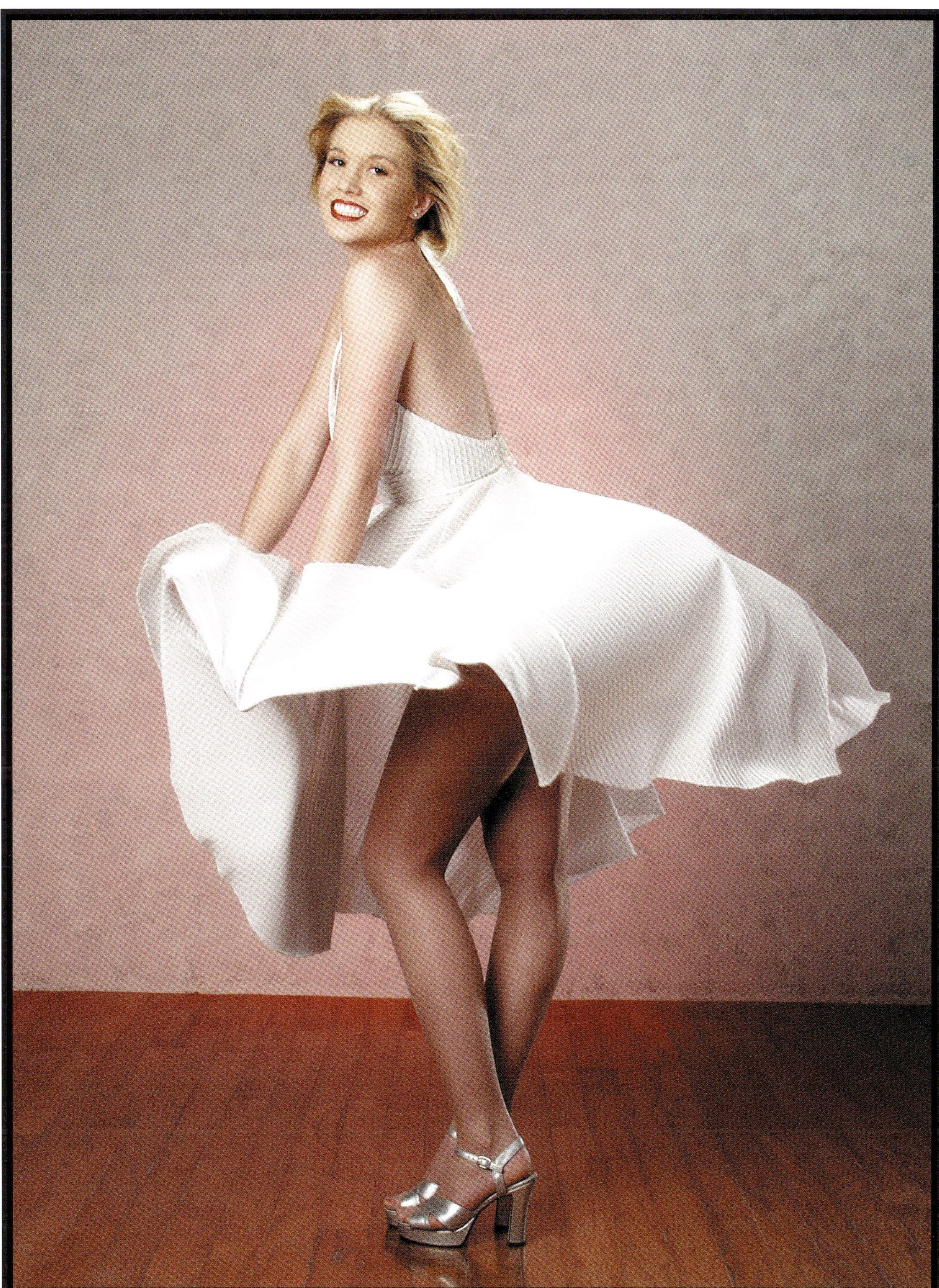

Body Panoramic

Conceiving a spectacular portfolio of your work involves planning out images before you shoot pictures.

This particular shot of Ginia was one of those images that I envisioned in my mind. The idea came from looking through photo magazines I came upon a series of panoramic images and the idea occurred to me that I could pose a model with a panoramic camera (or at least imply that it was taken with a panoramic camera).

In reality, the image was made with my Hasselblad 201F camera with my favorite 110mm lens. I cropped the image to appear as though it were taken in a panoramic camera. The actual negative size of this picture is 2 1/4" long x 3/4" in height. I knew I would need a model that appeared very leggy and quite thin.

I perused my model files and found a model named Ginia who I had recently tested with. Ginia had fine features and photographed beautifully. I knew she would be perfect for the image with her sophisticated, exotic look. I photographed Ginia in both B&W and Color because I was not sure how I would use this image. The color was Fuji Provia as I like the way skin tones reproduce on this fine film. The black & white film was Ilford FP-4. Although I was very pleased with the color images. I also had a great black & white shot. I went on to hand-color the final B&W print using Marshall's Oil colors. I liked the surrealistic effect the hand colored image portrayed.

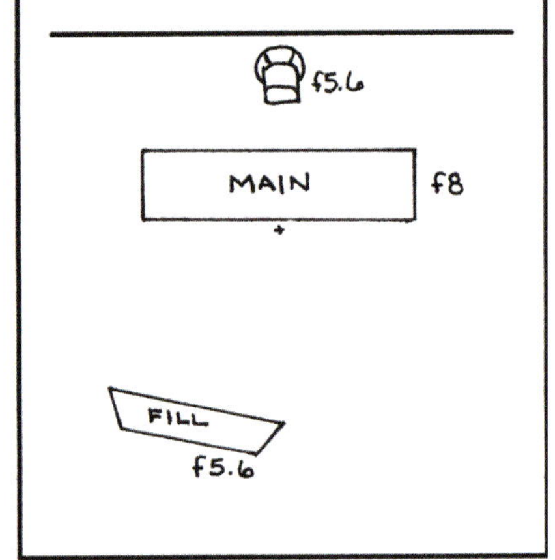

When I executed the shot, I draped the shooting area with pastel colors of a material called Fantasy cloth available from Backdrop Outlet. I photographed Ginia in different positions but always kept her in a long pose. That was my goal when I pre-planned the shot Who says an image has to be proportionate to an 8x10? Why can't an image be square, round or some other shape?

This is one of my favorite images in my portfolio because it is sensual but in good taste and has been published in many magazines. It is also one of the lead images on my web site, and has been used both as a promotional post card and on my business card.

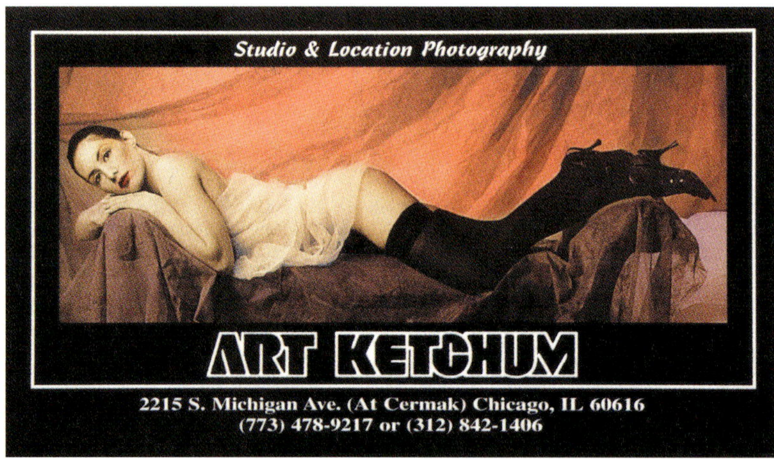

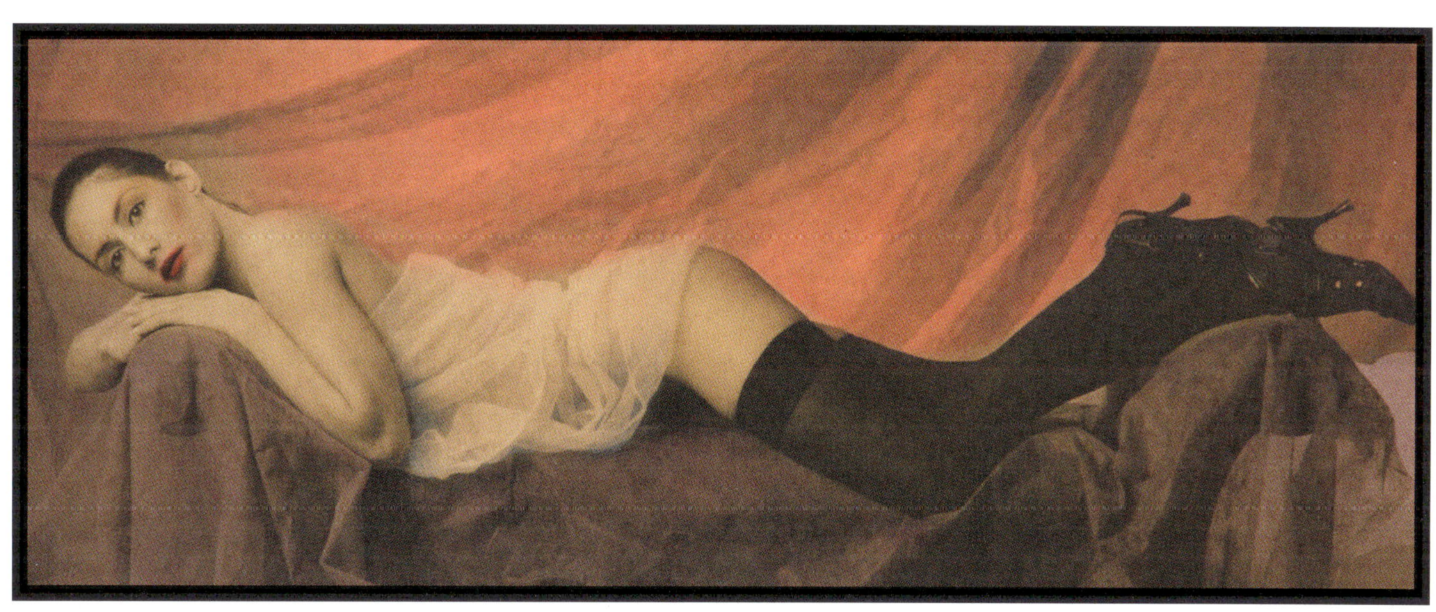

Body Builder

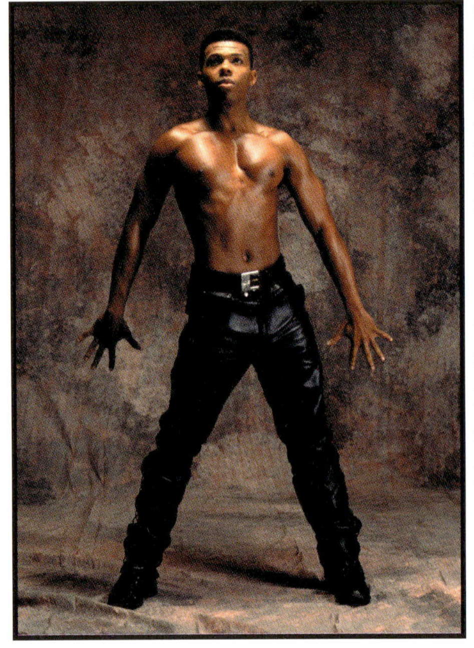

One thing I do to keep myself on the cutting edge of this profession is read publications that relate to our industry and look through the vision of other artists and photographers. I start by building an idea file. The idea file is nothing more than a collection of images that you intend to plagiarize in some way. *I bet that statement raised the hair on the back of some necks out there.* Let me clarify that statement. There is no original idea. Every idea is a blend of other ideas and things we see in our everyday lives. After all, did some inventor start out to invent the automobile? No! Some ingenious person decided he would attach a motor to a carriage; hence the horseless carriage was born. Other people added to the idea and as a result we have today's automobiles.

Our brain categorizes different ideas. If we draw upon our experiences, we will recall some of those thoughts when we have a model in front of our lens and use those ideas to create a fantastic image. Unfortunately, my brain can not hold that much, so I rely on my idea file. My idea file consists of a briefcase with 100 to 150 images I have clipped from magazines or photographic books. When I have a model in front of my camera, I go to my idea file and see if some pose, lighting idea or other element in the printed image will apply to my shoot. Many times I will combine two or three ideas to build my image, creating a brand new idea.

Anthony, the model in these shots, stopped in one afternoon to ask me if he could test with me. (To test is to exchange time for photos). Neither model nor photographer charge for their time or service. Why would you want to shoot pictures for free? Well, normally you don't. But testing is an excellent trade of your time and film to build yourself an amazing portfolio without having to pay for high quality models. When I test in B&W, I provide the model with one free 8x10 of their choice. In color, I give the model the transparencies I do not intend to use.

When looking at Anthony, I saw that he had a strong upper body. I decided to capitalize on that concept and create a dance -type pose with Anthony in tight jeans or leather pants. I wanted to create a strong hollywood-type lighting similar to what Horst, Hurrell or Willinger did in the 40's when they photographed the movie stars.

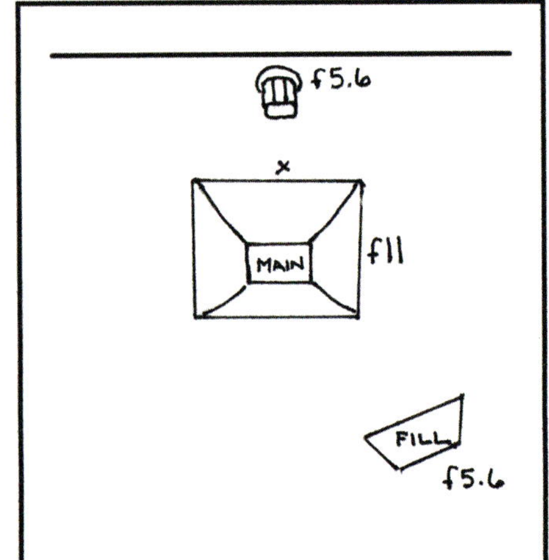

Lighting; I set up one 30x24 soft box over the Anthony's head to light his entire body. After testing with a polaroid on my Hasselblad, I realized I needed some fill light in front because Anthony's dark pants were melding into the background. I set the fill light from the front two stops lower than the overhead main light. I positioned a background light with a 40 degree grid set for two stops lower than the main light.

Finally, I asked Anthony to put some baby oil on his body. This gave his skin the sheen that added dimension to the finished image. Two variations on the same image.

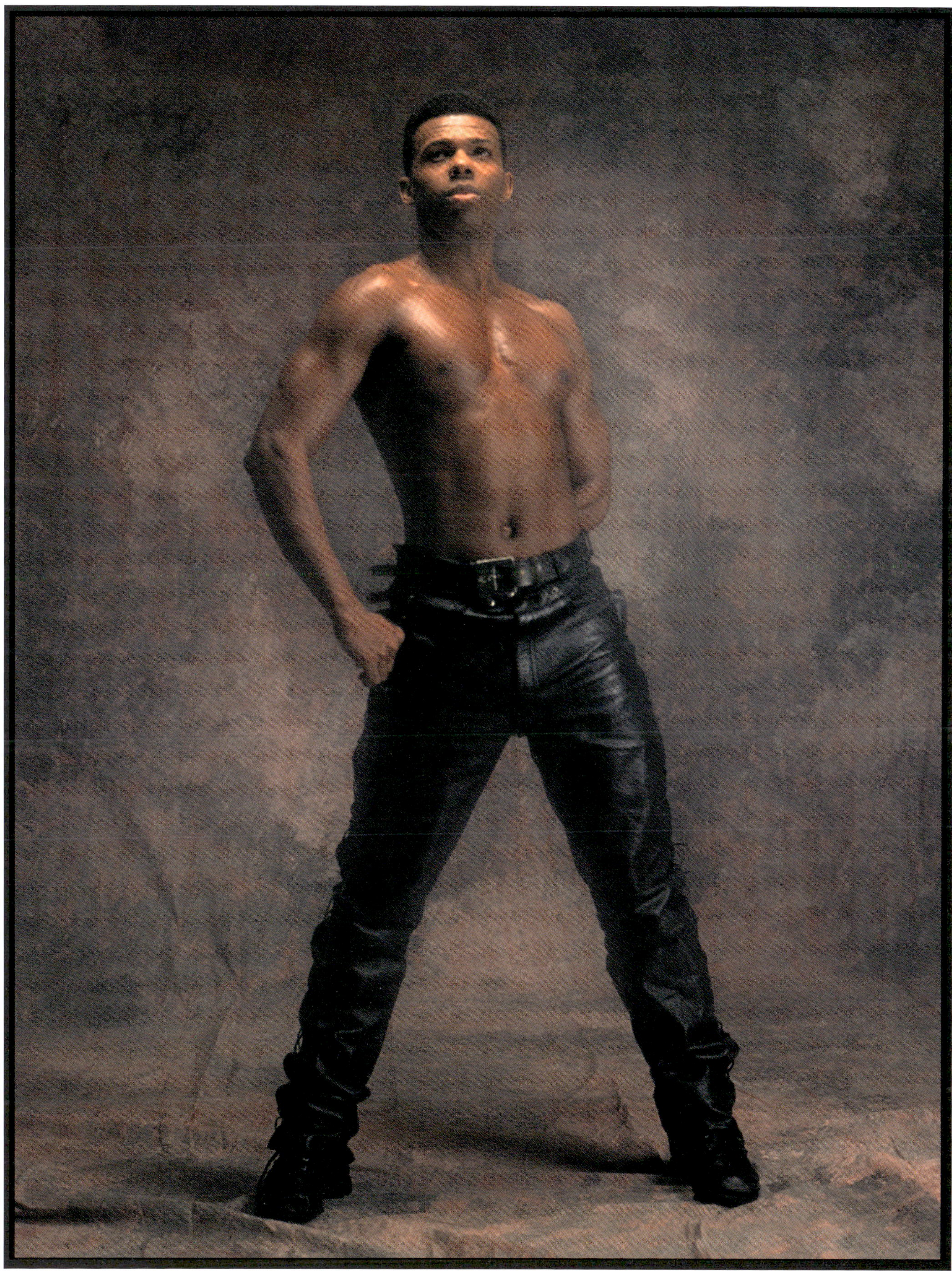

Natural Light

When I first moved into my commercial studio in a Chicago industrial area, I noticed how the light came through the south side windows in the afternoon in one part of the building. I thought this might make an interesting shooting area with the right model.

Some weeks later when I was scheduled to shoot Marilyn, I asked her if she had something elegant to contrast with the rough texture walls for my natural light shot. Marilyn showed me a beautiful silk blouse that I thought would work nicely for the shot. I positioned Marilyn so the shadow did not create a large block of shadow on her face. I metered the shot with my Sekonic L-308 meter using the incident dome on the meter to get a very accurate incident reading of the face and set the camera accordingly.

I directed Marilyn to try a number of different poses like the models do in fashion magazines. After this image was created, another tenant moved into the building so I did not have access to this wall again. What a shame! But I am always searching for new exciting locations.

This image was produced with a Hasselblad camera, 110mm F:2 lens, camera set for F:2 at 1/250th with Fuji Astia Film.

Mentors

It is my belief that we all need heroes, or mentors, to model our lives after. When I was a kid, my heroes were cowboys. Television and movie cowboys. As I grew up, I realized I did not want to become a cowboy, so my heroes faded away.

As my love for photography grew, I started reading every photo book that interested me, and my new heroes became my mentors. I studied the works of Edward Steichen, Alfred Steiglitz, William Mortensen, Richard Avedon, Helmut Newton, Deborah Turbeville, Art Kane, Robert Farber, Bert Stern, and so many others I could not even begin to mention them all.

Many of these superlative photographers became my mentors, as I wanted to create lasting quality photographic images like these famous photographers did. I learned by studying their images and in many cases, copied their techniques and shooting styles.

We all learn from others. I chose to learn from the real masters of the craft, the photographers who are known all over the globe for their enduring, timeless images.

My suggestion to aspiring photographers is to copy the works of others and, in the process, you will develop your own style.

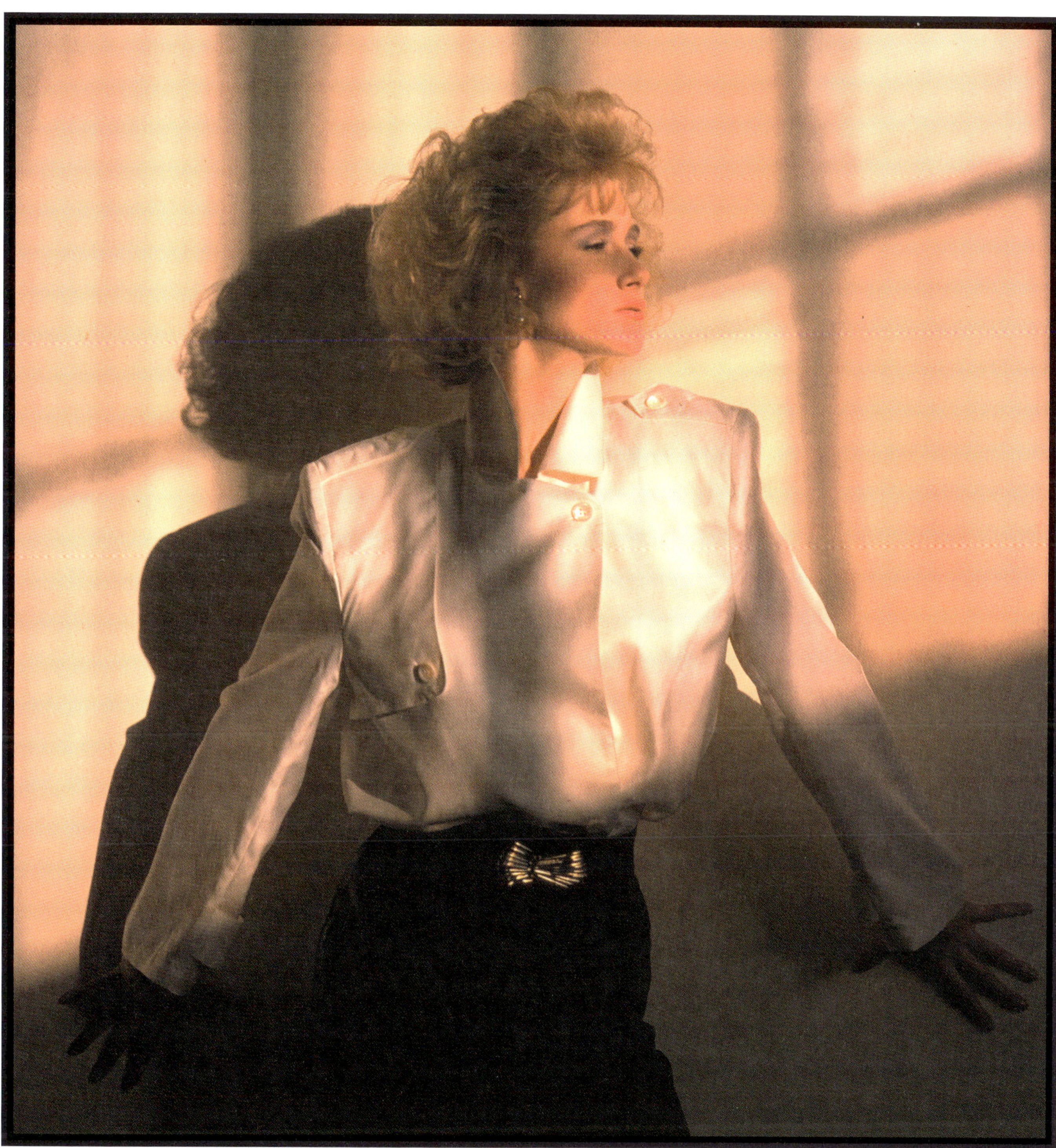

Airborne Dancer

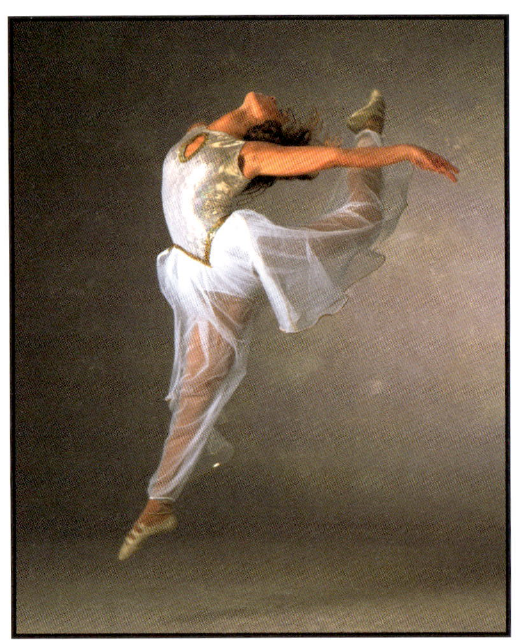

Jump image used in the client's catalog.

Of all the photography I do, one of the most challenging assignments is shooting for a company that over the years has put their trust in my photographic ability and talent to help build their sales. In commercial photography, the name of the game is not to create pretty pictures but to sell the product. When shooting a commercial assignment, we test each exposure and model's outfit on polaroid film. With the help of the company president, costume designers, posing stylist, make-up artist my photo assistant and myself we look at the polaroid and ask ourselves, will this costume sell? If the answer to this question is yes and the president thinks the same, then we proceed to shoot final transparencies.

This particular dance image was produced to create a stylized, action image of a dancer in mid-air. It took 24 jumps from the model to be sure I had the best image I could get. (All this and bracketing, too). As with any commercial assignment, I bracket by shooting one image at the recommended meter reading and a second exposure 1/2 stop more open.

The chosen lighting for this image was ratio lighting with a 3 to 1 ratio, main light F:11 and fill light set for 5.6 and a half. One and a half stops difference between main and fill lights. Background light was set off center to create a dark corner and was set for F:8 with a 12" reflector. We had to have a custom background 20 feet wide and 30 feet long made by Backdrop Outlet because we wanted the model out 10" from the background. This kept the light on the model separate from the background lighting, which made the background light consistent on all images. With groups and jump shots, we needed this width to make sure we did not shoot off the background. The hair light I normally use had to be set at ceiling height for fear of the model hitting it when making the jump.

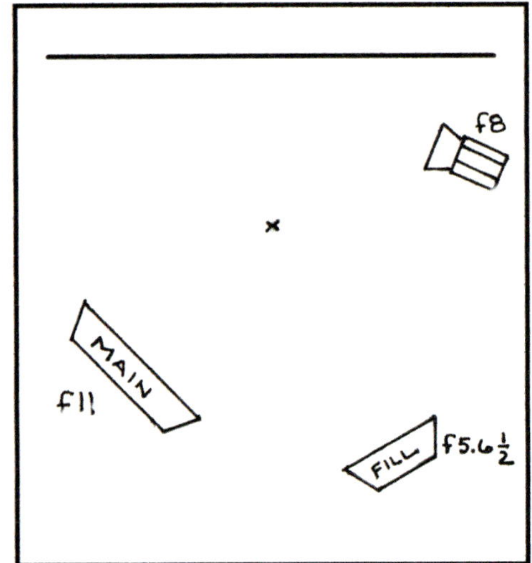

I also shot a few B&W images and later hand-colored an 11x14 Black and White print using Marshalls oil colors to provide a gift to the president of the company in thanks for their continued support. The image on the right is the hand-colored black and white image.

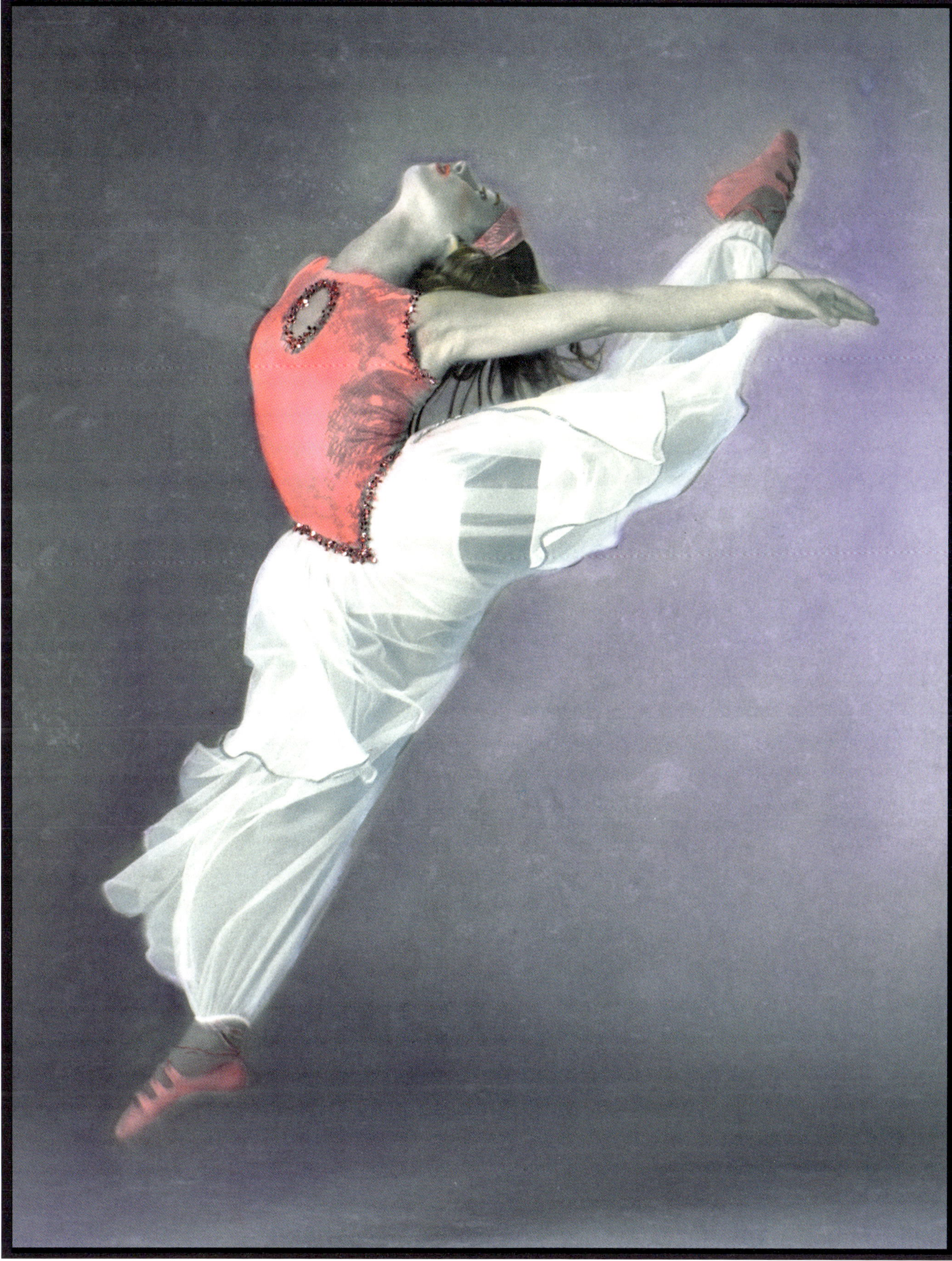

Colored Shadows

With the digital revolution in full swing, I decided to take the plunge and bought a new Olympus Camedia E-10. I wanted to see for myself if digital images could replace the 2 1/4 and 35mm images I have been producing for years. I was pleasantly surprised at the quality and convenience this new photographic tool provided.

Since I wanted to see if this new camera could be used for my commercial accounts, I decided to shoot some model composites. Nadiya was one of my first test subjects with the new Camedia E-10. I shot a total of 80 images, after a little computer work in Photoshop converting files to Tif, I found the images to be equal to the ones I could produce with my 35mm cameras.

I was eager to try some of my more unique lighting setups with digital. Nadiya showed me her outfits, and I chose to have her in the red and black long evening gown. The reason for choosing this outfit was to use my colored shadow technique.

Some years back, I purchased an Australian fashion magazine and noticed one of their contributing photographers was creating a shadow behind the model, except that the shadow was the same color as the outfit she was wearing! At first glance, it was really striking. After all, shadows are black or gray. They do not come in colors. Who has ever heard of colored shadows?

I set-up the subject with a hard light to create the a shadow and proceeded to light the shadow. Once I figured out the process, I realized that if you light the shadow with a colored gel and the light is set two to three stops lower than the main light, you will get *colored* shadows.

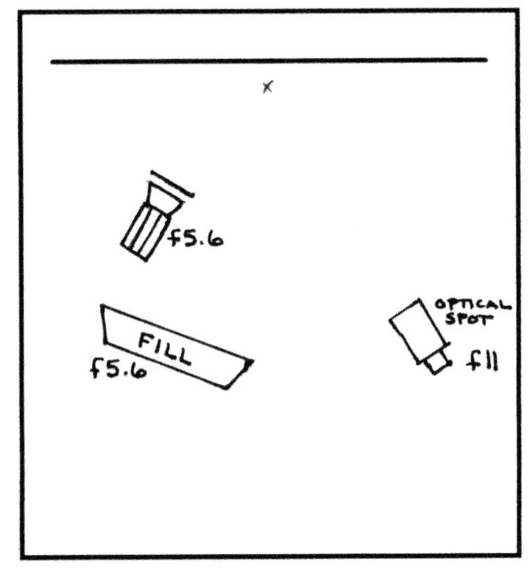

The principal here is that the white main light will cancel out any lower intensity colored light on the subject and only those areas where a shadow exists are left colored.

The Nadiya image you see on the cover and in this section was created with an optical spot projector as the main light, using a cookie cut in the shape of a chain link fence. Cookies can be purchased from any professional lighting store and generally cost less than $10. I set up the optical spot at 90 degrees to the right of subject and the background at 90 degrees to the left of camera and subject. Since I did not want the design on the cookie to be in focus, I intentionally defocused the optical spot so that the image would not be too busy.

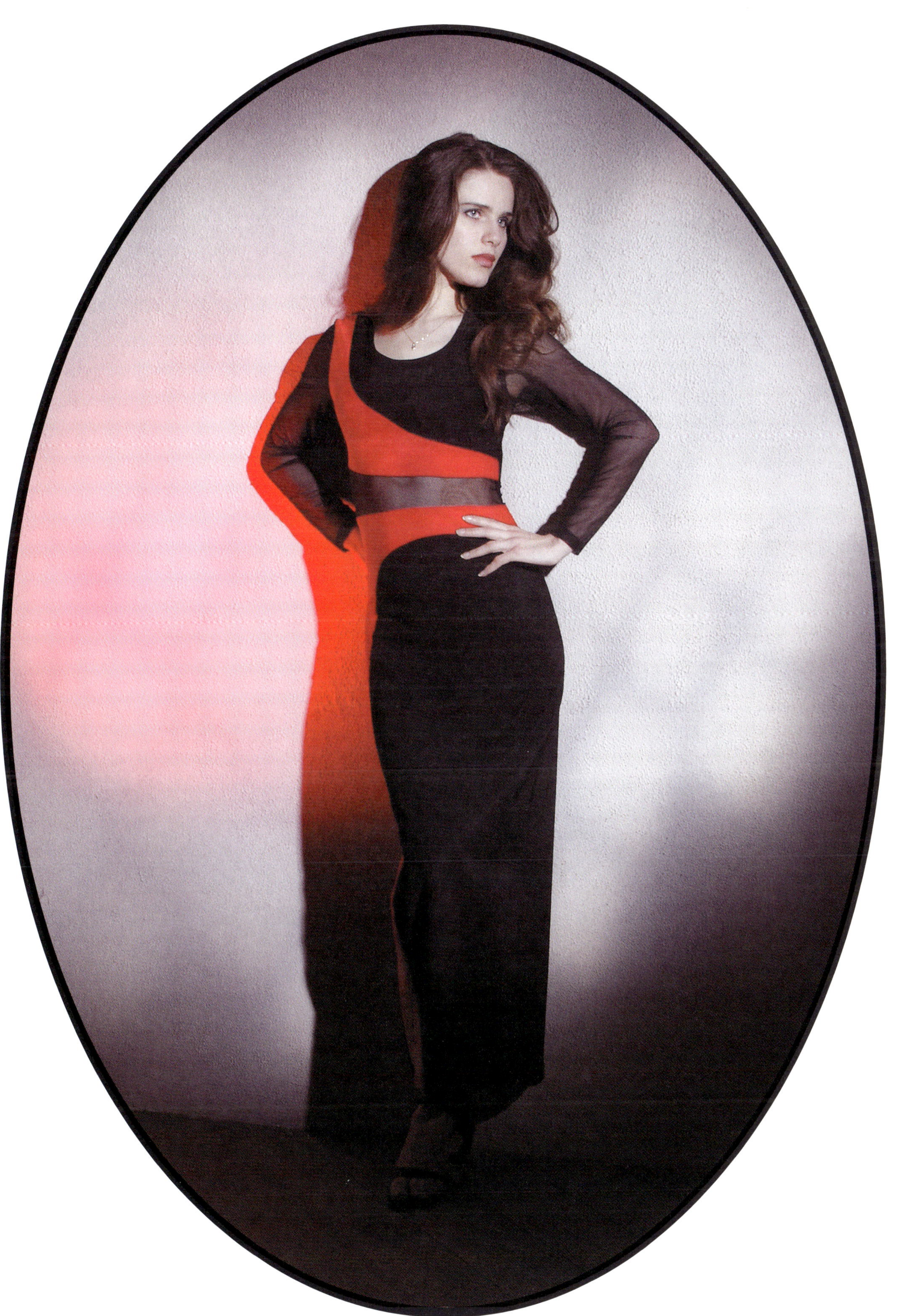

Mesh Dress

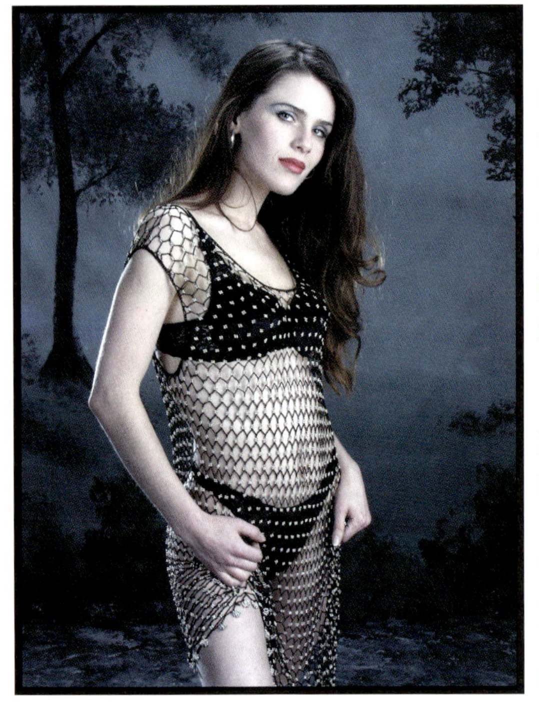

This image of Nadiya was taken digitally for the Backdrop Outlet catalog. Nadiya showed me this outfit along with the previous black and red dress. I thought this would be really wild on a scenic background. When I showed Nadiya the background, she told me a story in Ukrainian folklore about the mythical god who came from the forest and turned into a beautiful princess. I know she really liked this concept, and I felt we had a very hot image with her stunning mesh dress.

Lighting for this image was created with one large soft box as the main light and an umbrella near camera position. The main light was set for F:8 with the umbrella fill light set for F:4 1/2 creating a 3 to 1 light ratio. Ratio lighting maintains the shape of the body and creates modeling in Nadiya's arms, legs and face, giving a more dimensional look. I added a rim light. The rim light was set one stop lower than the main light. It is noticeable when you look at the right side of Nadiya's body. Rim lighting adds more dimension and separates the subject from the background. A hair light was also used to provide more illumination to her hair. The hair light was set one stop brighter than the main light.

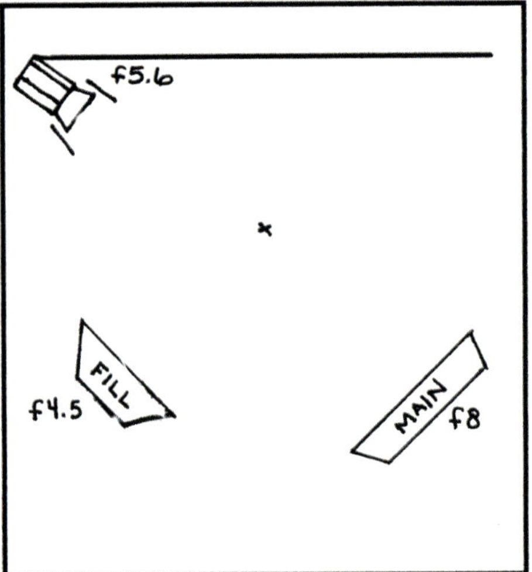

Pose is very important when shooting any image, but especially so with full length images. Knees looks better when bent as knees are generally not the most attractive part of a body. By bending a knee toward the straight knee, you beautify one knee and help hide the straight knee. A bent arm will also look more flowing and natural than a straight arm.The technique of bending limbs in posing helps create the S curve. This makes for more flattering images.

The Importance of Make-up

One of the most important elements in creating sensational images of women. is the correct application of make-up. I don't pretend to know how to apply make-up, nor do I wish to learn this specialized craft. But I do know good make-up when I see it.

I work with many experienced models that know how to do their make-up themselves and in many cases newcomer models and high school seniors who are not experienced in make-up application. In these cases, I recommend we get a make-up artist at the shoot to make sure the images I shoot are worthy of the models portfolio. There are many good books on this subject if you need more information on make-up for photography.

Finding a make-up artist is not difficult, as every hair salon has people that do this type of work, and in many cases the make-up artist will trade for photos to build her portfolio. I have a selection of at least a half a dozen make-up artists when I and the model are in need of one. Most charge from $100 to $125 for make-up and hair styling. The cost can be well worth it for the aspiring model trying to create the most professional image she can to help build her career.

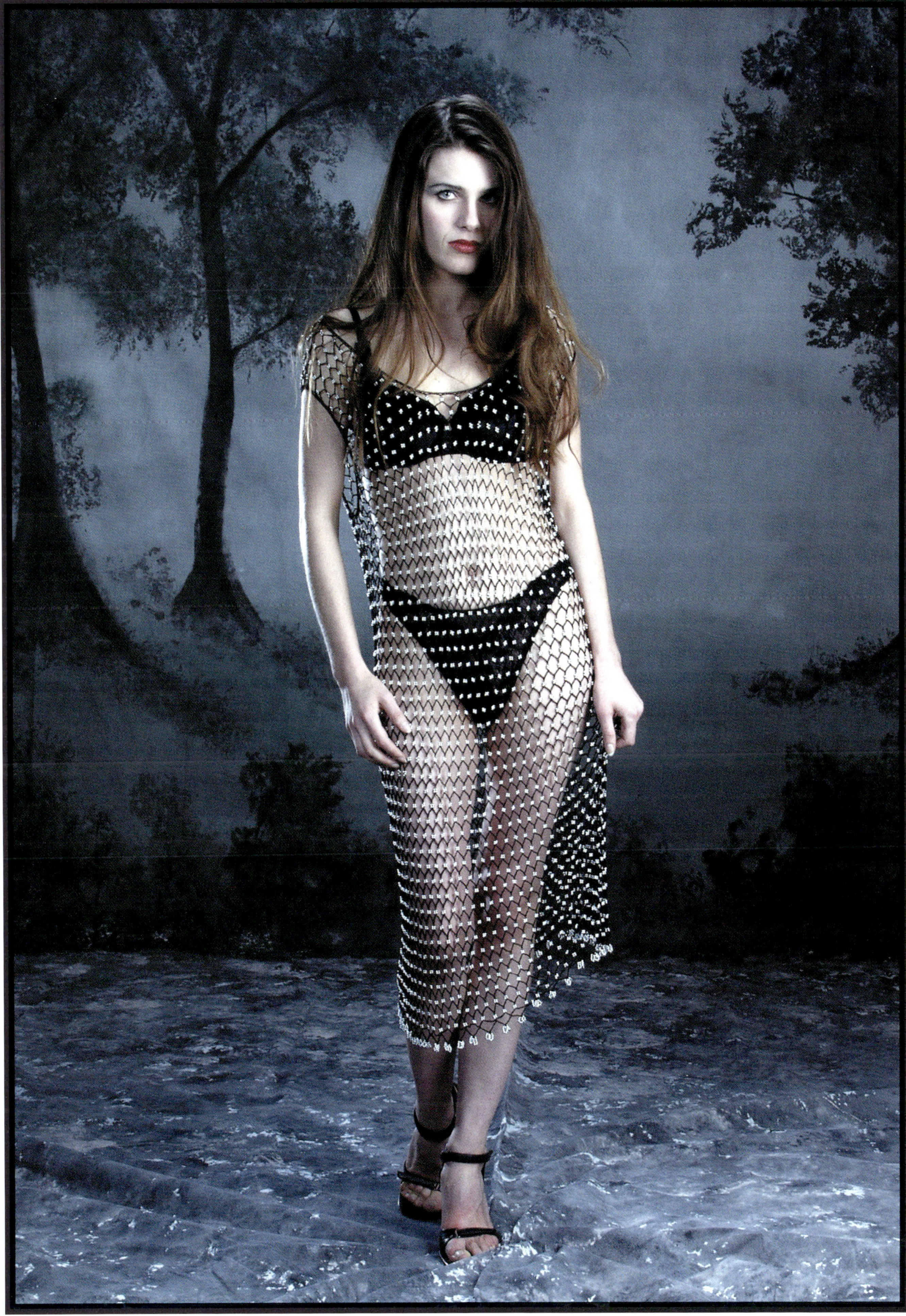

Beauty and the Beast

Every so often I get a dream assignment. The images on this page were part of that assignment. Over the years I developed a relationship with an association in Chicago that produces photography for the beauty industry, showing the latest hair and beauty styles. The client decided to produce a black & white calendar as a promo piece for all of their members. My studio was complete chaos for that day with over 40 people coming and going. However, the client and I put together a very successful promotion.

After that project was completed, I suggested we start on next years calendar using landmarks to show it was produced in Chicago. The client liked the idea. I called a stylist named Sandy who is an excellent hair stylist and make-up artist, and we planned out 6 different scenarios for the new calendar.

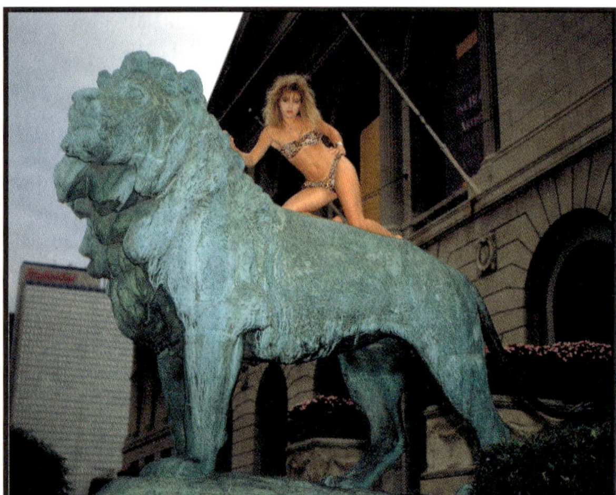

Other poses from the same shooting.

One of Chicago's best known landmarks are the two lions that guard the entrance to the Art Institute. I decided to have a model in a bikini sit atop one of the Lions. In my mind, I envisioned the shot with the model sitting astride the lion hugging the bronze mane. The make-up artist, the model, and I arrived at 5 AM, on a Sunday morning to avoid traffic problems and have spectators watching the shoot. After the model was dressed and her hair and make-up were completed, she stood by in a trenchcoat waiting to climb up on the lion. As the first light of dawn approached, I set up my Hasselblad camera on a tripod and used my little Sunpak 383 flash for fill flash lighting. Reading the background light falling on the model, I set the flash for one stop less light, allowing the daylight to be one stop brighter thus creating a background light and hair light. Also, the fill flash created that sparkle in the eye called a catch light.

The camera and lighting were set. The model used my cupped hands to step up to the lion. When she got onto the lion, I realized she looked miniscule in the pose I envisioned. It was time to change the game plan and plan a new pose. The illustration shown demonstrates how I posed the model to look best for the calendar. One of the things I like about doing photography on location is that it teaches you to think on your feet. In almost every situation, you must be able to improvise at a moment's notice.

Everything went as planned except a bus with one passenger stopped to watch what we were doing, when a car almost slammed into the stopped bus. We knew it was time to get out before more trouble arrived

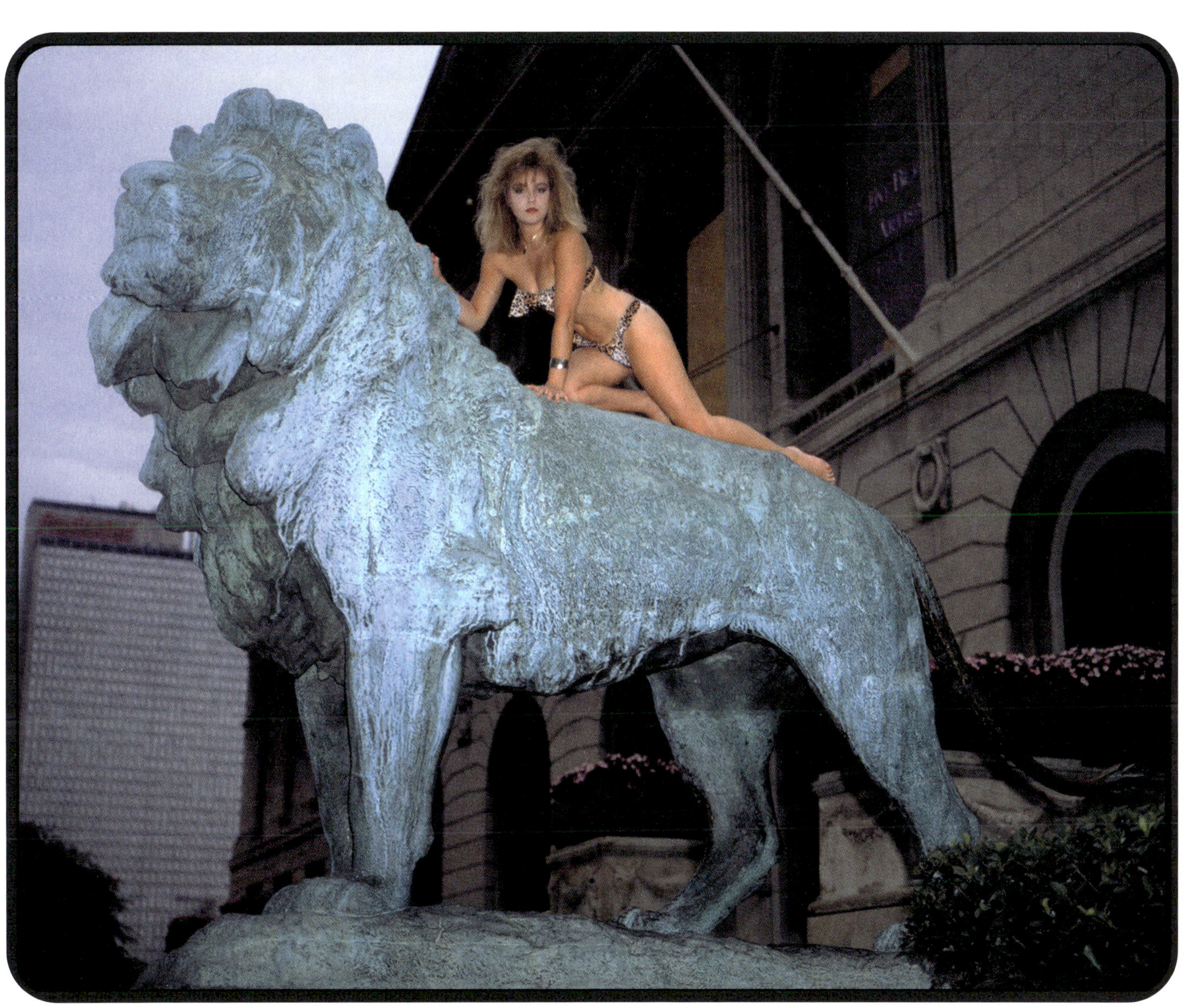

Perfect Poise

This second image of Natalie and Boyfriend was her idea to create an image similar to the Calvin Klein type ads.

Natalie modeled in a workshop that I was doing in my friend, Ron Anthony's, studio. After seeing the images in Natalie's portfolio, I knew I wanted to do some prints for her (and for myself) that would impress the agencies and get their attention.

I went through my idea file looking for concepts that would work with her tall, thin figure. When I came across an image similar to the one you see illustrated, I showed it to Natalie. She was anxious to see if she could copy it. We draped the set with fantasy cloth and sheer to create the wispy feeling I wanted. I knew this shot had to be a high-key lighting effect to make it a clean and uncluttered image.

By the time Natalie was prepared for the shot, we had the set ready to go with the fabrics and pedestals in place. Two of us helped Natalie into position by holding her arms and lowering her body onto the pedestals under her back. Once she felt comfortable on her back, she lifted her legs to the other pedestal. We were ready to shoot. The most difficult thing for Natalie in this shot was holding her head in this unusual position. In a workshop where 12 photographers wanted to get this shot, we had to put a box under Natalie's head between shooters to help relieve the stress in her neck.

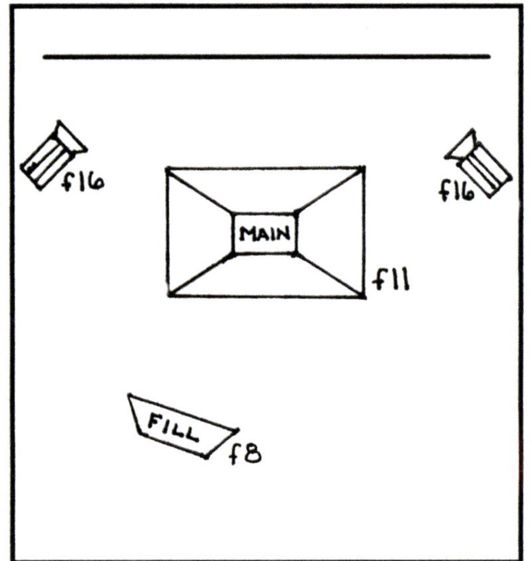

Choosing the right person for this image was crucial. Imagine a model with thicker thighs, short hair, large bosom. Picture a shorter model....None of these scenarios would have made the image work. What I am trying to impress upon you is that you have to choose the appropriate person for the correct image. Just because someone is beautiful does not mean they will work well in all shooting situations.

Lighting: Four light set-up. Two lights on the background set for F:16, medium soft box directly over the model, lighting her from above set for F:11, on the model's upper torso and not allowing this light to fall on the models knees or legs. The fourth light was a fill umbrella near the camera to add fill to the body,. set for F:8. Otherwise, the side of the body would turn out too dark.

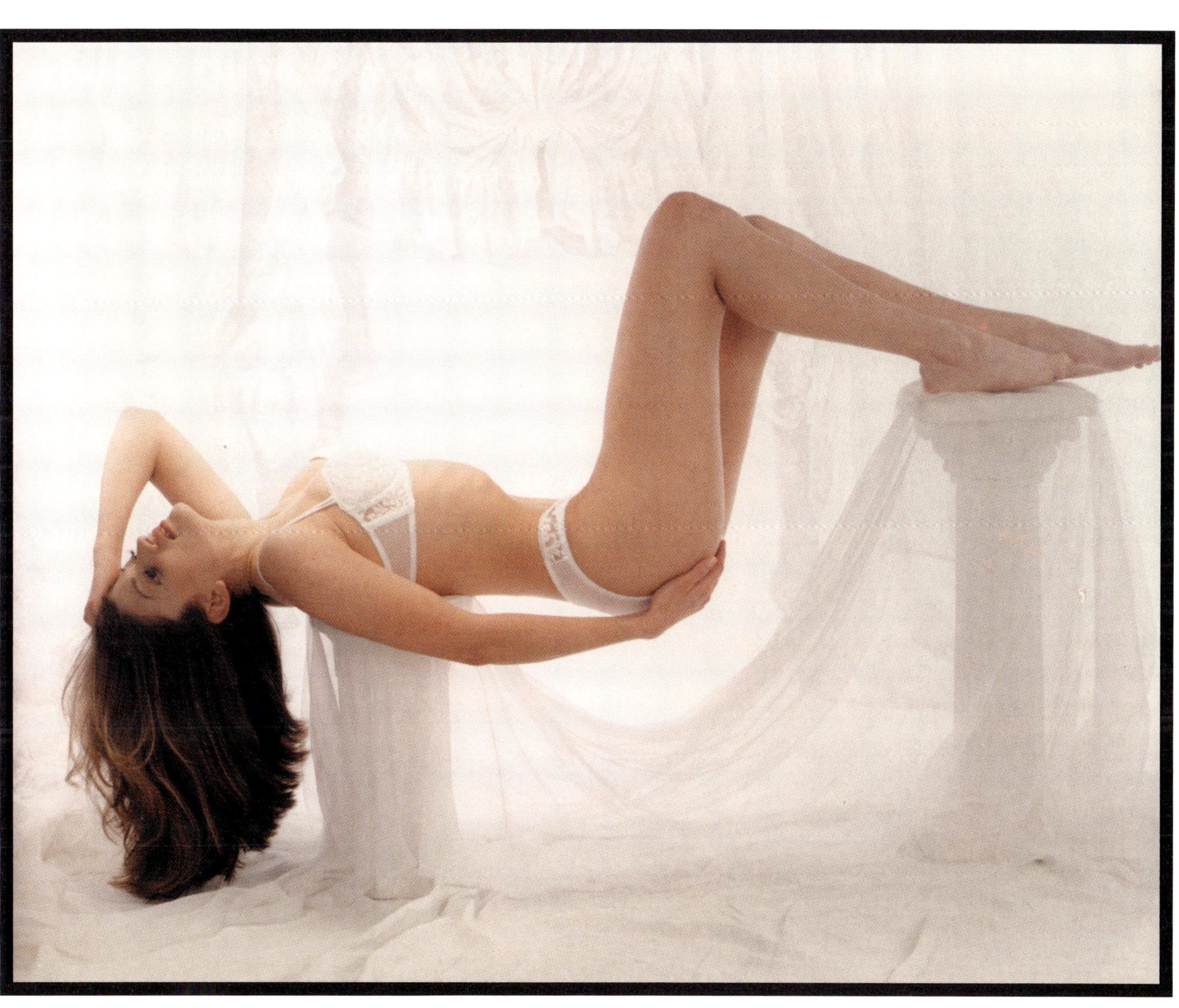

Telephone Poles

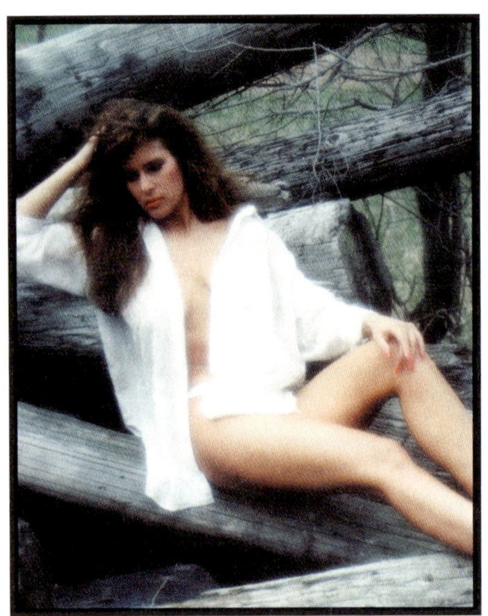
Another image from the Telephone Pole shooting.

I am always searching for background locations that will make interesting photos. When I had the opportunity to photograph Sue, I proposed the idea to do some outdoor lingerie images. She was agreeable to the idea if we had a shooting location that was not too public. When the day of the shoot arrived, Sue, the make-up artist, and I went to a private fishing preserve I knew of. Fortunately no one uses it during the week allowing me to shoot without attracting a crowd.This type of location is difficult to find in a metropolitan area.

Sue is a professional and easy to work with. She brought many different outfits, and I chose the man's shirt. I used a nearby pile of telephone poles for a background. This made for a dramatic image of Sue reclining on the coarse wood. The reclining pose looked the best to me, although we shot many others.

Lighting: This image was created using totally natural light. There was no need for reflectors. When shooting in an outdoor situation, I generally use the fastest shutter speed and let the lens aperture go as open as it possibly can. This allows background to go out of focus at the wider aperture and provides very sharp images at the higher shutter speeds. I always read light in these outdoor situations with my Sekonic L-308 meter using the incident dome for the most accurate readings.

This image also has my edge diffusion filter for the out of focus effect at the outer edges of the image. This is a homemade filter, starting with a skylight or UV filter and using Sally Hansen Hard As Nails clear nail polish at the outer edge of the filter. This particular brand of nail polish has no yellow tone.

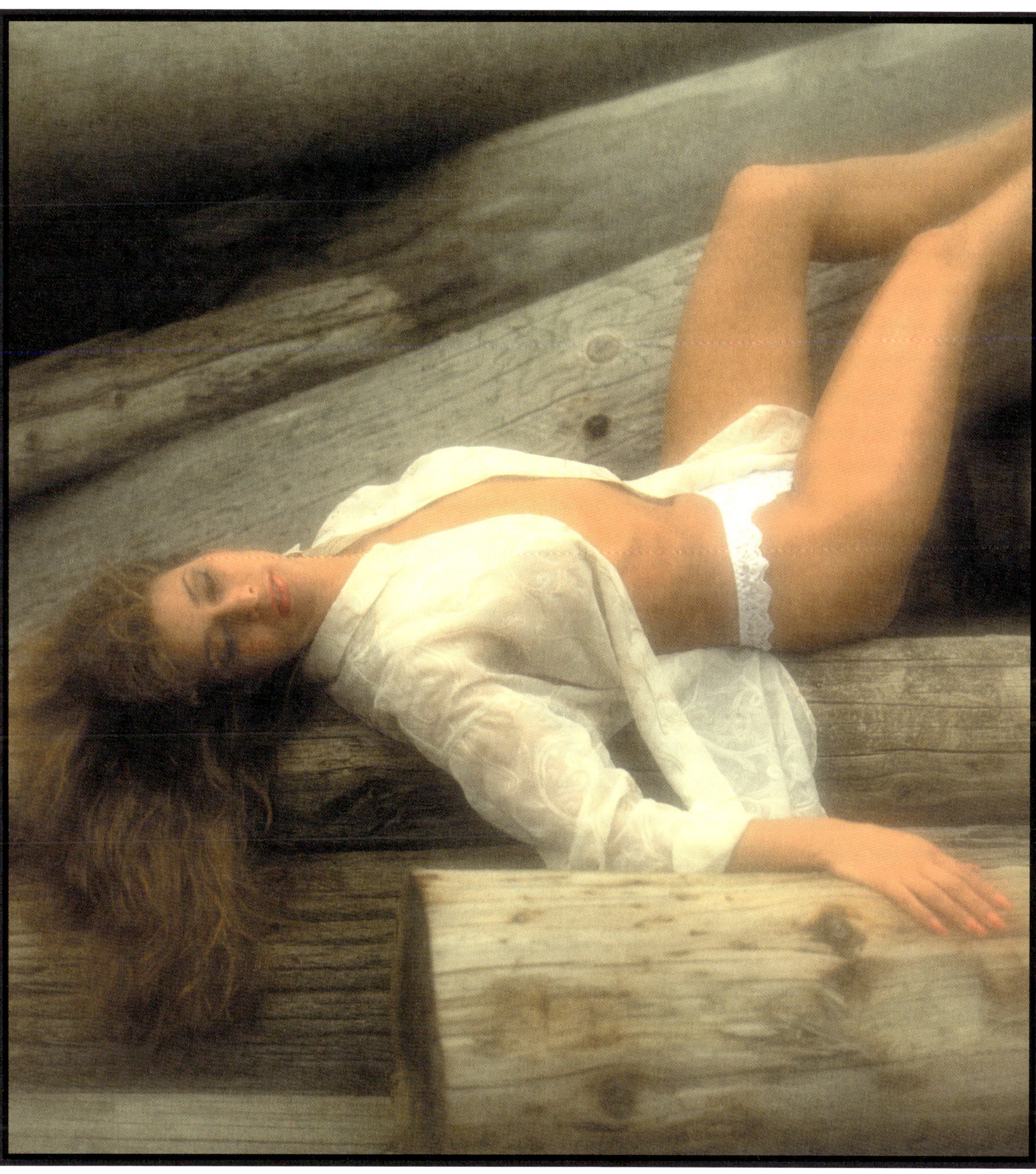

Butterfly

Partial body shots are a favorite of mine. I sometime like to create an air of mystery in my photography. It is not always necessary to show the entire body to make a point, or to create a finished image.

When shooting a model or subject, look at the person with a critical eye. If the model has great shoulders, great legs, hair, or eyes. plan a shoot around the model's strong points. In the case of the butterfly on the model's stomach, I had to have a model with washboard abs. I called one of my agency friends and told her what kind of model I was looking for. The butterflies were in my studio because I had just completed a shooting for a small company that imports and sells them mail order in glass encased displays for home decor. This type of image is appropriate on greeting cards and posters.

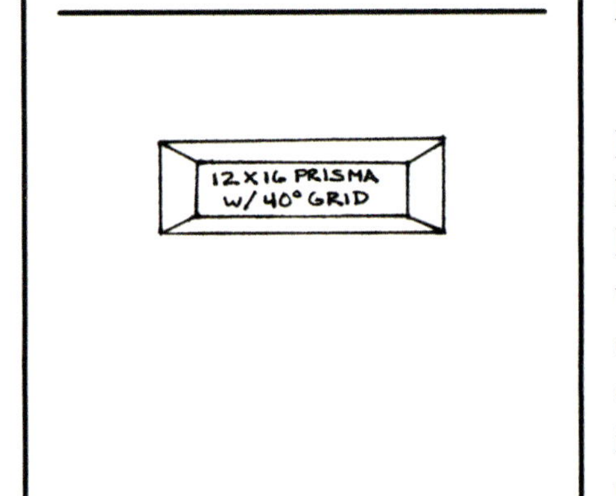

Lighting: An easy, one light set-up. I used my normal little Balcar prisma-light soft box with 40 degree grid on the front of the box. This soft box measures about 12"x16" and is about 4"deep. The box is mounted on a Bowens adjustable boom and this allows me to wheel it into position quickly. The 40 degree grid keeps the light directional and allows me to feather the light. Note; the light fall off on the models lower torso. Keeping the interest where the butterfly is, and making the brightest area of the image in that area. Also note that with the grid attached, there is no light falling behind the models body on the background. Exposed at F:11 at normal sync speed.

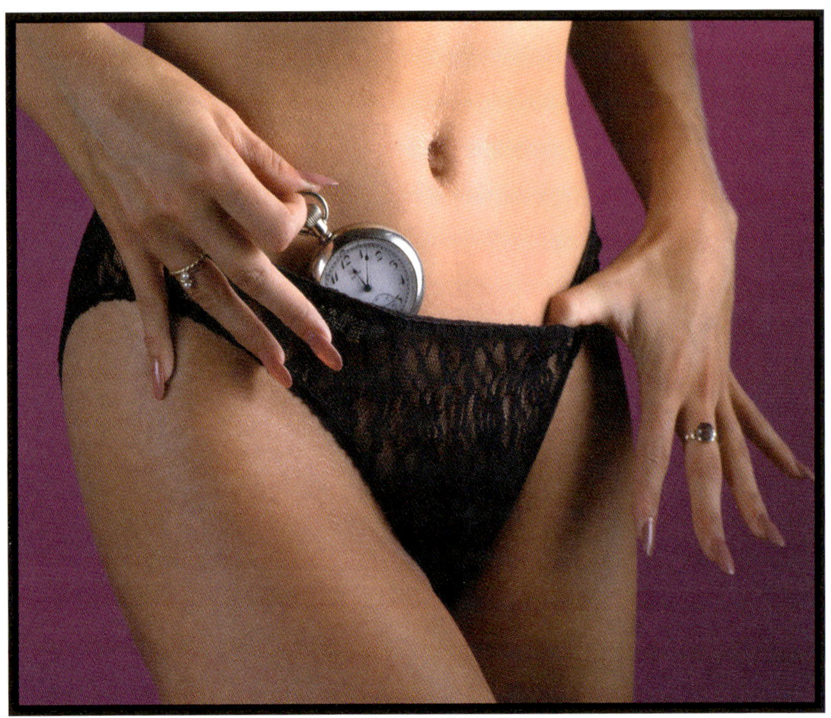

Time to Play

A second image was created with the pocket watch with the identical lighting but in a vertical position. Think of the titles that might be added to either of these images for a greeting card or poster.

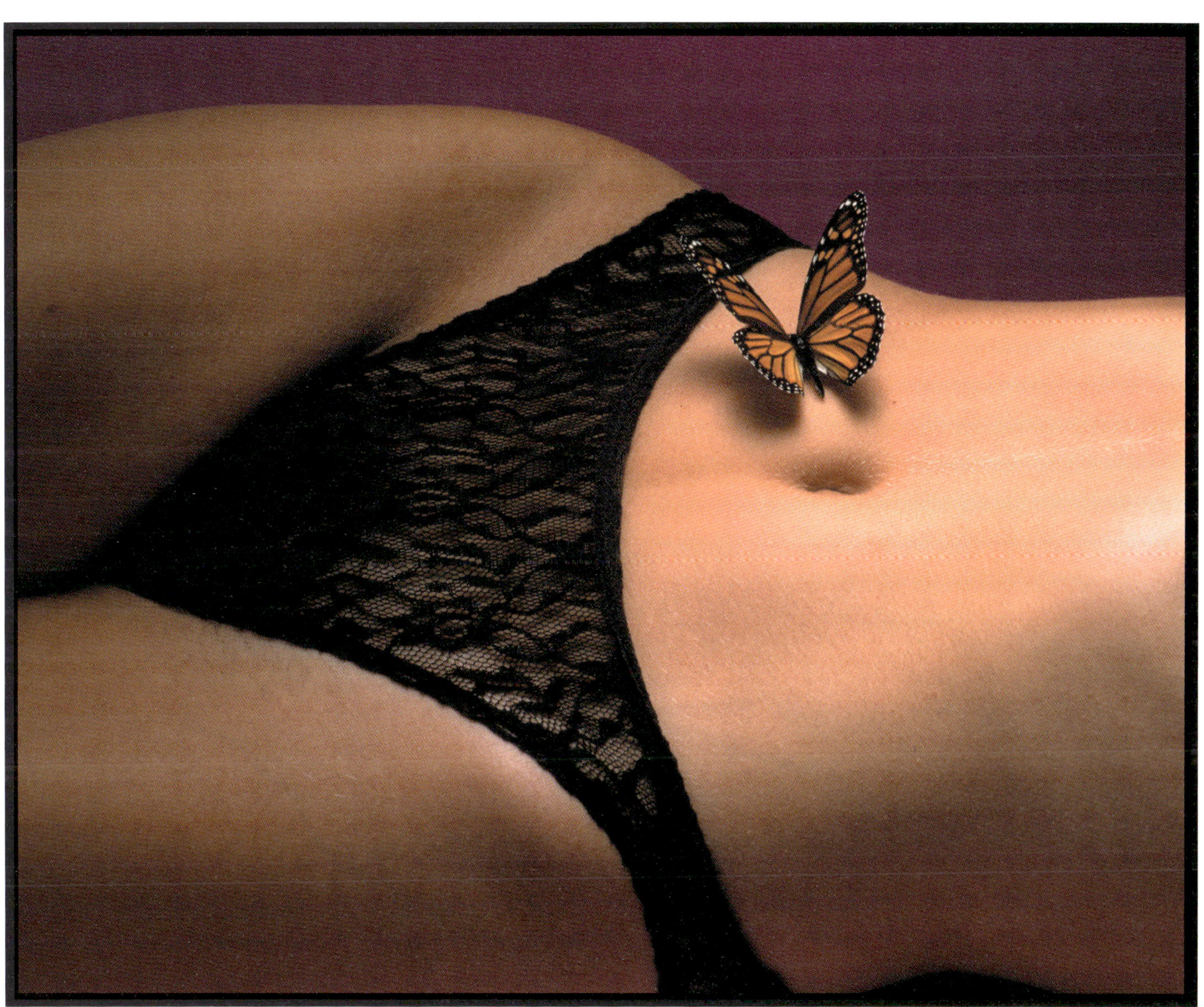

Derriere

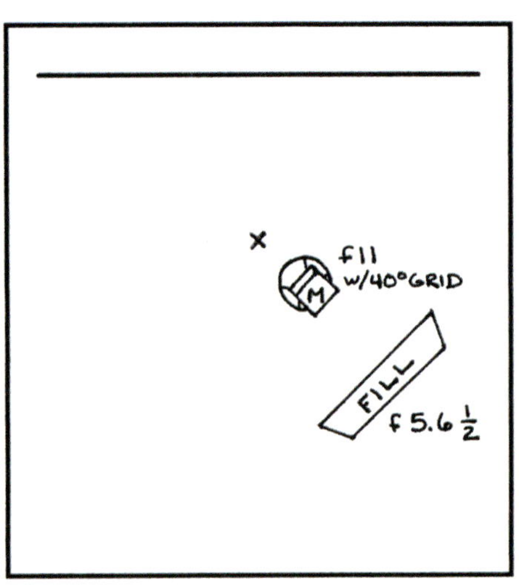

The derriere shot was created when my model showed up with a costume of unique white stockings with black bows. I asked if we could do a partial body showing only her posterior and legs. She liked the idea, as most models can use a leg shot in their portfolio.

Lighting: Using a small soft box that I normally use as a hair light; it now was being used as a derriere light. I added another soft box in front to add some fill light. Otherwise the light fall-off would be too extreme. The rule of thumb here is to set the front light about two stops lower than the overhead light.Most of all, remember to choose the right model for your image. The wrong derriere could be a disaster!

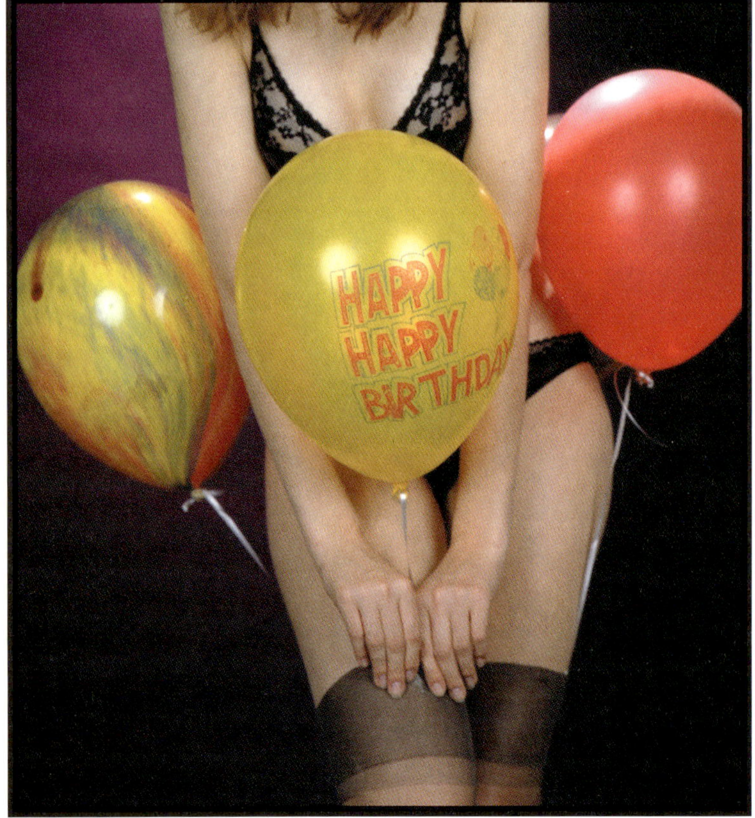

Happy Happy Birthday

The image of the model with stockings being held up by helium balloons was an idea I had seen in a publication of another balloon shot. I felt my image would create a whimsical attitude to another greeting card or poster type image.

I obtain many ideas from other ideas. It has always been my philosophy that there is no such thing as an original idea. All concepts are derived from other concepts, thoughts or inventions.

Lighting: Two umbrellas set for equal power totaling F:11, also a rim light set 45 degrees behind the model to create more separation between subject and background. The rim light set 1/2 stop lower than the main lights.

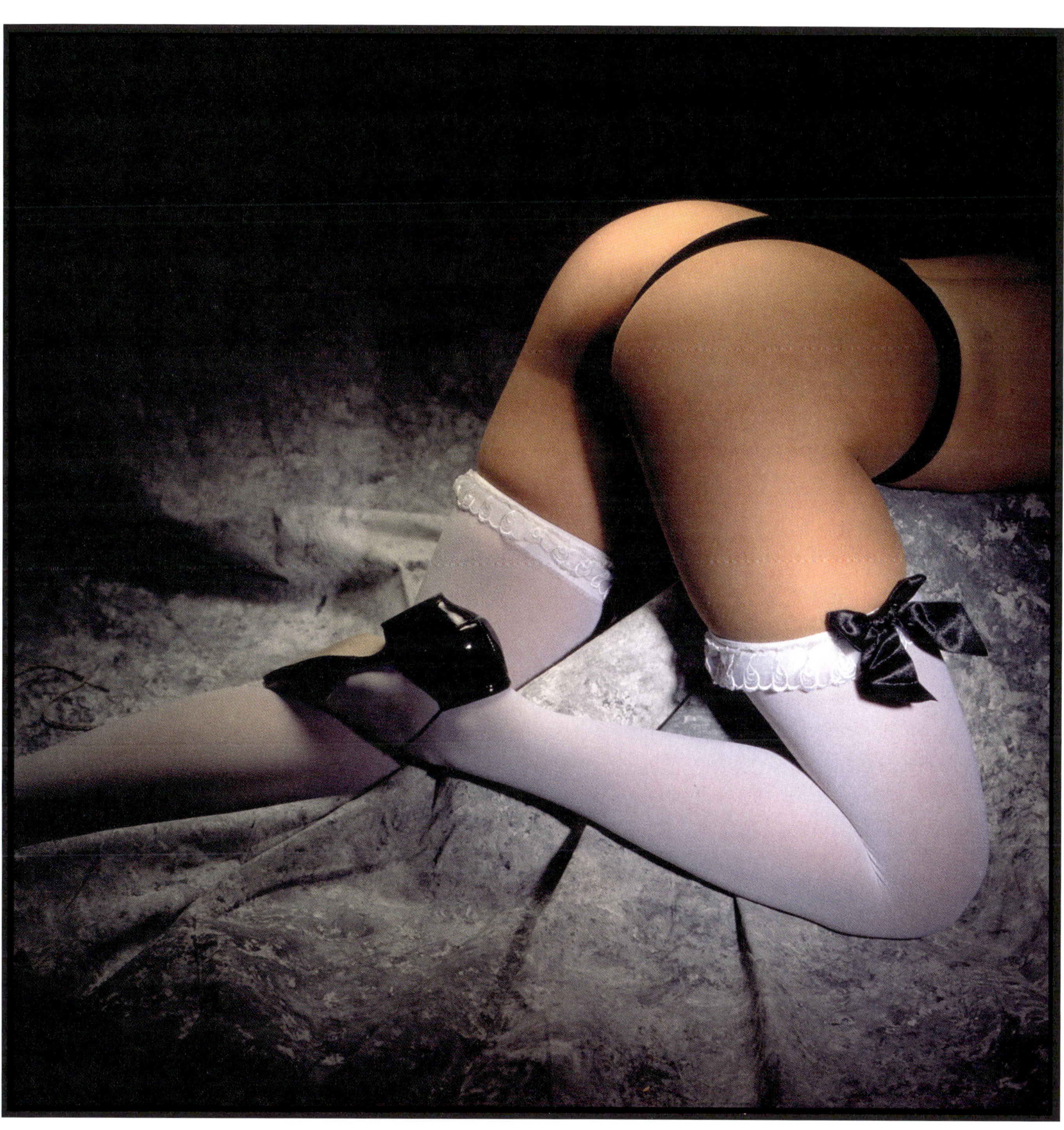

Cover Shot

The most important image of any publication is the cover shot. When my client and their ad-agency asked me if I could produce an image for their 2002 catalog that would say dance by showing only a face we had a real challenge.

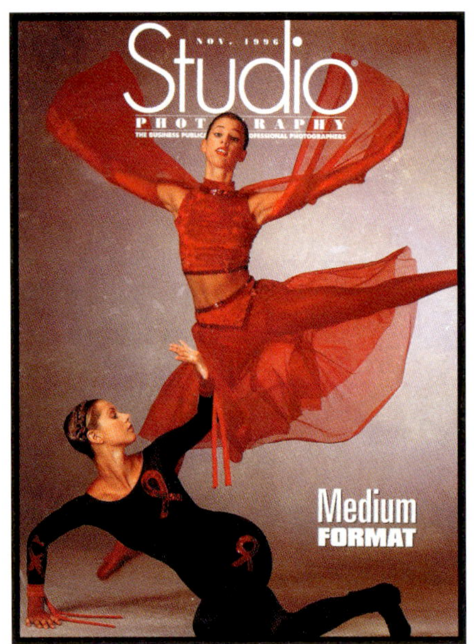

Studio Photography published an article on Art Ketchum's unique style, and how he shoots his dance photography images. Cover photo by Art Ketchum

The design concept was the brainchild of Nicholas & Associates, with the help of an award winning dancer named Kim, two great make-up and hairstylists, Karen and Chiquita and August, a fabulous choreographer, we built a team, along with Glenn the owner of the company and his super staff to create this image for their most recent catalog.

My assistant, David and I set up 6 lights; Two background umbrella lights, one rim light, two fill lights to light the model and a face light with 3 degree grid for an additional one stop of face light.

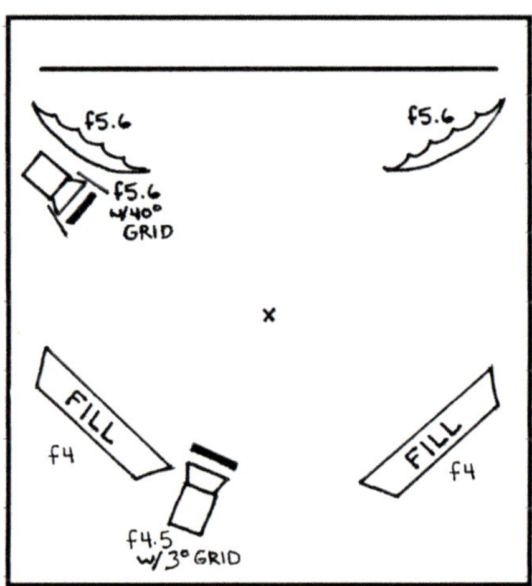

Photographed with a Hasselblad 201F camera, 150mm lens at F:4 to intentionally throw background out of focus. Using my custom made edge diffusion filter.

Costume '98

When working with clients, you rarely have the opportunity to do partial body shots. Most clients are selling a product. If that product is a costume, the client wants the entire costume to show so it will sell to the market they are promoting to. In the case of Suzanne in the highly colorful costume, the client wanted a tight close-up for a cover shot. I positioned the model and using my 110mm F:2 Sonnar lens with a Hasselblad 2X tele-extender creating a 220mm lens on my Hasselblad to move in really close. This created a dramatic shot that would show all the details, sequins, and fabrics on the costume.

The shot was very effective, proving to be one of the company's best covers and most profitable catalogs. All of the images in the catalog, including the cover image, were shot on Fuji Velvia for the maximum color saturation. The client ran full page ads in many national dance magazines, along with creating a 5 foot x 7 foot display transparency for their trade show display.

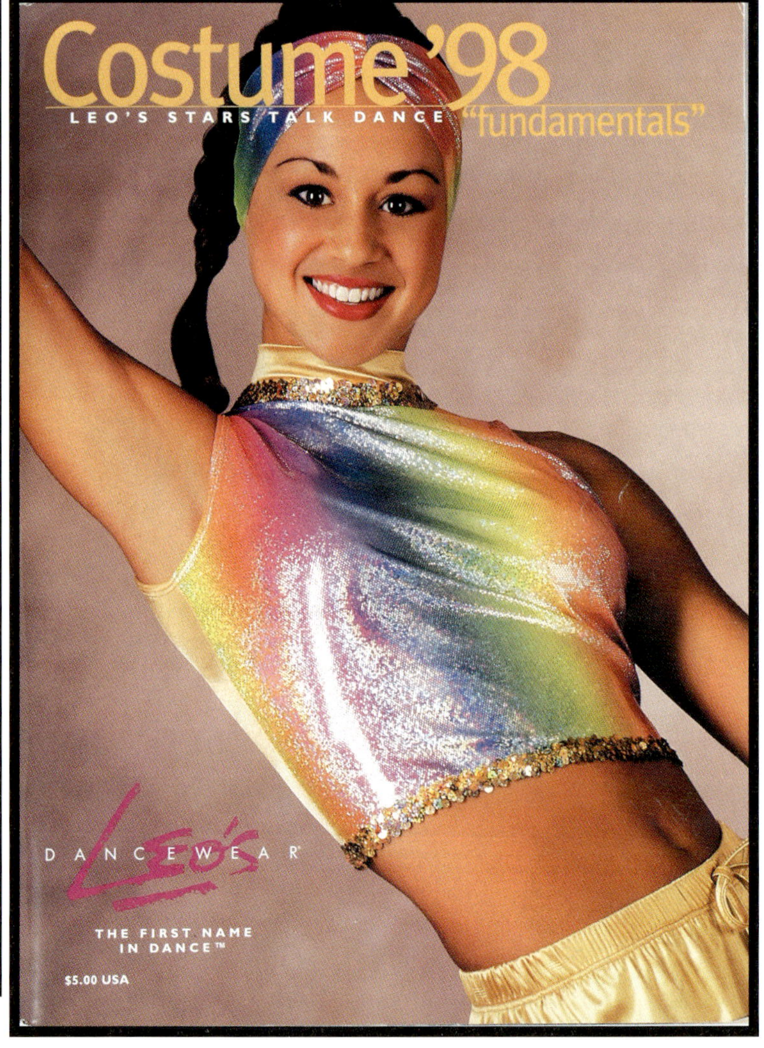

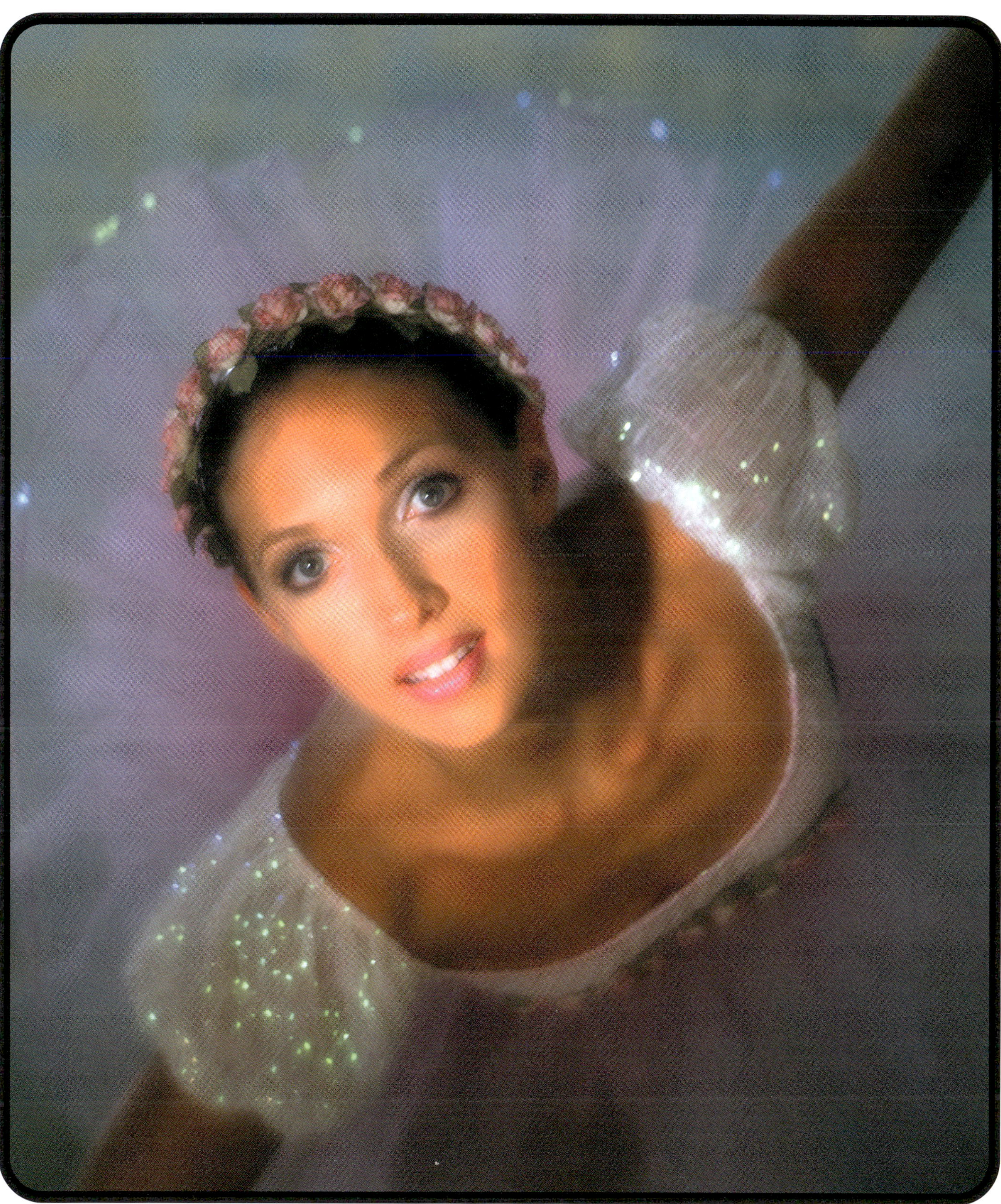

Seductive

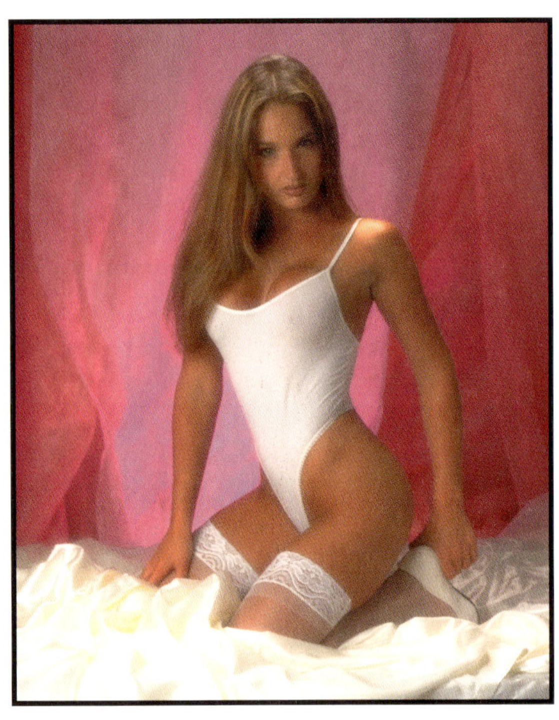

If ever there was one catalog that every attractive model would like to appear in, it would have to be the Victoria Secret Catalog. To be a model selected for inclusion in the Victoria Secret catalog would be a very high honor and would provide much notoriety and fame. When I met Laura and saw her in a bathing suit shot, I suggested she do some lingerie images. Laura has classic good looks and was able to pull off some fantastic lingerie shots that would make any art director consider her for their catalog.

One of the most common looks in a model's composite or portfolio is the lingerie shot. The reason for this is to show a model's figure. A figure shot is necessary for almost any fashion-type model composite. While a figure shot could be a leotard or bathing suit, lingerie is desirable because lingerie is worn with evening make-up, and an elegant look is created. Evening make-up with a leotard or bathing suit would look ridiculous. Another reason many models include lingerie images in their portfolio is that lingerie modeling pays double rate.

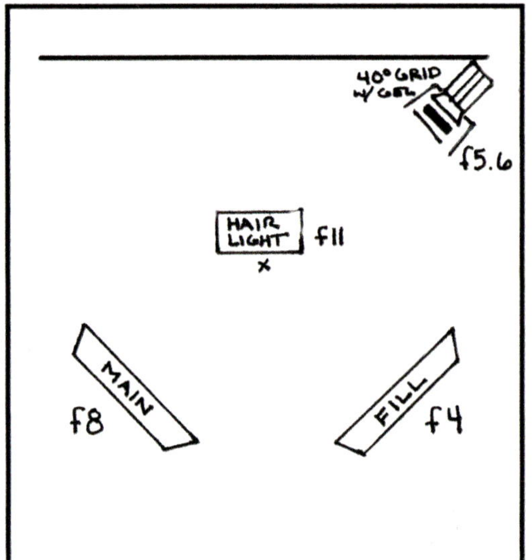

Laura brought many different outfits. I chose to use the two illustrated in these images because I felt they created a classy (not trashy) attitude. I set up each outfit differently as I wanted each outfit to have a unique look.

All of the images of Laura were lit with 4 to 1 ratio lighting. However, in the case of the black background image, the background light with magenta gel was turned to light her backside and set one stop lower than the main light creating a rich pink glow on Laura's hair and body.

Lighting: Four Light set-up, two large soft boxes, main light F:8, fill light set for F:4 and 1/2, hair light set for F:11 and rim or background light set for F:5.6.

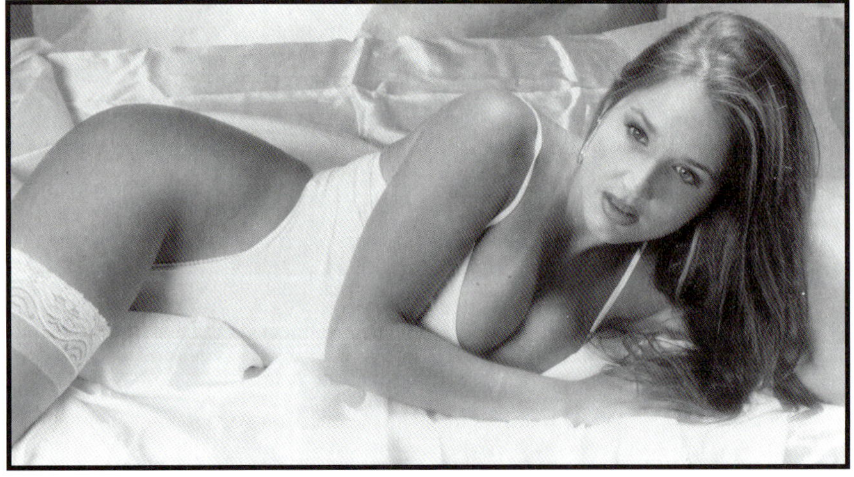

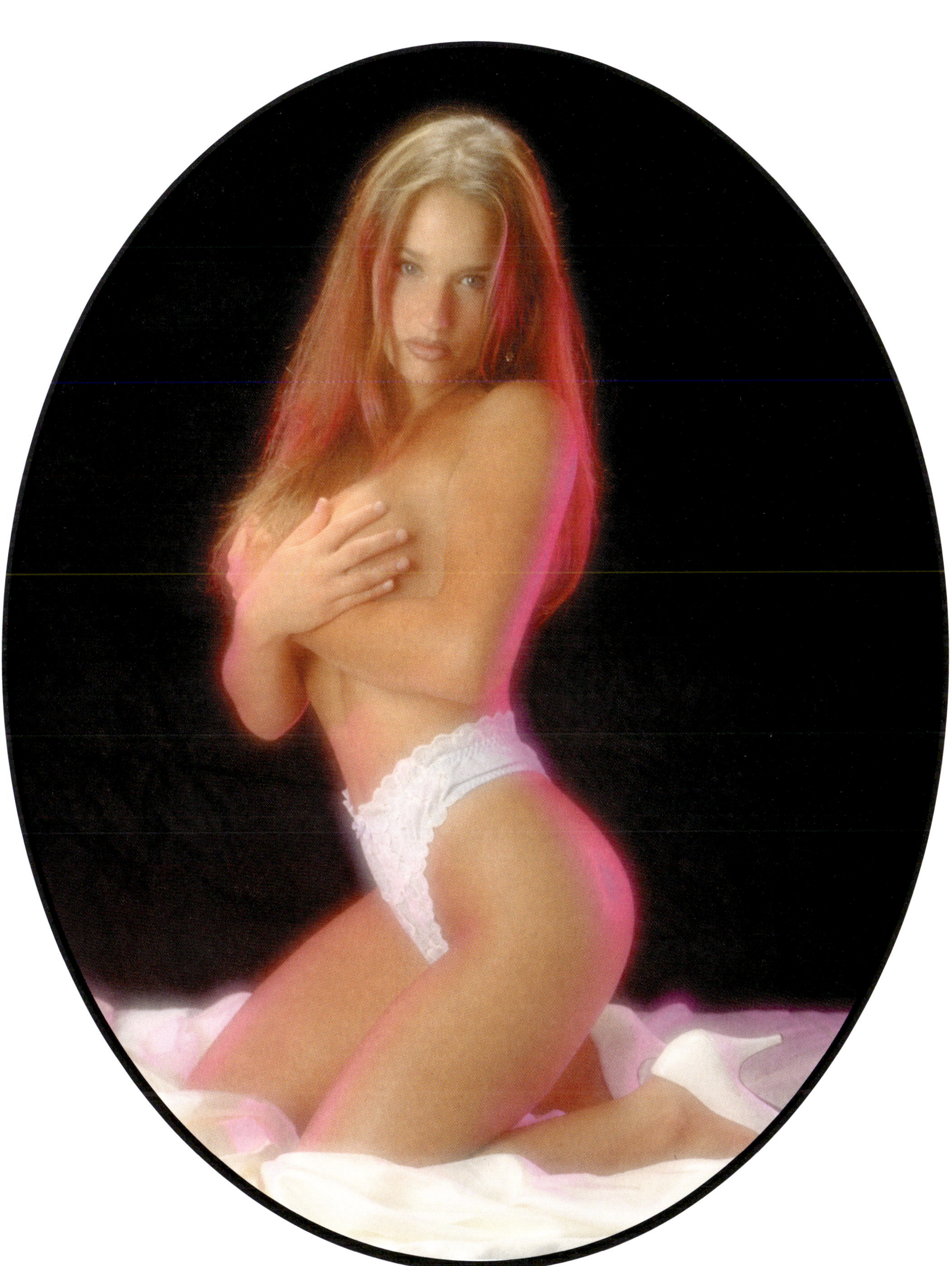

The Bike and the High Heel

One of my favorite photo projects is to create images that would make stunning poster images. I love posters, especially photographic posters. The types of images that make desirable poster photography also fall into the area of greeting card photography. When I think up some bizarre idea, I write it down in my idea book. Then when I am shooting, I see if any of my ideas might be implemented for my poster shot.

When Jill came in to shoot with me, I noticed she had some fishnet stockings and black ankle strap high heels. I suggested a shot that would be fun to do. I pulled my dusty road bike down from the ceiling, did a quick wipe down and proceeded to set up the shot you see here.

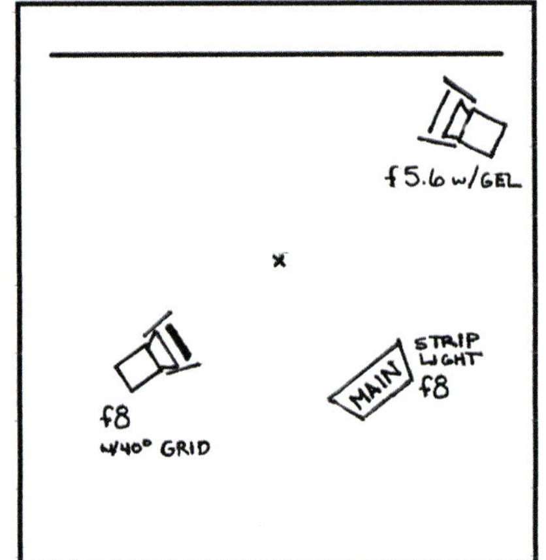

The dynamics of this image suggest that people ride bikes dressed in fishnet stockings and high heels. I think the shot is an attention grabber, and I find a particular humor in this image. I used this shot to create a dynamic 11 x 14 poster for my business. I sent out my new poster to many art directors and clients who I wanted to impress.

The poster was printed with matte black background. Only the image area was varnished giving the poster a unique look. This created the impression that two different black inks were used in the printing process.

Lighting: Three light set up, two lights lighting the leg and bike at 45 degrees left and right of the camera with umbrellas. The third light is lighting the red background with 40 degree grid attached to a 7" reflector. Each light was about 3 feet from the model's foot.

Promotional Poster

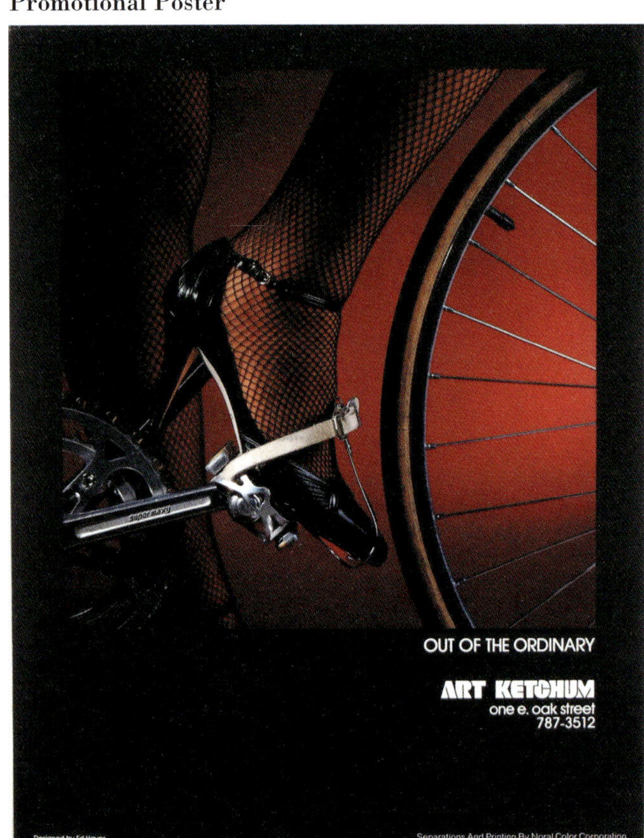

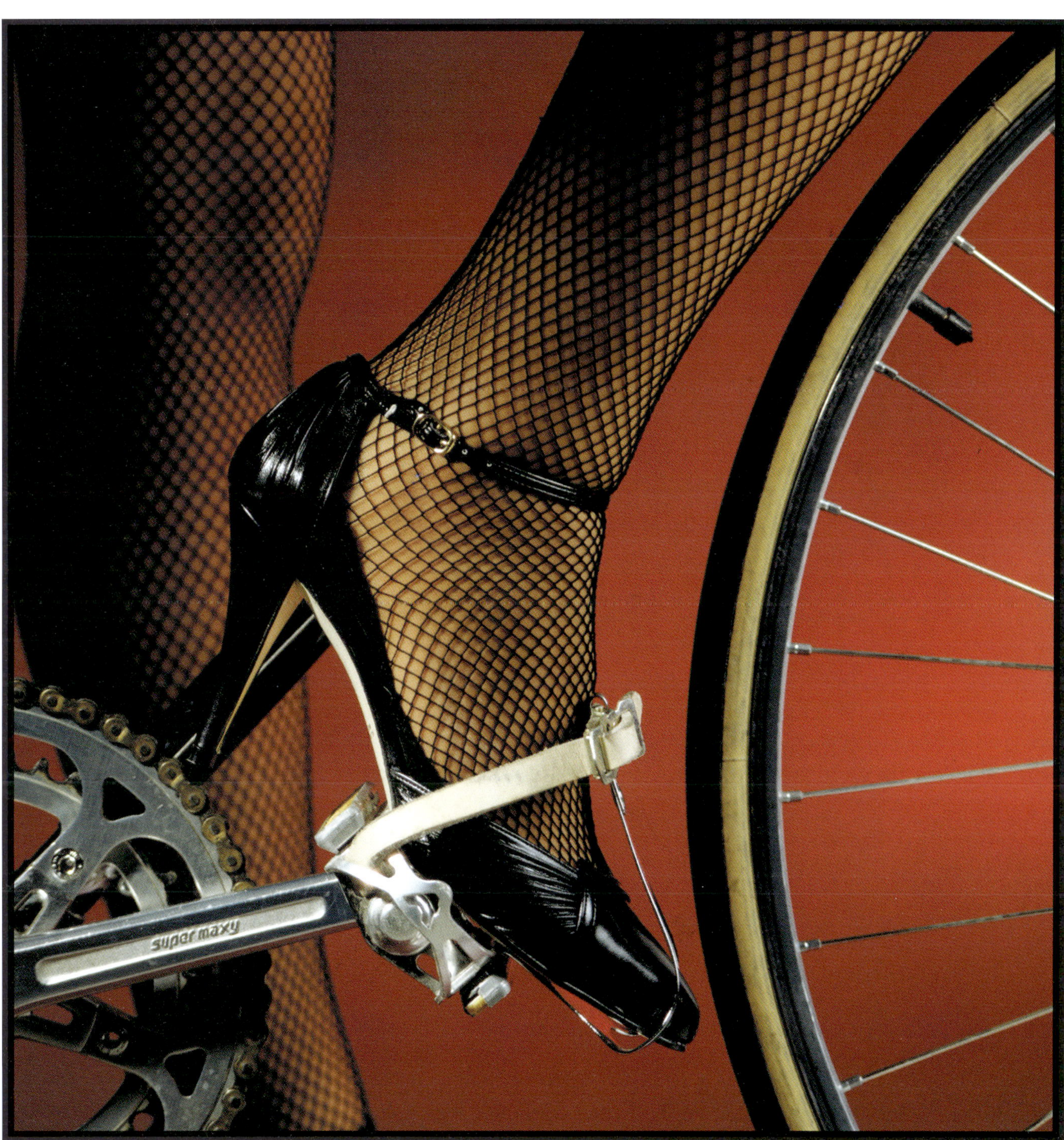
super maxy

The Mission Shots

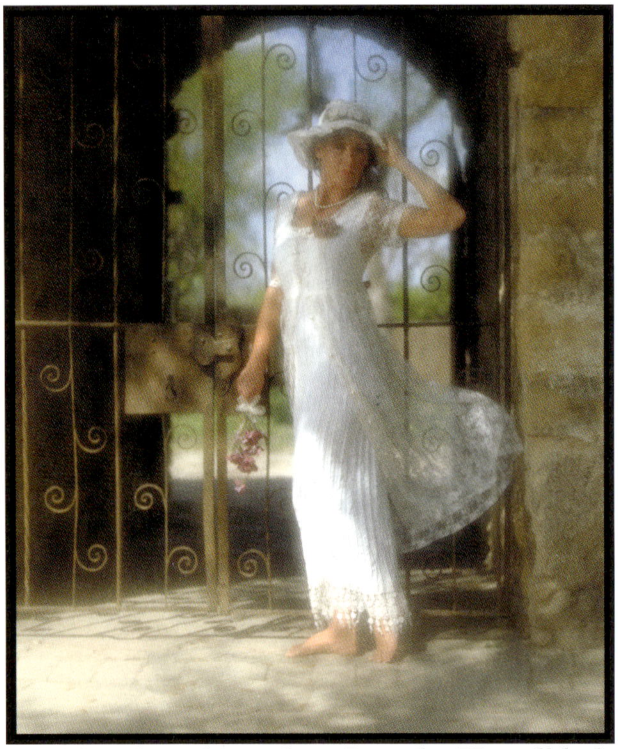

For the white dress shot, I used a Hasselblad #2 Softar filter and my edge diffusion filter to add romance to this image. Edge diffusion filter explained on page 30.

Often in my travels I have the opportunity to shoot pictures of beautiful models in exotic locations. When I planned a workshop in San Antonio, Texas, I wanted to do some photos at the Alamo. A local friend suggested I try one of the other missions as a shooting location. I mapped out the missions and chose the one I thought would photograph the best for backgrounds. San Antonio has 5 missions; some are small, and others are immense. One of the advantages of shooting in a location like the missions is the endless possibilities to create unique images.

In the course of doing workshops all over North America, I have developed a network of models across the country who wish to model for me when I come to a particular area. I also have a list of talent agencies who know my work. One of my model friends who worked for me in my first workshop in Taos, New Mexico called when she heard I was doing a workshop in San Antonio. Having worked with Lydia previously, I knew she was talented. An experienced model is always preferable to a newcomer.

Lydia is a model that comes to a shoot well prepared. She brought along clothing she had designed herself. With the many rustic walls, gates, woodwork, and geometric shapes, I could choose a new background by moving just a few feet in either direction. Both images illustrated were taken within 100 feet of each other at the mission.

Lighting; Natural light was supplemented in the case of the white dress with a Photoflex white pop out reflector. In the case of the blue dress the distance was too great for any reflector. In all cases exposure was set for the highest possible shutter speed enabling me to shoot with a more wide open aperture. Metered by a Sekonic L-308 with incident dome. Camera Hasselblad 201-F with 110mm Lens.

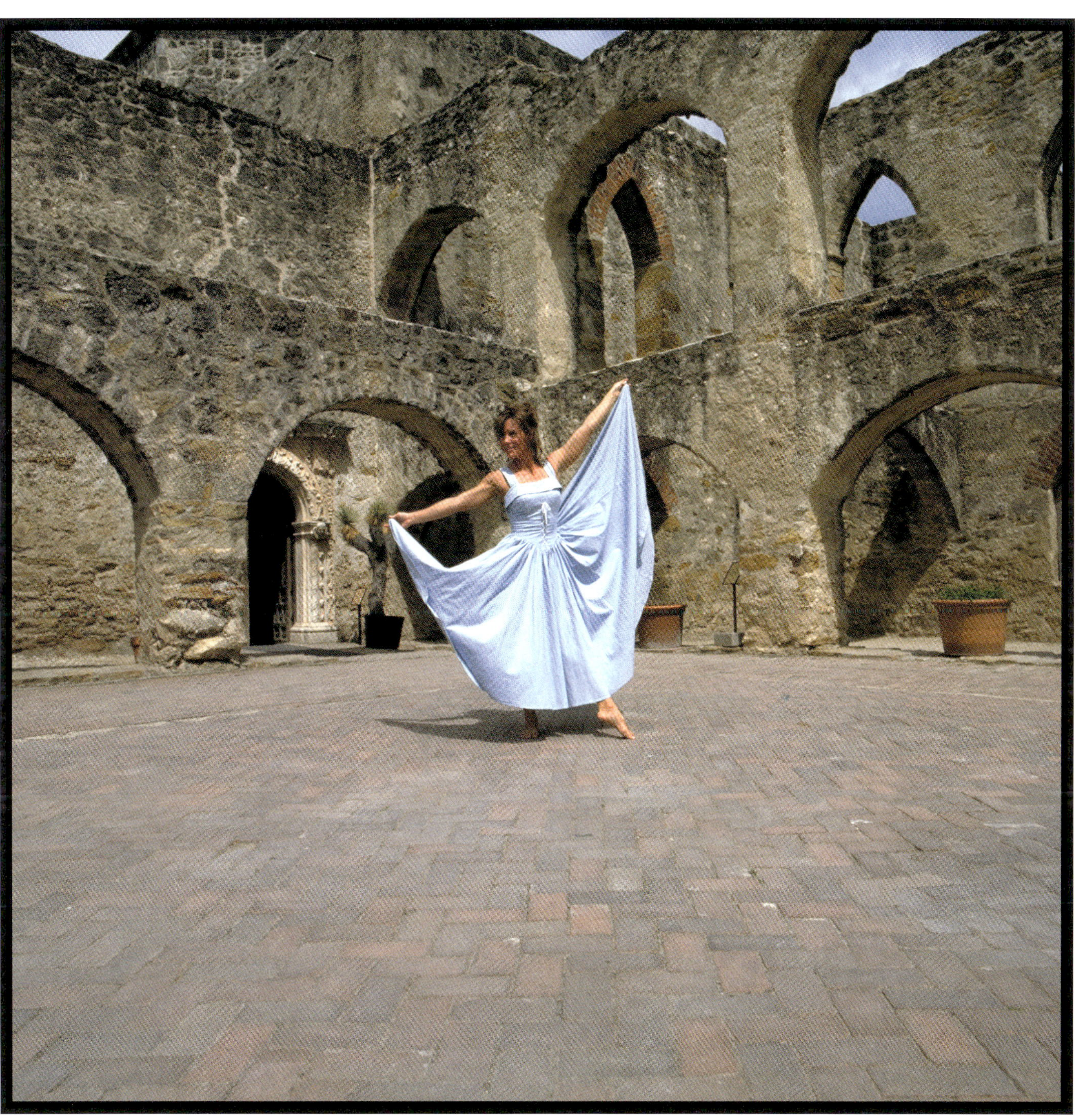

Rustic Wood Glamour

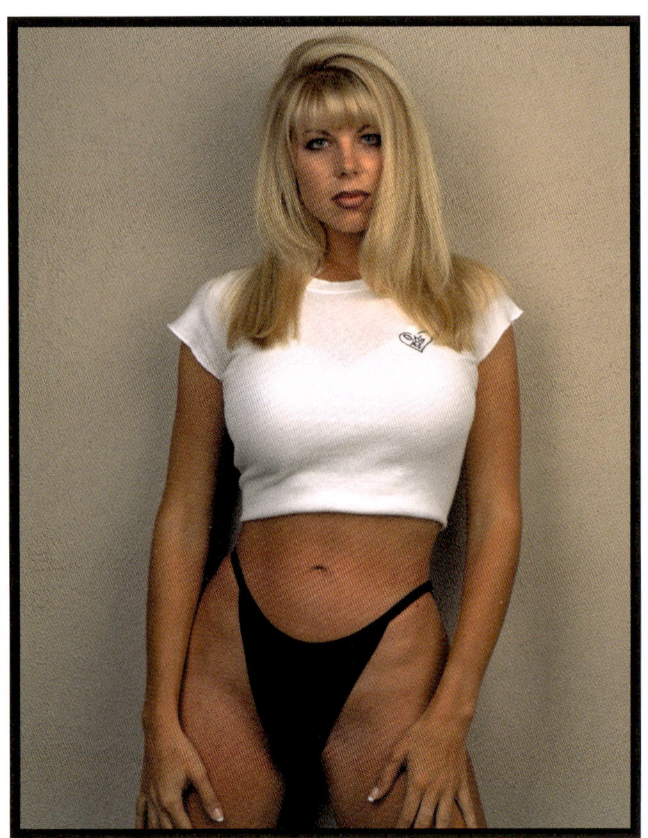

A few years ago when I built my studio I wanted one of the walls to be a western scene. As luck would have it, a movie called Hoodlums was being shot nearby. The company that produced the movie spent millions of dollars on sets that replicate New York in the early 1930's.

After the movie was completed, the production company was preparing to break down all the sets and put things back as they were before they arrived. One of the sets next door to my building was a shanty-town built with modern materials made to look like the 1930's. I contacted the property manager of the movie set and found I could have any of the lumber as long as I removed it within 24 hours. I borrowed a pick-up truck and pulled apart all the good lumber for use in my studio. Now I had enough lumber to create my western set. I have used this western wood wall and floor in many different images. My friend and assistant, Clay Davis, helped me build the adjoining stucco wall designed after the walls in the Southwest. The second image of Kristin was shot on what we call our Taos wall.

Both the wood wall and the stucco wall can be made to look different with some creative lighting. By having these walls in my studio I can create the illusion that we are shooting on location.

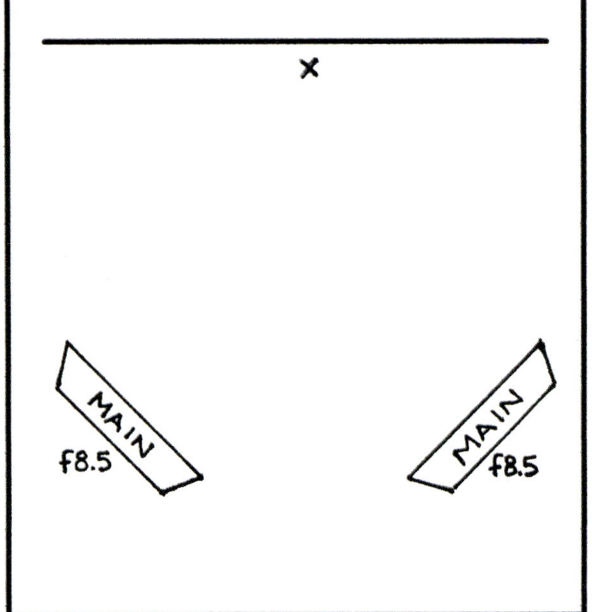

Lighting; Flat lighting using two large 54"x48" soft boxes set equally in power to provide an F:11 aperture setting and eliminate any strong shadow that ratio light would create because the model is next to the background. Both shots were lit the same way.

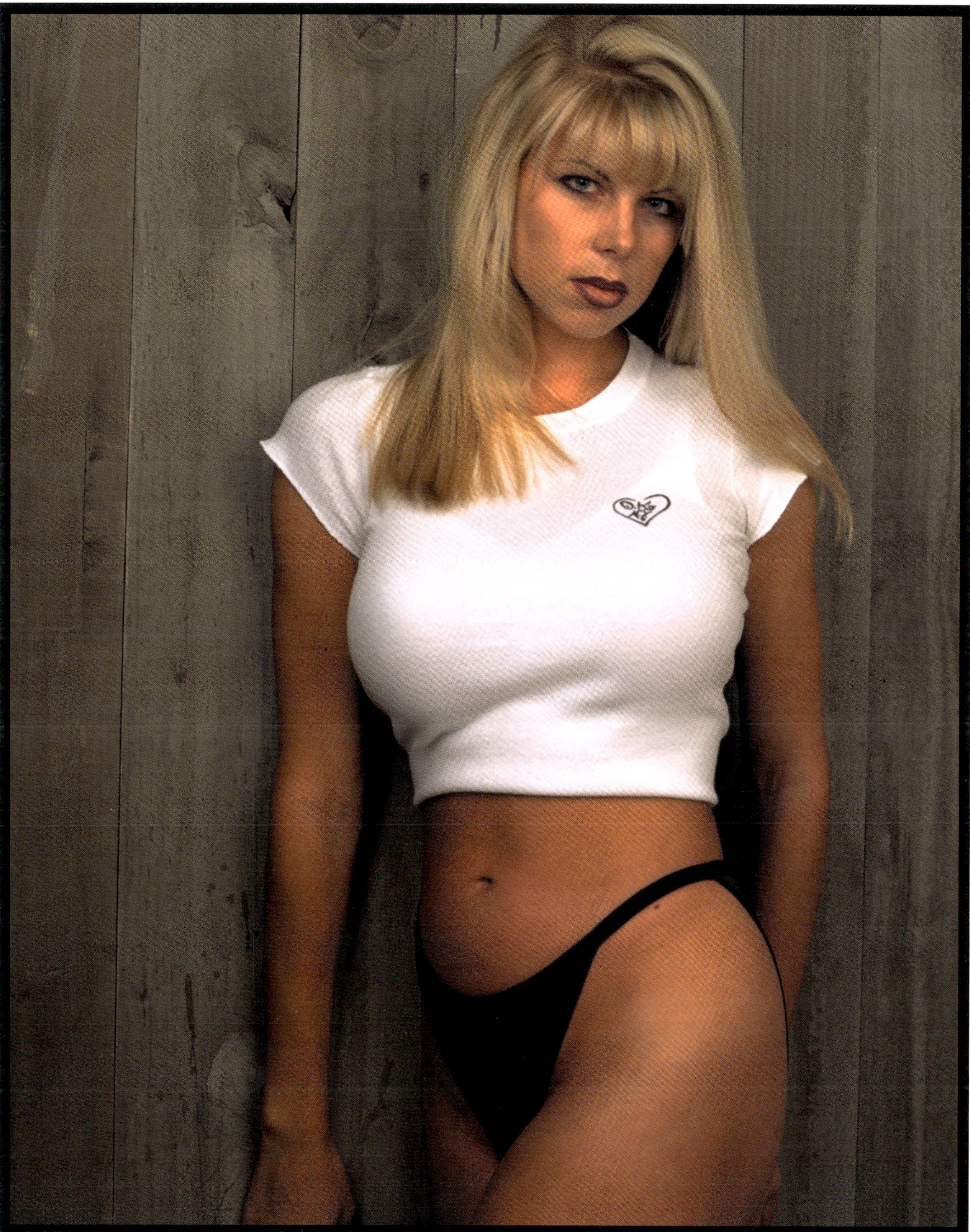

Babbling Brook Reflections

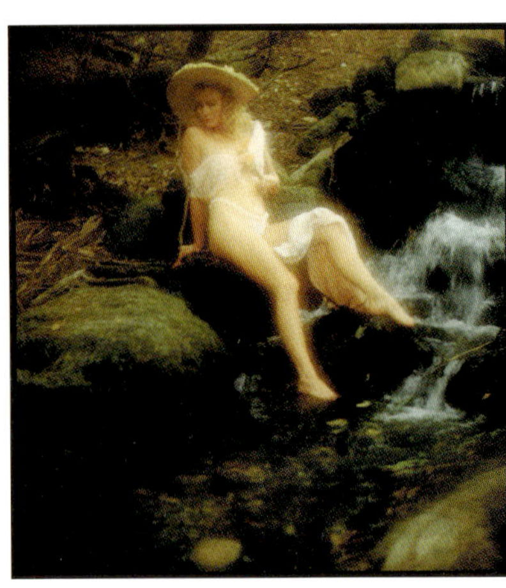

A few years ago, I was asked to produce a calendar for a company in Chicago that provides dancers for bachelor parties, private shows and parties. The company wanted to promote their actors, actresses and dancers in lifelike situations that would show off their talents in exotic and beautiful settings. These images were produced with an excellent dancer I had worked with previously. I knew of a location not far from where the dancer lived, and chose to shoot there. It was a private hunting and fishing club that had many different backgrounds. There were some small streams that flowed from one lake to a larger lake at the end of the park.

I positioned myself within the greenery, ferns and rocks, midway into the small stream and took a position for shooting about 200 feet away. Selecting a 250mm lens on my Hasselblad with tripod, I hoped to create a romantic feeling to the images you see here. I metered the subject with an incident meter while I was close to the model. Light would be perfect no matter where the camera was positioned because reading the light with an incident meter at or near the subject is more accurate than any in camera or reflected meter. If I had used an in camera meter or reflected light meter the darkness of the greenery would have caused an over exposed image.

I wanted the stream to be flowing, so I chose very slow shutter speeds for these images. Exposure was approximately 1/15th at F:8, I bracketed the amount of drag on the shutter but did not change exposure. If that sounds confusing, it isn't. If you know your exposure is correct, there is no need to bracket the amount of light to the film. But in this case I wanted to see the water at different shutter speeds to create a flowing feeling. However I was afraid if the model moved too much the slower shutter speeds would partially blur her.

If the correct exposure was 1/30th at F:8 and I bracketed to 1/15th at F:11, the exposure to the film would be the same, but the water would appear more blurred using the slower shutter speed. I would highly recommend shutter bracketing in a situation like this, as the swiftness of the stream will make a difference in the end result. Film; Fuji Provia.

From among the model's many outfits, I knew the light colors would work the best with the dark foliage. As there was no way to add light to the subject because of the distance from camera to subject. In these images I used Hasselblad softar #2 filter. When using diffusion filters, you create halation in the highlight area of the photo. Both the model and her white outfit are the highlight areas of these images. Diffusion filters create a romantic effect. I feel diffusion is mandatory for this type of image. However, I feel you can go too far with diffusion. When you cross over the line and use too much, the image appears to be out of focus.

To make sure you get the correct result when creating a romantic image like this.... ask yourself if diffusion will help the final shot. It is better to shoot it both ways than not get it right. You cannot duplicate this type of diffusion in printing.

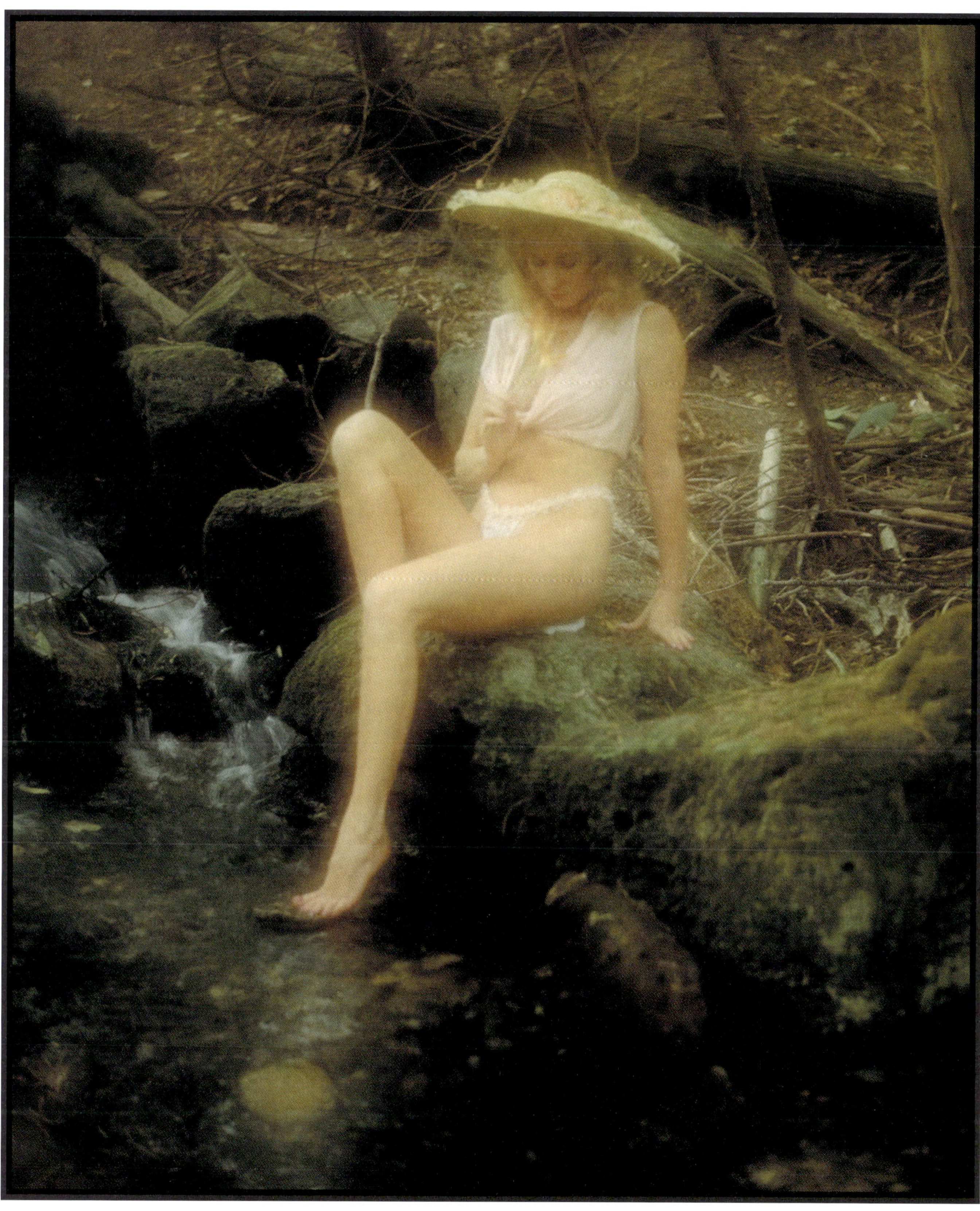

BACKDROP OUTLET
VOL.8
1997
Textured Canvas
PATTERNED MUSLINS
NEW
TRI-FOLD Muslins
Exciting NEW PROPS
MOTTLED
FANTASY CLOTH
More posing extras
PHOTO © ART KETCHUM BACKGROUND SHOWN SAND CASTLE
1-800-466-1755
BACKGROUNDS, PROPS AND STUDIO ACCESSORIES

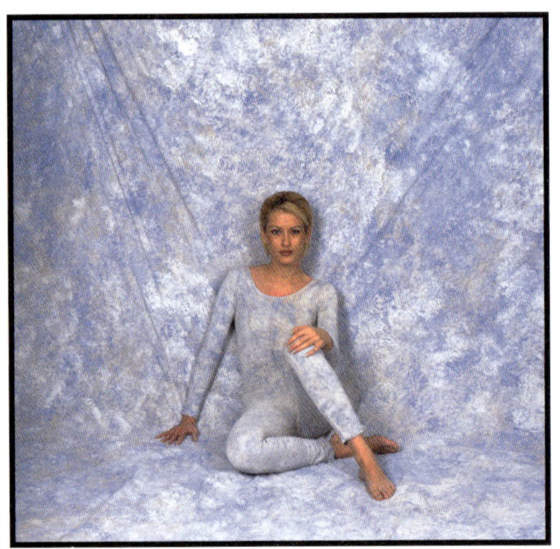

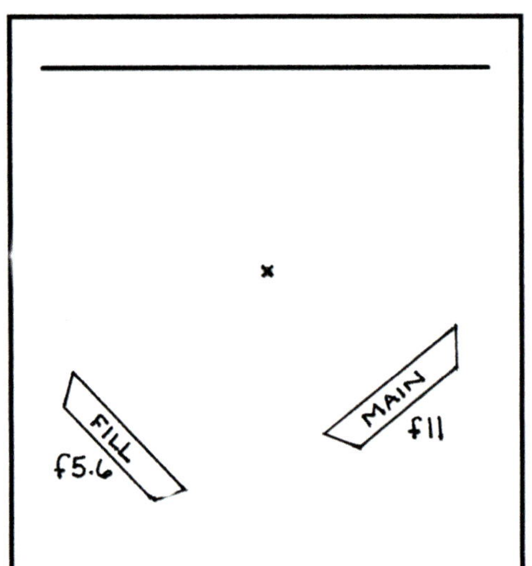

Lighting Diagram for the main image on facing page of Shelly in Chair.

Camoflauge

One of the unique things about the photography profession is that there are those rare people who have a creative eye but are not always capable of creating fine images due to lack of experience and technical know-how.

My daughter,Karen, helps me out with ideas for images. She suggested painting a plain white unitard exactly the same as the background we were planning on using. This would create a continuous monotone effect with only the features of the model standing out. Karen bought two full body unitard's and had the background artist paint the blue background and the unitard so that they both looked alike. The other unitard was a hooded unitard and was painted a mottled tan color in case the blue color did not look good on film. As it turned out, both colors worked beautifully with their matching backgrounds. This shot was used for a cover shot for the Backdrop Outlet catalog, and appeared in hundreds of ads promoting their business.

I knew of a model I had employed previously who would make the image a winner. When Terri arrived, we had her try on the blue unitard. This turned out to be a 5 hour shoot because we had so many different ideas to try. In every shot, the model had to be close to the background to keep the colors the same. If the model were 5 or 6 feet away from the background, then the background would have to be lit with the same intensity as the model or the background would appear darker. due to light fall-off. When I positioned Terri against the background, the blending of the unitard and background looked phenomenal on my polaroid test shots.

Lighting; for the main image on the facing page are two large plume 54"x36" soft boxes with identical White Lightning lights mounted on each light and set for a 4-to-1 light ratio to provide the necessary modeling of light to create depth in the picture. The smaller images of Terri are set for flat lighting, this is necessary so there would be almost no visible shadow, even though the model is next to the background. All of the images illustrated were shot at F:11 at sync speed.

The main image to the right, Shelly in the blue unitard was created in a workshop. I added the vase, chair and flowers painted the same as the background and unitard to create an even more dynamic monochromatic image. I wanted a pose that would add to the total effect and directed Shelly into the pose shown. Using the correct model in a particular shot is the key to making your photography spectacular.

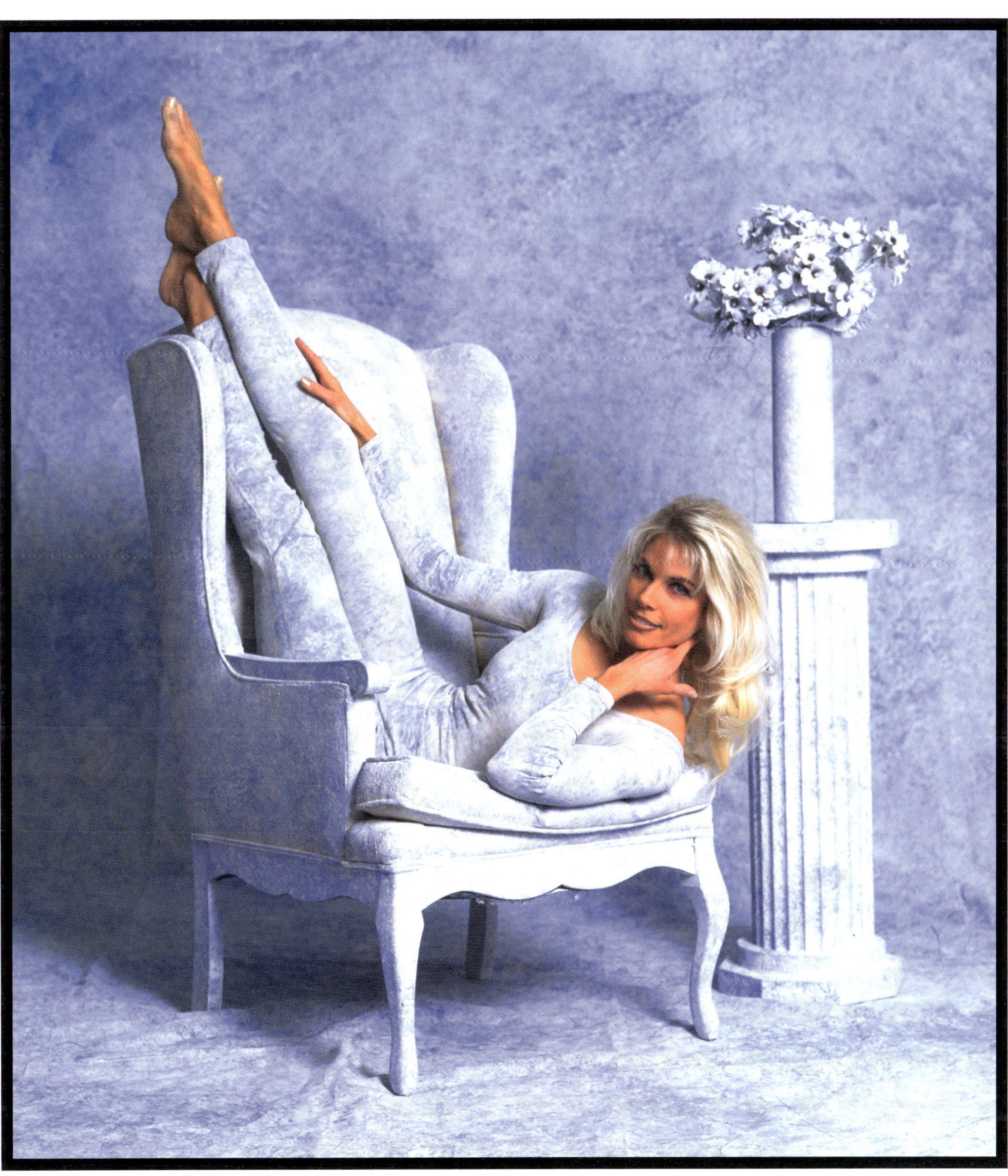

Pensive Window Light

Over the course of 20 years of photographing people, I am always amazed by certain models. Maggie is one of those models who can't take a bad picture. She comes to every shoot with a professionalism and energy that makes it a pleasure to photograph her. I first met Maggie when she found out I provide pictures for models who work in my classes. My first impression of Maggie was that she was just another pretty face, and I did not expect the quality of modeling that I received.

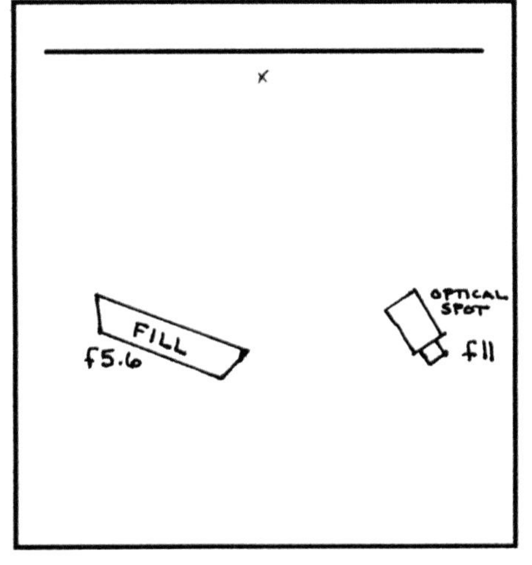

You will find Maggie's images in the Backdrop Outlet catalog and in my portfolio. While I have photographed over a thousand models in my career, I cannot judge a person's photogenic quality by just looking at them. For as many people who I thought would be fantastic, far too many have proved me wrong. They did not emote anything in front of the camera. By the same token, I have met people who are ordinary looking but when a camera is pointed in their direction they take on a new personality. Maggie comes alive on film.

The image of Maggie standing against the wall with her skirt and tied tee shirt was created with two lights; an optical spot projecting the window frame pattern on the background. The spot light metered F:11; a second light or fill light with an umbrella to the left of camera, designed to lighten the shadow area. The fill light was set for F:5.6, two stops lower than the main light.

Creating Sensuality in your Photography

Sensuality is a quality or trait that is difficult to define. Webster's dictionary describes sensuous as appealing to the senses and sensitive to the beauty of others. While I may not always know how to define sensuality in every sense of the word, I do know it when I see it.

Being a talented photographer, understanding lighting and having a beautiful subject in front of your camera is not enough to create sensuous images. When you peruse the images illustrated in this book, you will notice that many subjects have something extra that gives them that elusive quality of sensuality.

Creating a sensual image does not mean having the model or subject expose themselves. It is creating an image that my model and/or my client will be pleased with. Bringing out the sensual side of the subject comes from watching body language, smiles and gestures, and using these sensual traits in your picture taking. A smile can say it all. Body language is displayed all over this book. Especially watch shoulders. As your subject moves their shoulders in various positions, you will see changes in body language and sensuality. Look at the different ways legs can be posed to add sensuality to your finished image.

It is my belief that every person, young or old, male or female, wants to look sensual. It is your mission to create sensuality for them.

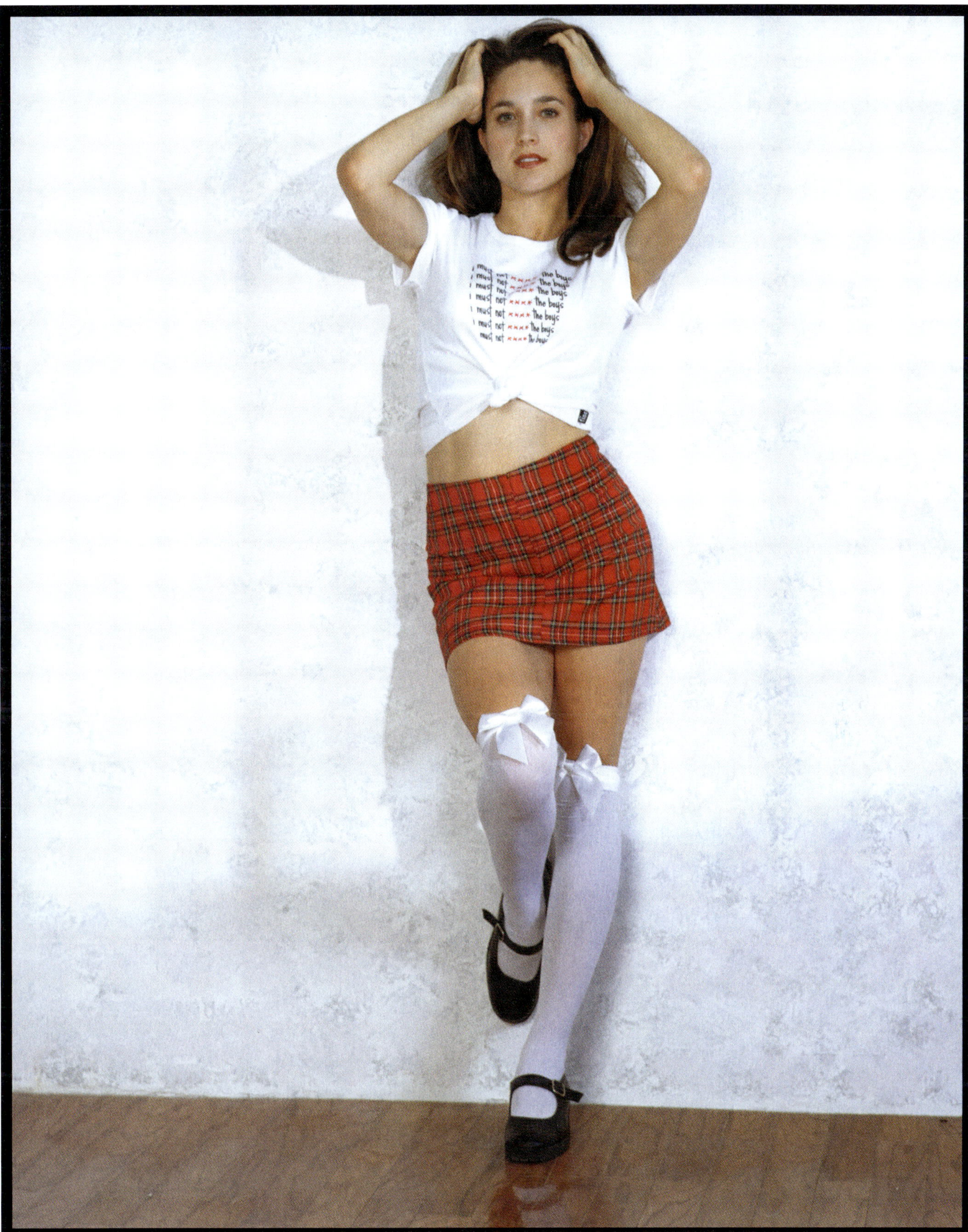
i must not **** the boys
i must not **** the boys
i must not **** the boys
must not **** the boys

A Gentleman's Gentleman

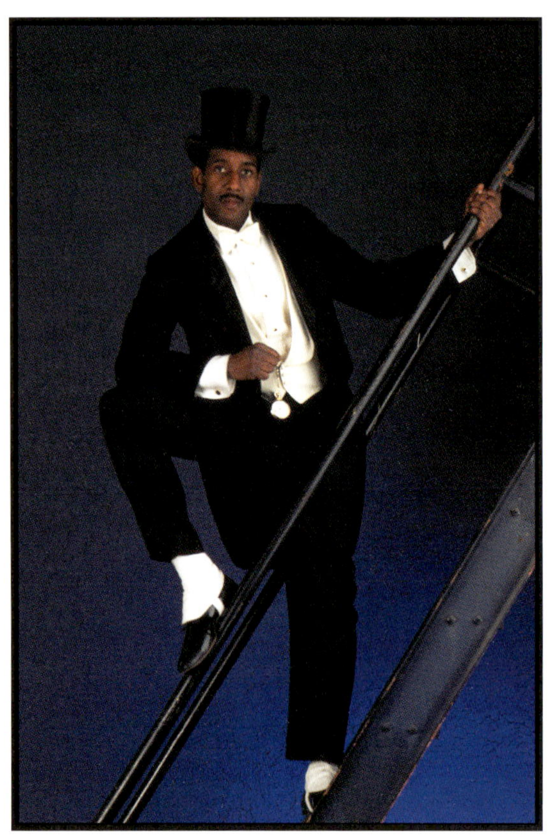

Some of the greatest benefits of being a photographer and writer are meeting other talented photographers and models. A few years ago I had the opportunity to do a workshop for the Professional Photographers of New England in Hartford, Conn. The program was well received, and I came in contact with many photographers who have since become friends.

One particular friendship evolved when I met a photographer from West Springfield, Mass. named Walt Steinmetz who attended my program and acted as my assistant. Walt insisted that I see his studio. I was totally unprepared for how fantastic it was! The studio was located in an industrial neighborhood in West Springfield. When we drove up, I was skeptical. However, the work hanging in the reception area was magnificent. The studio looked like something you would find in New York City like Avedon's, Penn's, or possibly Helmut Newton's studio.

Walt had bought a portion of a railroad work terminal, and it was immense. There were 42' ceilings, lofts everywhere, showrooms for different types of photography, make-up rooms, eight huge shooting bays, along and a syc wall (a built-in continuous white structure with curved walls and floor). Separate sets of lights in each bay with radio remote's enabled Walt to shoot as many as 26 different high school seniors in a day with the help of an assistant reloading film. This was a fantastic studio operation. Most importantly, Walt was a master of the craft of photography.

Walt invited me back the next year to give my workshop in his studio. When I returned, Walt rolled out the red carpet, even contacting models for the workshop. It was a tremendous success!

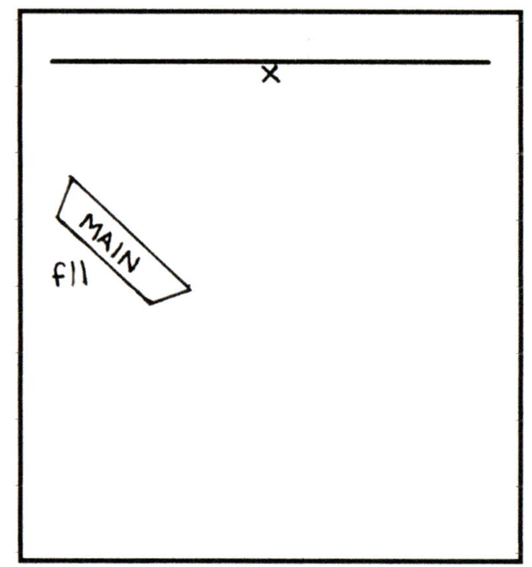

One of the models Walt provided for the workshop was a gentleman named Chauncy. He was as meticulous in his choice of costume as he was in his modeling, a real pro. Chauncy was charming to work with and capable of delivering some of the best modeling I have ever seen.

Chauncy on the brick wall was photographed using one large plume wafer 54"x36" set high and to the left of camera set for F:11. You can create superb images with just one light. The brick wall and Chauncy's outfit work together to make this shot a winner.

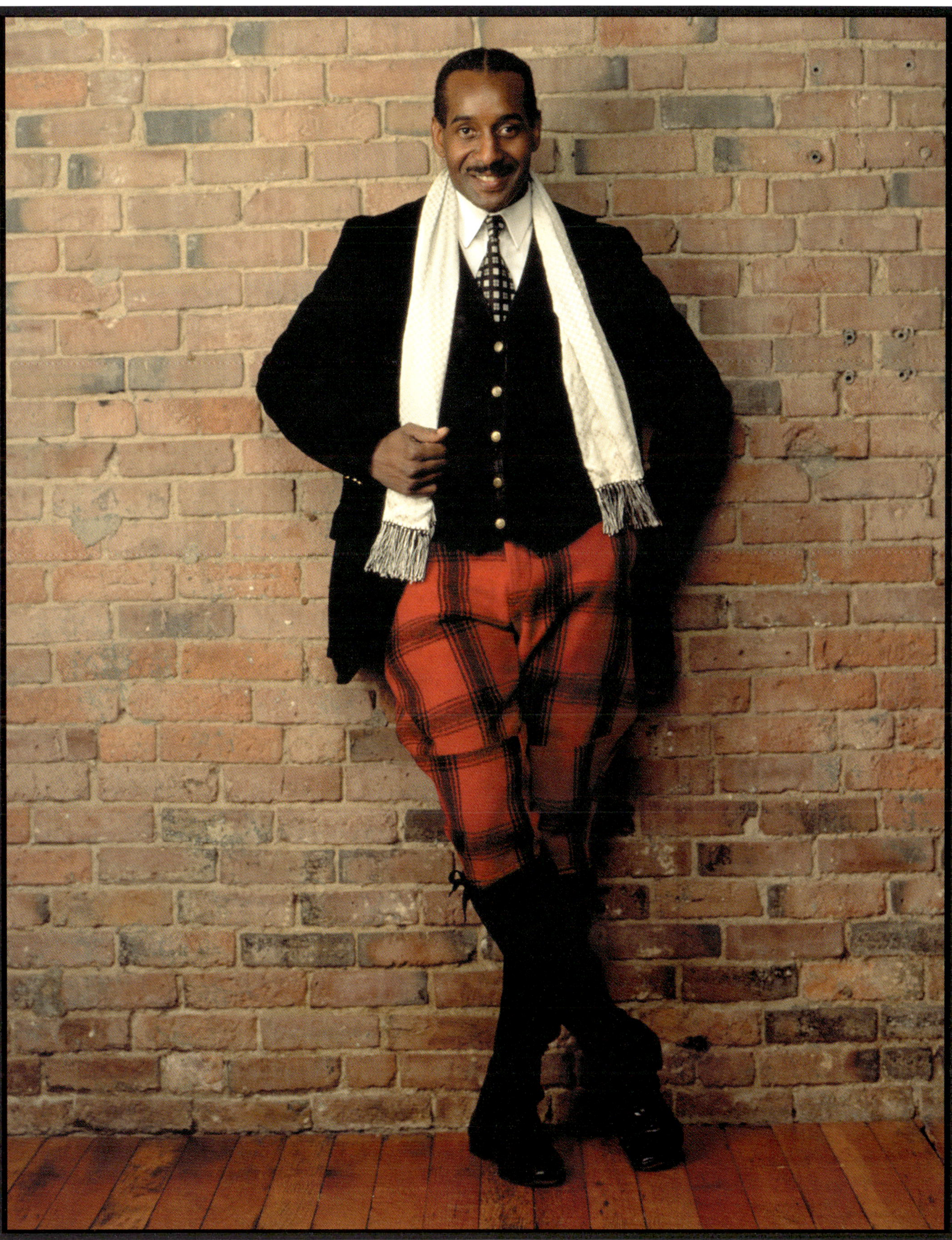

Vibrant Beauty

The high key image of Callan in her black and white outfit was shot as a model portfolio image. Being young, her vibrant beauty shows through in this clean white background shot.

I used a Bowens wind machine to give this image added life. Callan is 15 years old and possesses a natural beauty with excellent features and a magnificent complexion. I have had the opportunity to photograph Callan many times and with good reason as I am her grandfather.

Lighting for the High-key image was a main and fill light each light mounted on large soft boxes,the main light was set for F:11 and the fill-light was set for F:5.6 and 1/2 The 3-to-1 ratio lighting created more pronounced cheekbone and slenderizes arms and legs. The white background is lit with two lights and 30” white umbrellas to the right and left of the background set for F:16 creating a clean white high-key background.

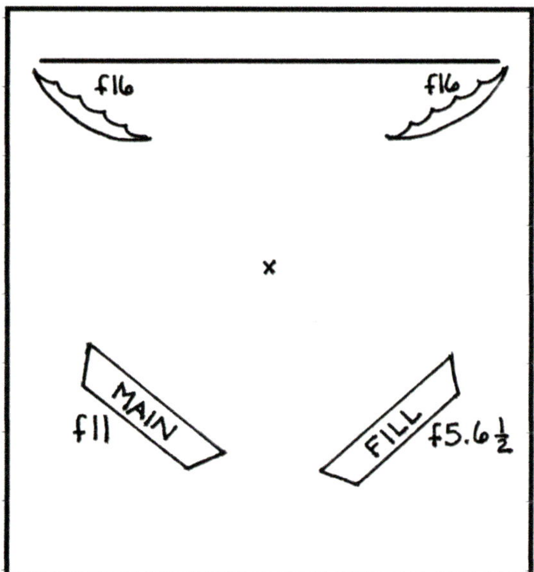

Callan’s face shot on my stucco wall with an optical spot lighting attachment.

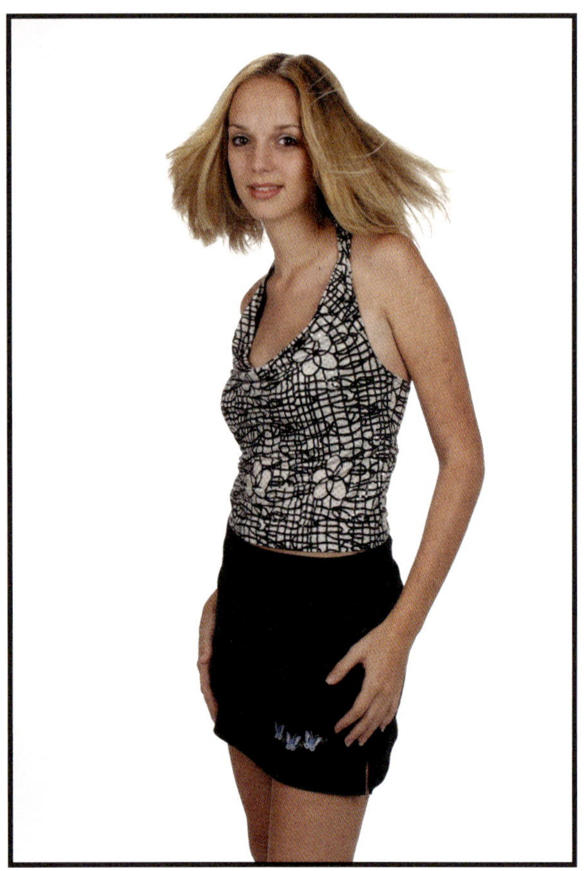

A second image from the same shooting.

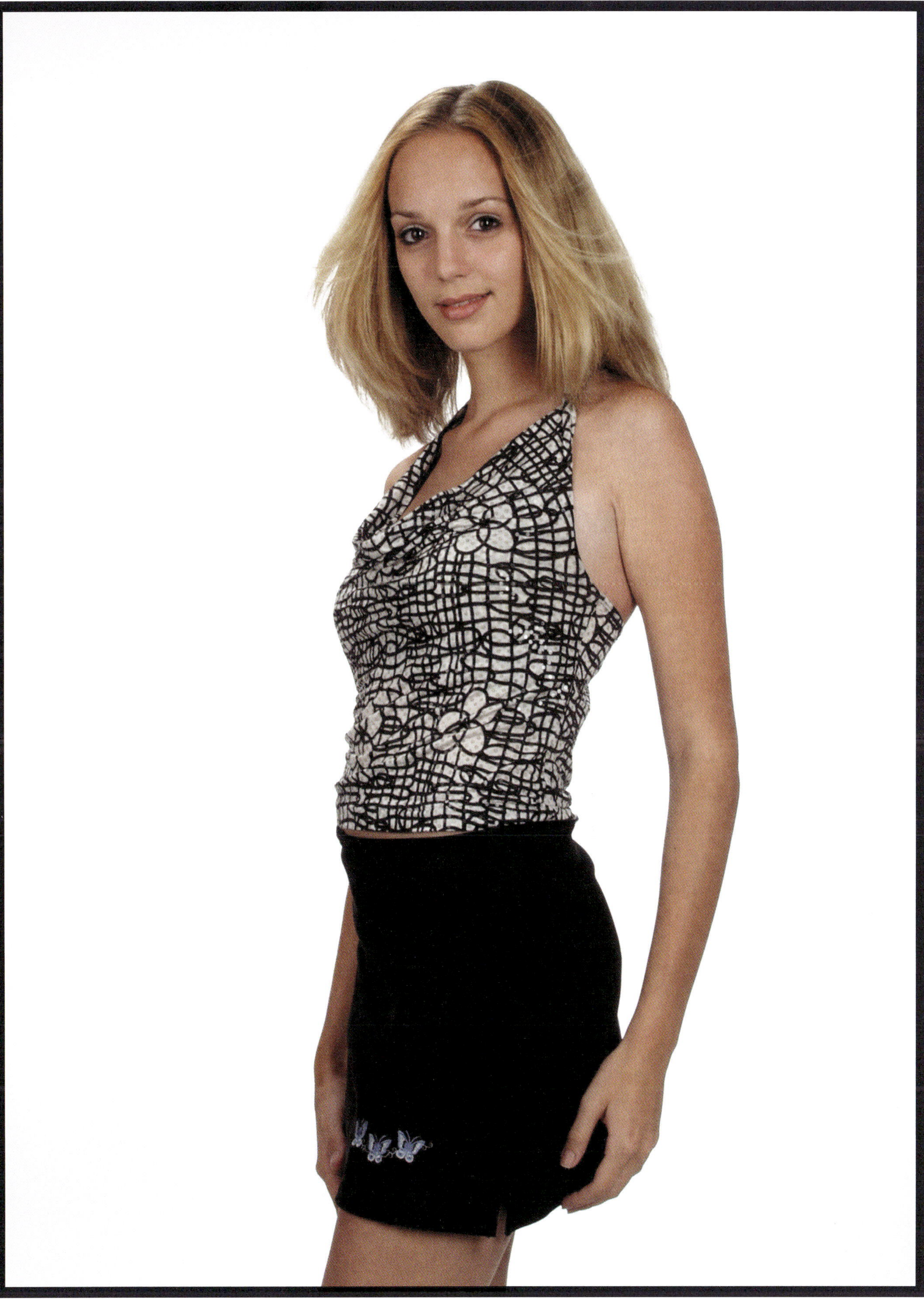

Window Light and Mirror

Several years ago I photographed Meghan and a friend while they modeled in one of my Chicago workshops. They were high school freshmen and amateur in their modeling skills. Recently, Meghan called to ask if I would photograph her again because she wanted to rekindle her modeling career. When Meghan came in, I was surprised at her newfound confidence and potential as a model.

I discussed some image ideas with Meghan, and she was eager to try them. Being 5'10" tall, Meghan is an excellent candidate for doing poses that show her in runway situations, as that is how most agencies would want to employ her modeling talents.

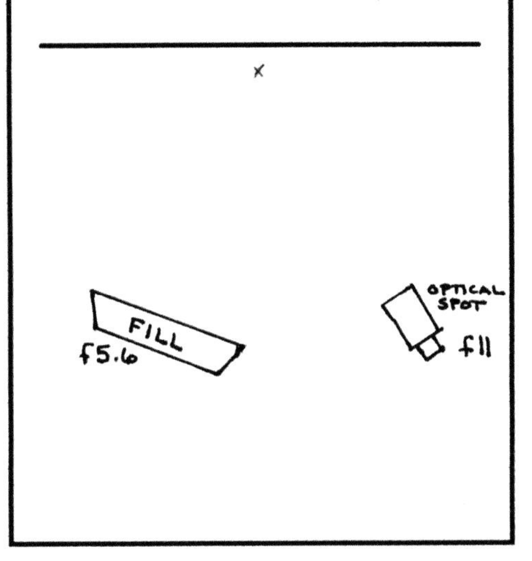

I wanted to create dynamic images that would make the talent agencies take notice of Meghan and of my work. I decided that Meghan in the black dress would look good in a natural room setting. By positioning Meghan on the floor with the mirror beside her, I created the feeling that she was in a real room, not a studio. Even though the shot was created on one of my studio sets, I decided to use a two light set-up with the optical spot and a window pattern set for F:11 with a second light (fill) set to F:5/6 and a half for a 3 to 1 ratio. The reason for the fill light was to lighten the shadow areas so they would not go black but would turn out a more pleasing gray tone. The pose was dramatically diagonal and leggy. I tried many different poses but ultimately selected the one you see illustrated here.

The Lab Connection

The most important relationship any good photographer can make in building a successful photographic career, is to establish a Lab Connection. Through all the years I have been a photographer I understand the need for a strong relationship with my photo lab. When you establish this relationship with your photo lab, you have the opportunity to see first hand how all of the photographic processes works.

When I shoot a commercial job for a client I want to know my lab is looking out for me and making me look my best. My lab provides me with the services I need to keep my clients happy. I can drop film off at my lab in the evening and within a couple of hours pick up my finished transparencies. I can check with Rich, the lab manager and see the charts of the film processing tolerances for any particular time within that day.

This is the kind of service that always makes me look professional, and allows me to shoot with the peace of mind to know I always have a team of professionals behind me. Whatever type of film I shoot, black & white, color transparency, color negative or digital imaging I can rely on my lab to produce the best possible end product to make my job easier and make my clients happy.

My lab in in Chicago is: Imperial Color 219 N. Carpenter St. Chicago, IL.60607. (312)421-3338. Call or write them for a listing of the type of services they provide. Also look for a lab in your area that is professional and capable of taking your photography to a higher level of professional excellence.

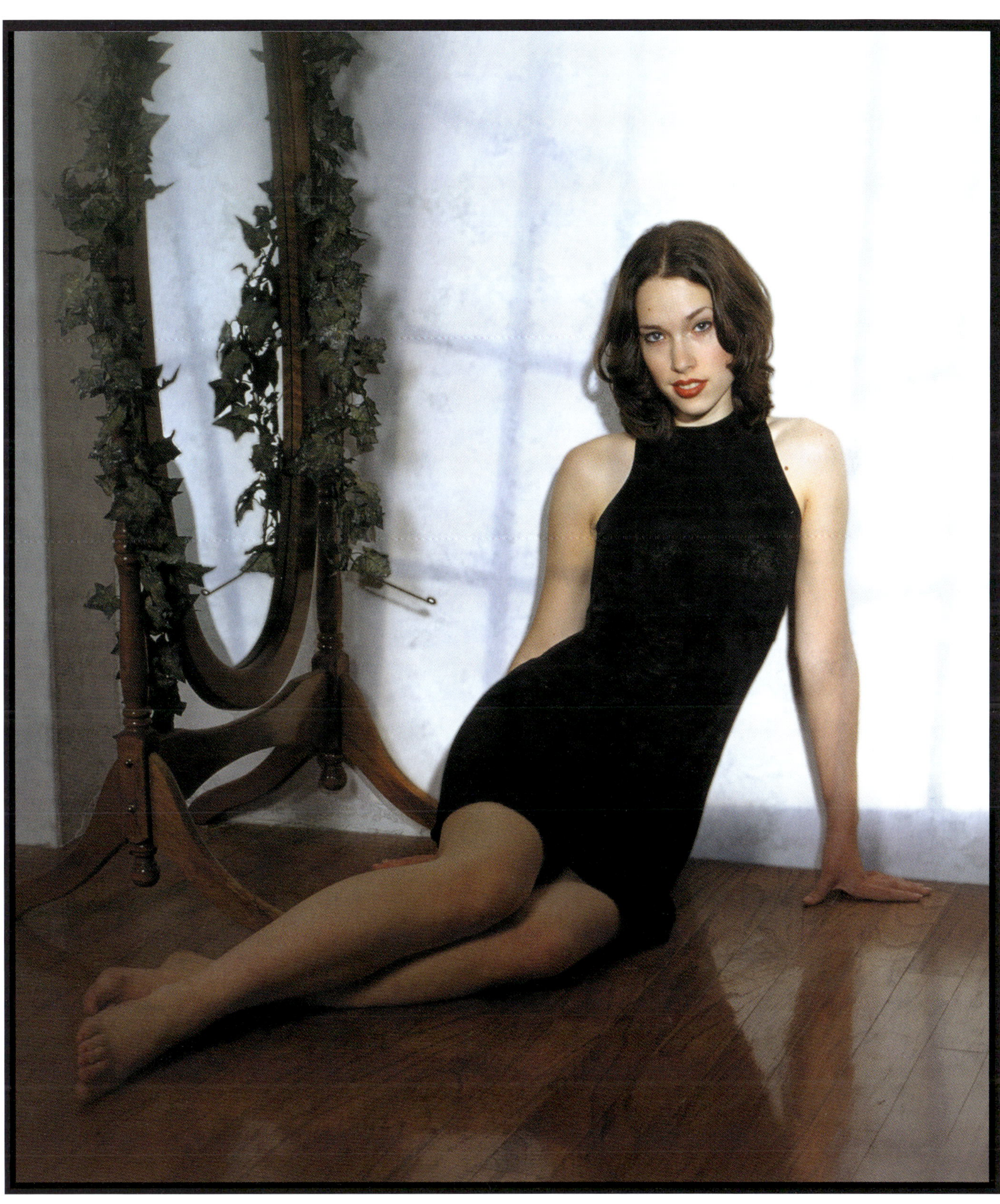

Classic Beauty

After shooting with Meghan on two different occasions, I suggested we do some artistic images that would be used in a new book I was doing on the female figure, as long as the images would not be too revealing.

I wanted Meghan's face to appear angelic in this artistic image, not provocative.. The shot was to be sensual and tasteful. The key to making an image like this work is the lighting, and your choice of model with the correct face and figure.

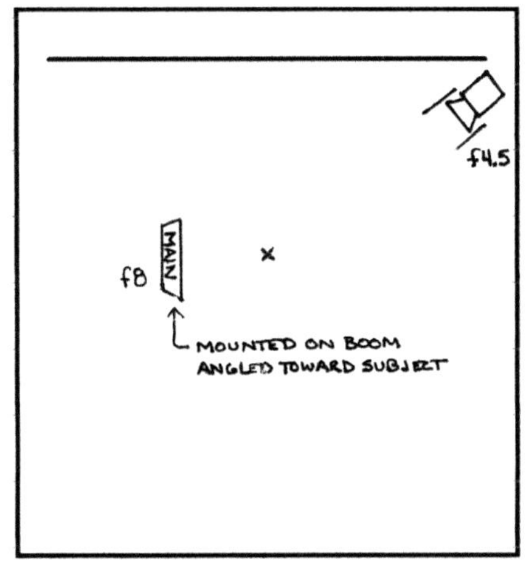

The important light in this image, is the rim light. This light brightens Meghan's hair and her back side. The rim light was a White Lightning X1600 with barn doors. This placed the light where I wanted it and prevented it from reflecting into the lens of my camera creating unwanted flare. The rim light was placed 45 degrees behind the subject aimed at her back side. The key is to set this light one and one half stops lower than the the main light. Main light F:8, Rim light F:4.5. The main light is a White Lightning X-2400 with my small Balcar Prisma-Lite soft box with honeycomb grid mounted 2 feet over the models face. The main light lighted the face and hair. This same light being set high over the models face would fall-off as the distance from light to subject increased to create less light on the arms and body.

Choosing and Utilizing Backgrounds

Choosing a background is as important to your photography as the film is to your camera. I take pride in trying to choose a background that will add excitement to the image I am trying to create. In past years I would use background paper to create different effects from using white paper for high-key images to using colors including black and all shades of gray. Any background that is well chosen for the particular subject you are shooting can greatly enhance your finished image.

Today I use all types of fabric backgrounds; Muslin for its versatility and wide variety of choices available; sheer is one of my favorites for its filmy, cloudlike quality, and is available in 9'x21' sizes and can be combined with other colors, lighted with colored gels and is translucent for greater depth in your photography. Sheer can also be used in front of a muslin background for creating a totally different look. Sheer is available from Backdrop Outlet Co in dozens of colors and is quite reasonable in price.

Fantasy cloth, velveteen,mylar,lace,sheared,vinyl,theatre drapes and metallic's are all alternative backgrounds that are inexpensive and will change your photos dramatically. The one thing about fabric backgrounds that appeals to me is their portability and reluctance to scuff or stain from usage.

The more often you change backgrounds in photographing different subjects, the more creativity in your finished images. The same rules apply in outdoor photography. Changes in backgrounds will make your images look new and exciting.

Any background can be made to look different by placing your subject at various distances from the background. The further the subject is from the background, The darker the background appears to the eye. I generally shoot with my subject about 6 feet from the background.

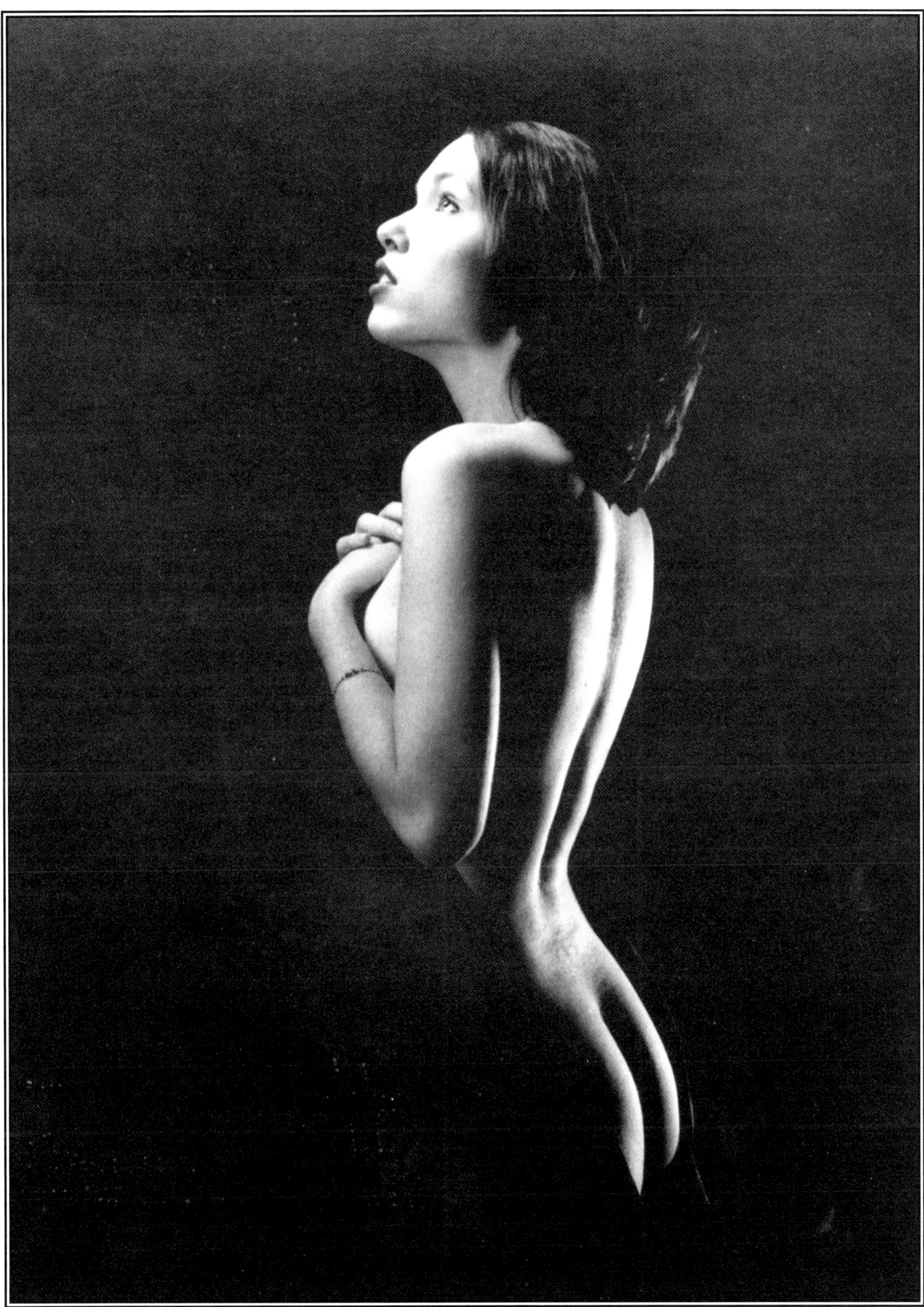

Savannah Cotton Exchange

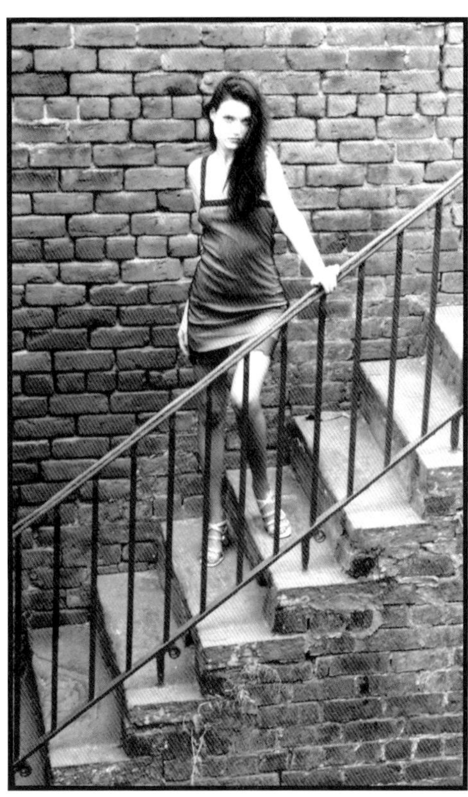

The image of Elizabeth in front of the Savannah Cotton Exchange is one of my favorites. During the process of creating this image, all the elements fell into place perfectly.

I found Savannah an absolute delight, a photographers dream location! I met a talented local photographer and asked him if he knew of any models who would model for me, as I had an extra day to spend before returning to Chicago.

I was referred to Elizabeth, who agreed to model. I asked her to bring clothing that she could model on the streets and in the alleys of Savannah. I wanted high fashion...something that was sexy and a little "bitchy". My assistant and I set up in many different locations, but in my opinion the Cotton Exchange was the best location. Although Elizabeth was not exceptionally tall, the illusion of height was obtained with the help of a wide angle lens and a low camera angle. This image was photographed with a Hasselblad Superwide camera. This camera has a built-in 38mm lens on a 2 1/4 square format camera. The superwide is a great architectural or scenic camera but can be used for shoots such as this.

When using wide angle lenses to create fashion images, it is not always possible to throw the background out of focus. I recommend choosing backgrounds that will not detract from your image. One of the things that make Savannah such a perfect city for photography is that wherever you turn in Old Town Savannah, there is a completely different background. With all the trees, the lighting at high noon is still soft and highly reflective with all the buildings bouncing light around.

We set up a photoflex reflector (silver) approximately 6 to 8 feet in front of Elizabeth to pump some additional light into her face. The end result is the image you see illustrated on the next page. We worked with the posing and lighting to ultimately create this leggy fashionable shot. Everything clicked in this amusing shooting to create an image that worked for both Elizabeth's portfolio and my book.

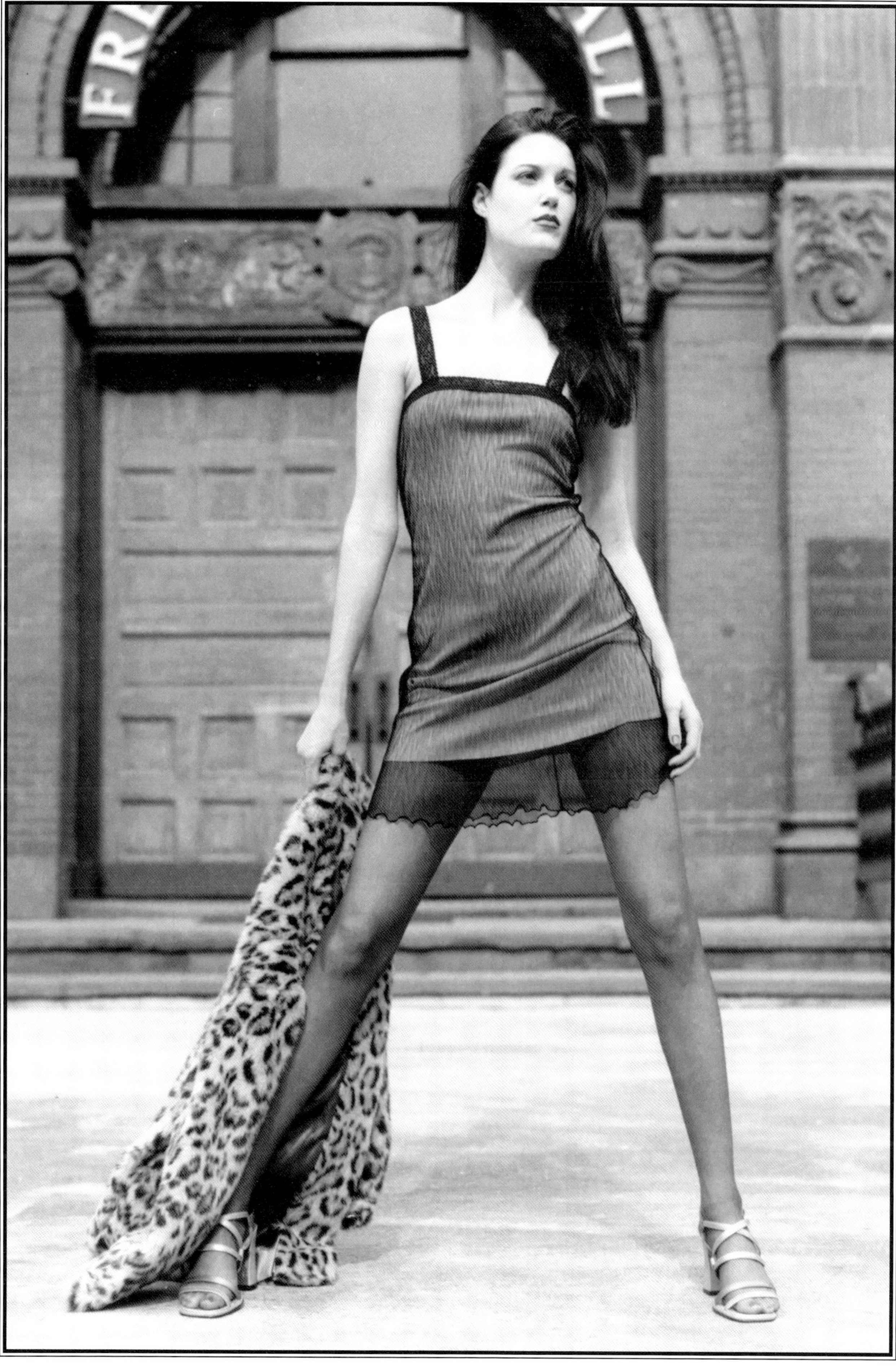

Nashville Naturals

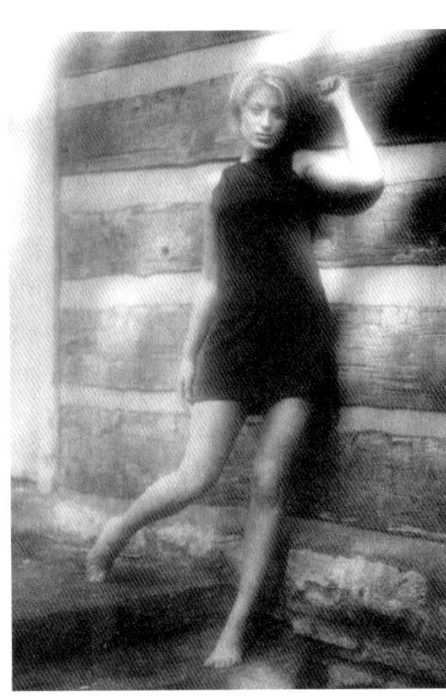

Kari-Lynn in the same shooting location as model on facing page. Black & White 100 ISO film with mild diffusion filter and photoflex reflector to brighten the face.

Of all the workshops I do across the United States, one of my all-time favorites is Nashville, Tennessee. First of all, the location is a one day drive from Chicago. Secondly, the city is a very friendly, beautiful place with true southern charm. Finally, Nashville is the home of White Lightning and my friend, Michael Harvey. Michael is marketing manager for White Lightning and one of the finest people I have had the pleasure to do business with. I have been a user of White Lightning products long before I ever started doing workshops and have had the opportunity to find out what this company was all about. They have been one of the most reputable, honest companies I have ever dealt with. White Lightning makes an excellent product and backs up every claim with quality and service.

With all the different brands of lighting equipment out there, why choose White Lightning? I can offer two reasons. The first is that they manufacture mono lights (no power packs). Reliability and quality are exceptional. The second is the configuration of the accessory part of the light. All Balcar accessories fit the White Lightning lights. This means there are more accessories that can fit this light than any other electronic flash made.

Going back to my first workshop in Nashville, I had the opportunity to work with an excellent model named Kari-Lynn. Later, Kari-Lynn opened her own talent and modeling agency. She now provides me with the talent I use for my workshops in Nashville. Kari-Lynn is one of those rare people who is an excellent model and a delightful person to deal with professionally.

The model on the facing page was provided by Kari-Lynn and was photographed with natural light using photoflex reflectors to add fill light as was the case in all of our outdoor shots in this location.

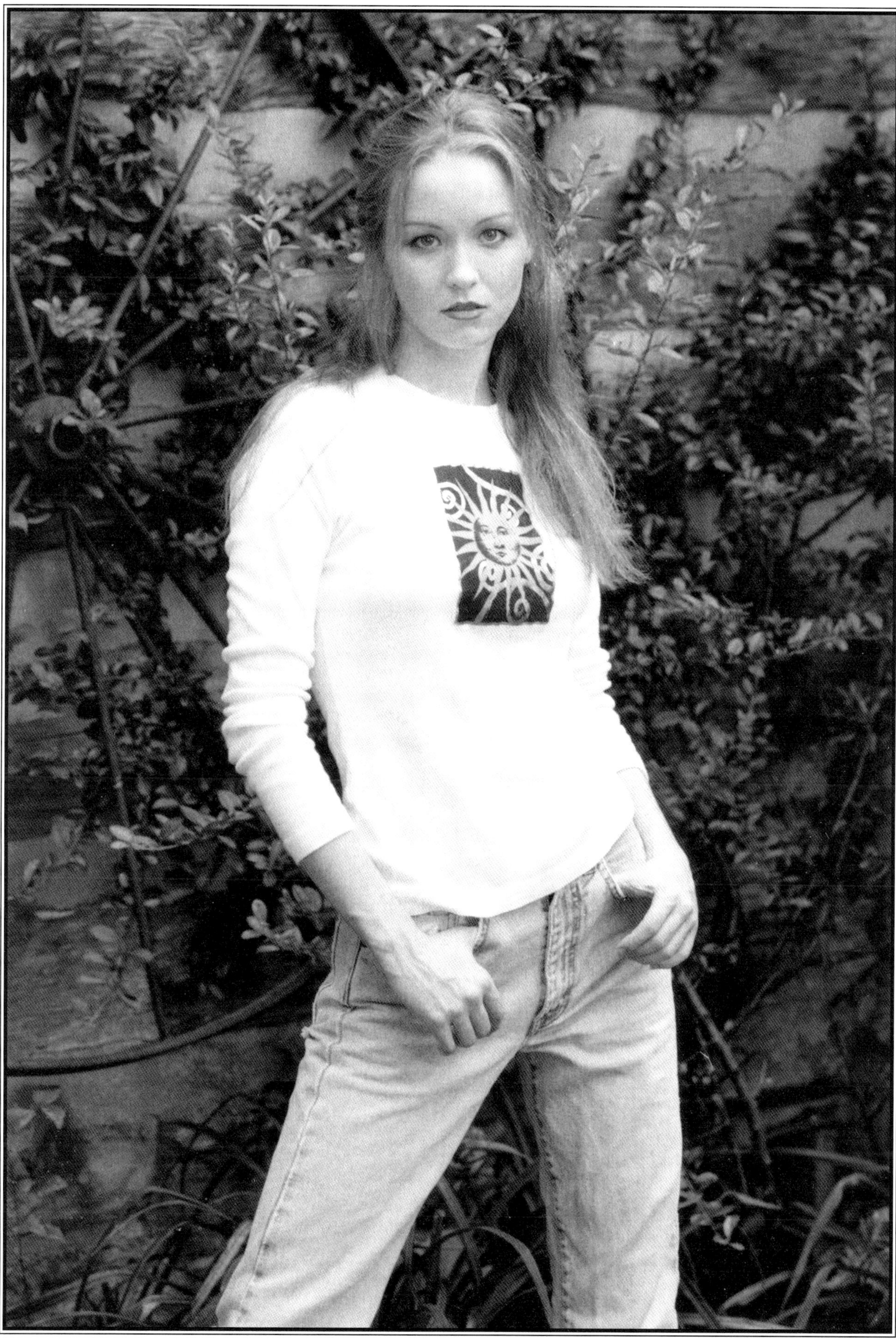

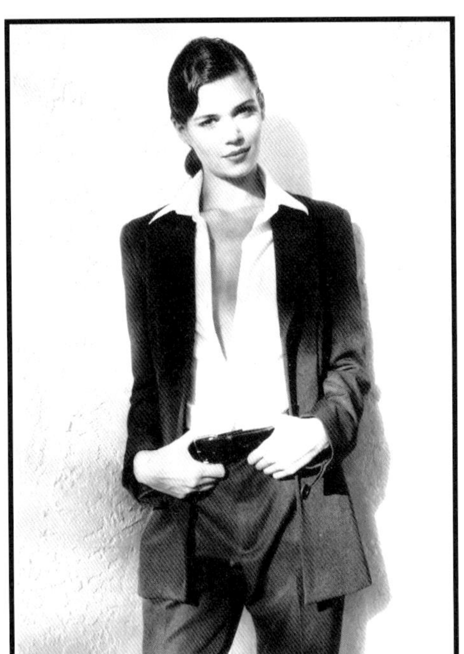

Orlando Hi-Fashion Diva

The model illustrated on the facing page was photographed during a workshop I was conducting in Orlando, Florida. She was provided by one of the top fashion agencies in Florida. Lighting in this image was totally natural light. The light bouncing off the white stucco walls created beautiful soft natural light in mid-day sun. The stucco walls created a natural high key outdoor lighting situation. The model's beauty makes this image work. Additionally, I chose to tilt the camera to add the diagonal dynamics that make the shot more interesting.

Building an Extraordinary Portfolio

As photographers, we tend to idolize the famous people shooters like the many names you read about in photo and fashion magazines. One of the reasons we think these photographers are as talented as they are is that they shoot the most beautiful women in the world. I would be interested to see how they handle the overweight real estate agent who needs a promotional photograph. What about the bald 65 year-old man who needs a new image for his corporate brochure? If you saw those images, I doubt you would be as impressed with the photographer's talent.

Please notice that this book is made up of beautiful people. You will not find unattractive people in this book. As I know from many years of experience in promoting my work, I show only the very best. Displaying only beautiful people in your work makes for an impressive portfolio. Each year I photograph from 100 to 150 models, but few find it to the pages of my portfolio. As I wrote in an earlier section of this book, you need the most stunning people you can find to create an award winning portfolio.

It is not hard to shoot the girl next door. Your family and friends will think you are talented. But an outstanding portfolio is achieved by shooting exceptional people. Look for the most photogenic people you can and your work will stand out as extraordinary. Average people do not make for extraordinary portfolios. Take a look at fashion magazines. Do you see average girls? NO! You will see people who are as perfect as humanly possible. When scanning these magazines, you may look at a shot and see imperfections. We can't all be perfect. Sometimes an art director for a fashion or beauty magazine will see differently than you or me. But look at the beautiful models in the Victoria Secret catalog. Then look at the shots you took of the neighbor girl and see if she compares to the models in the VS catalog.

The point I am trying to make is it is not wrong to shoot average people. We live in a world of average people. Both you and I want to make these people look as good as we can. We can manipulate lighting, provide flattering outfits, use diffusion to enhance the image. But unless you are a plastic surgeon, you cannot change someone's face, add height, or take off unwanted pounds.

You can create a fantastic portfolio by looking for and photographing the most photogenic talented people you can find.

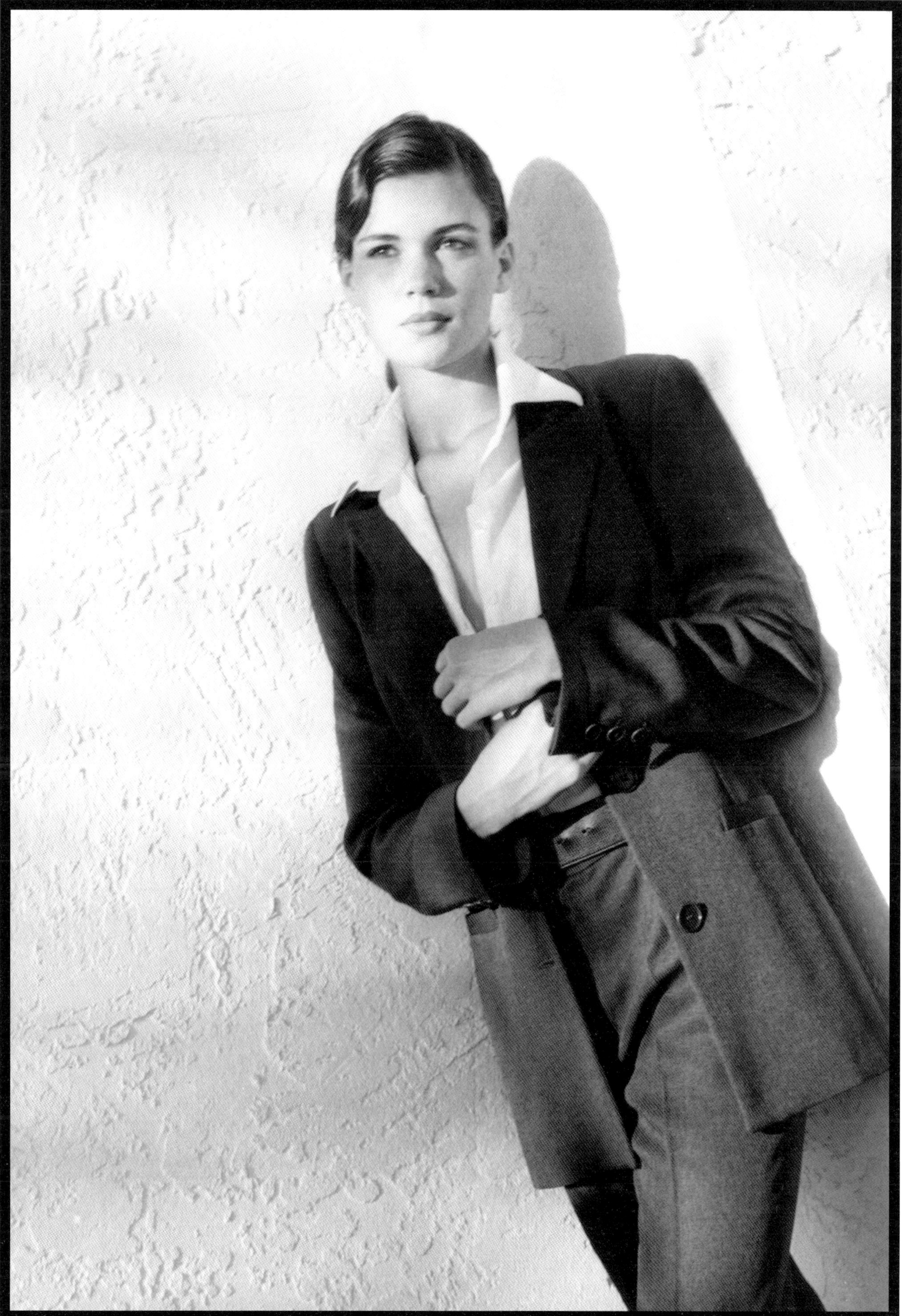

The Catsuit

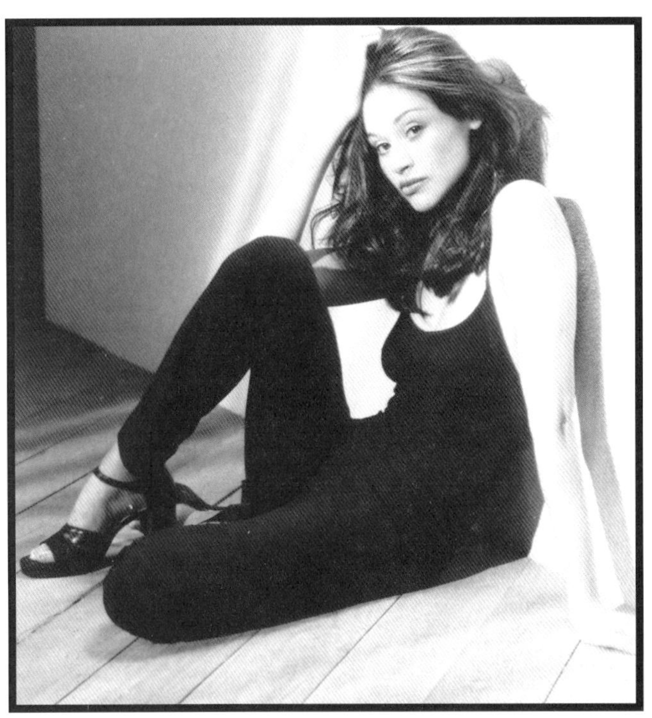

Recently the director of one of the leading talent agencies in Chicago asked me if I was interested in testing a new girl she had just listed. I agreed to have the model come over to my studio after the talent agent told me they were looking for fashion images for her book (portfolio). I suggested that Corrinne, the model, call me and set a time for our test shooting.

When Corrinne arrived, I was impressed. She definitely had the look, the height and was beautiful. My first thought was that Corrinne would be a flattering addition to my portfolio. When someone like Corrinne arrives for a shooting, I want to put in more effort because I know many people will see her book and therefore, my work. Also, she is the type of model who makes a photographer look talented, as her look is similar to the models you see in fashion magazines.

I decided to shoot Corrinne in her catsuit because I felt that the outfit, her dark hair, and her white skin made for a study in contrasts. Contrast makes black and white photography come alive. However, beware of using high contrast lighting with an average person. It can be disastrous! Setting up the optical spot as a main light with a random pattern cookie in it, I projected a pattern of light on Corrinne and added a fill light to lighten shadow areas. The fill was set two stops lower than the main light. I wanted a strong head shot that showed Corrinne's beautiful face and another shot showing her figure. The two photos illustrated here represent the images that I thought came out the best.

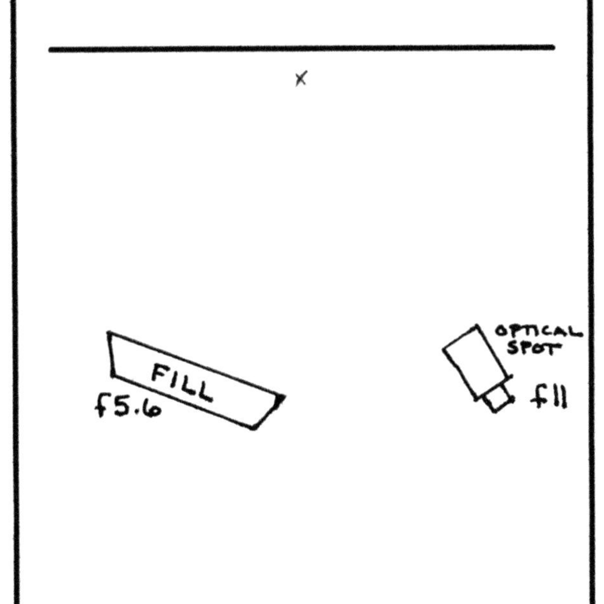

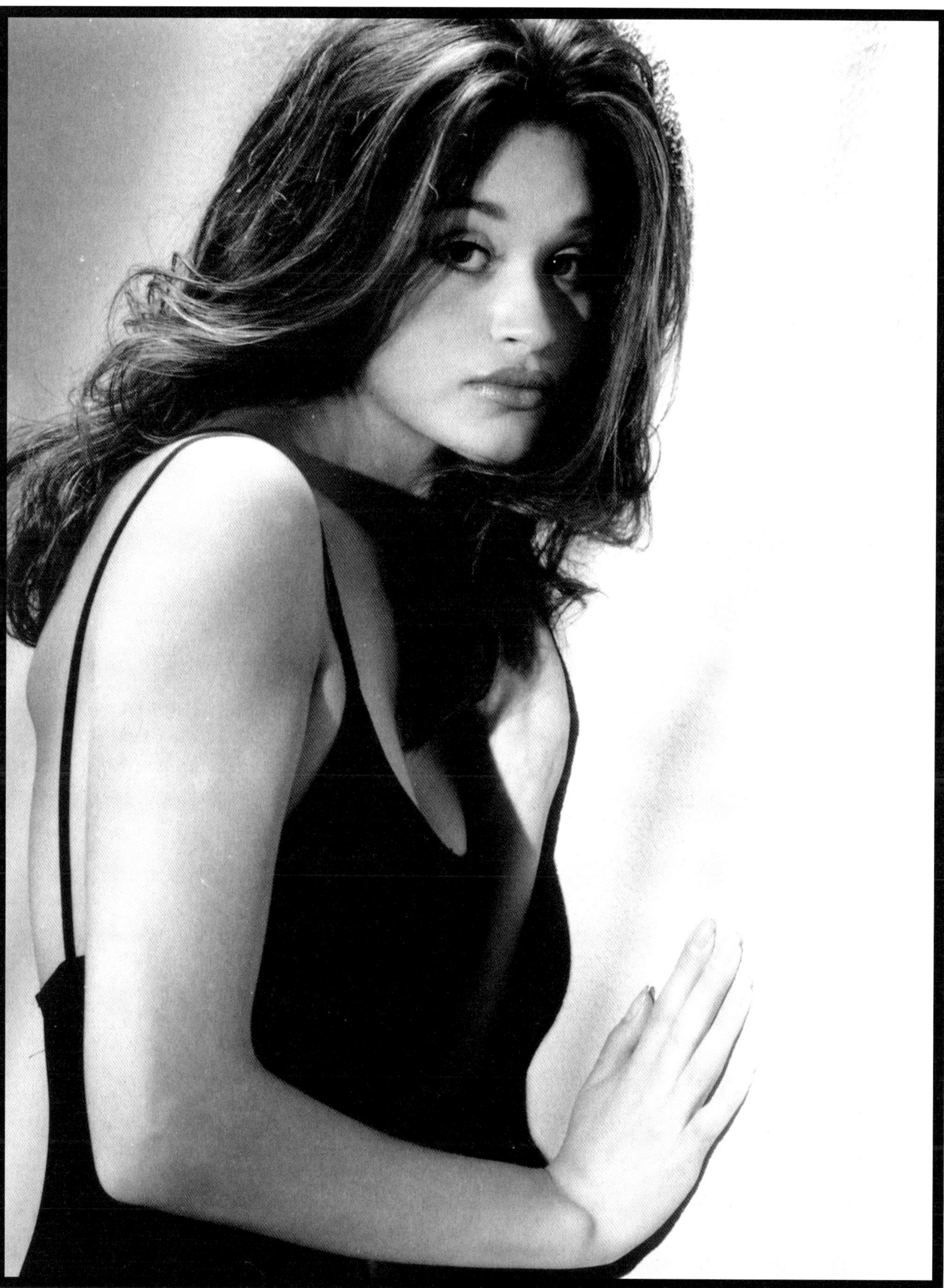

Stripes

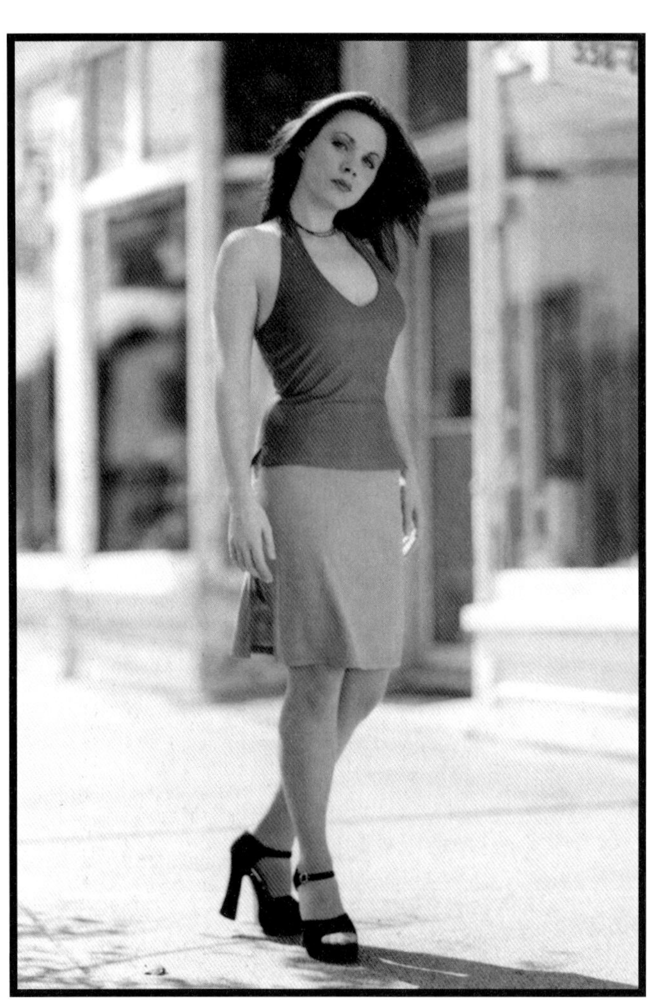

The image of Sabrina on the main street of Chincoteague was shot with Leica 90mm lens at 1/1000 at F:4 with a dark yellow filter to increase contrast.

Of all the cameras I own, (and I have more than I can easily count), my all-time favorite camera is my Leica M-6 because it is quiet, totally unobtrusive, and allows me to shoot in available light under extreme conditions. No camera feels or shoots like a Leica. While I was doing a workshop in Chincoteague, Virginia, in a make-shift studio that Bill Lemon (our assistant) Spencer and I had set up in a hotel meeting room, I noticed Sabrina leaning against a wall while waiting her turn to model. I could not resist grabbing my Leica and shooting about 15 frames in various poses. The Leica is always loaded with Ilford HP-5, ISO 400 film, and one of the examples from this quick, on-the-spot shooting is illustrated here.

Sabrina's face is her greatest asset. While she is not tall or busty, she is absolutely gorgeous. Using the Leica with Sabrina is a natural marriage as it allows me to shoot at high shutter speeds. With the aperture in an open position like F:1.4 or F:2, I can obtain high quality results. This image was shot at 1/500th at F:2 under natural light with all the midday lighting bouncing off the white walls, creating natural, gleaming light. No additional reflectors or fill flash were necessary.

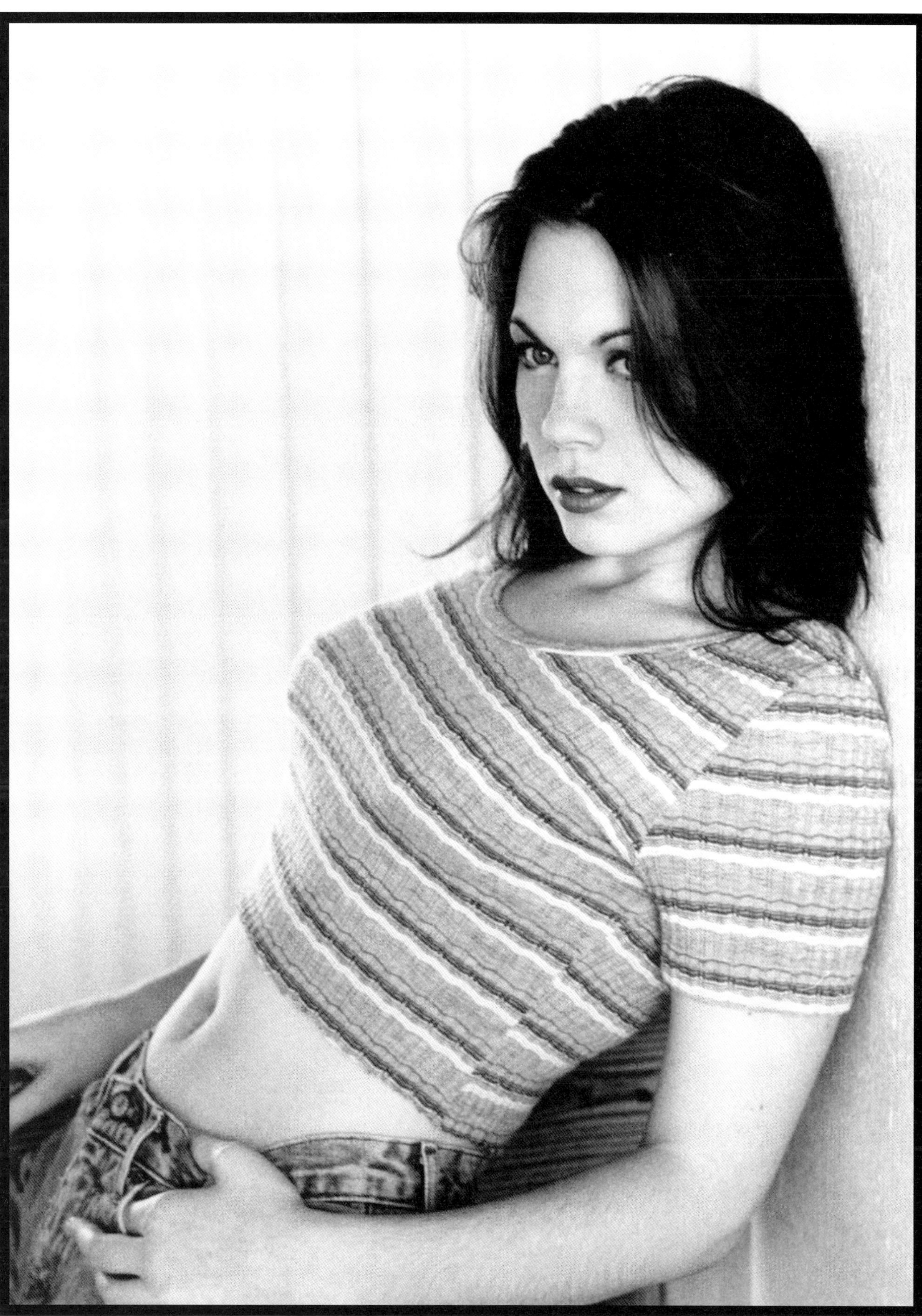

Fire

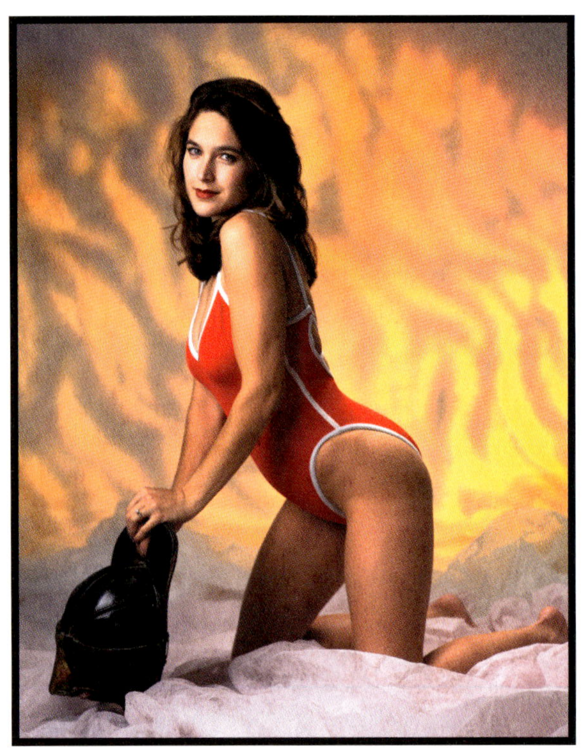

Maggie wearing the bathing suit with the fireman's helmet is one of my favorite images. The background I set up with the optical spot created a feeling of flames, giving the image extra punch. Ratio lighting (3 to 1) gave a bare arm and leg more definition and created a thin body. Flat lighting will add weight to a model. Be careful with two front lights set for equal intensity as it is not a flattering light when your subject is wearing something small like a bathing suit. In this case, the background was lit separately from the subject.

Lighting: Main light set to the left of camera using a large plume wafer set to F:8; fill-light set to the right of camera using an umbrella set to F:4 & 1/2, for a 3-to-1 light ratio. Hair light using a balcar prisma-light soft box with honeycomb grid set two stops brighter than the main light for F:16 because of the black hat. Note: the light on shoulders created by the hair light gives a sunlight effect. Background was lit with the optical spot using a cookie with flame cut-out. I also used a red gel on the optical spot to light the yellow background to creating the background colors in this image.

Photographed with a Hasselblad and 110mm lens.

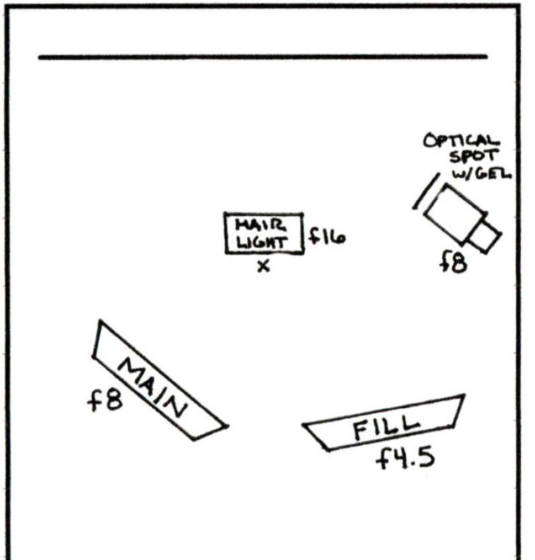

Bag of Tricks

I have learned that all talented photographers have a bag of tricks. The more you know and the little things you do to create a superb image are part of your bag of tricks.

I carry certain filters with my camera at all times. One of those filters is a warming filter. It is my belief that when you are shooting a caucasian person and showing a large amount of skin, as in bathing suit or lingerie photography, that person will look better with more skin color. This is an easy accomplishment with an 81A, 81B, or 81C filter. I find the 81A and 81B work best to give a white person some flattering skin color. This is one of the filters that is an absolute must in my bag of tricks. I have met many wedding photographers who use the 81A when shooting the bride and many times leave it on the camera for all of their shooting. Most people appreciate the warmth of this sensational filter.

When shooting Black,Hispanic, or Olive toned subjects, this filter is not necessary.

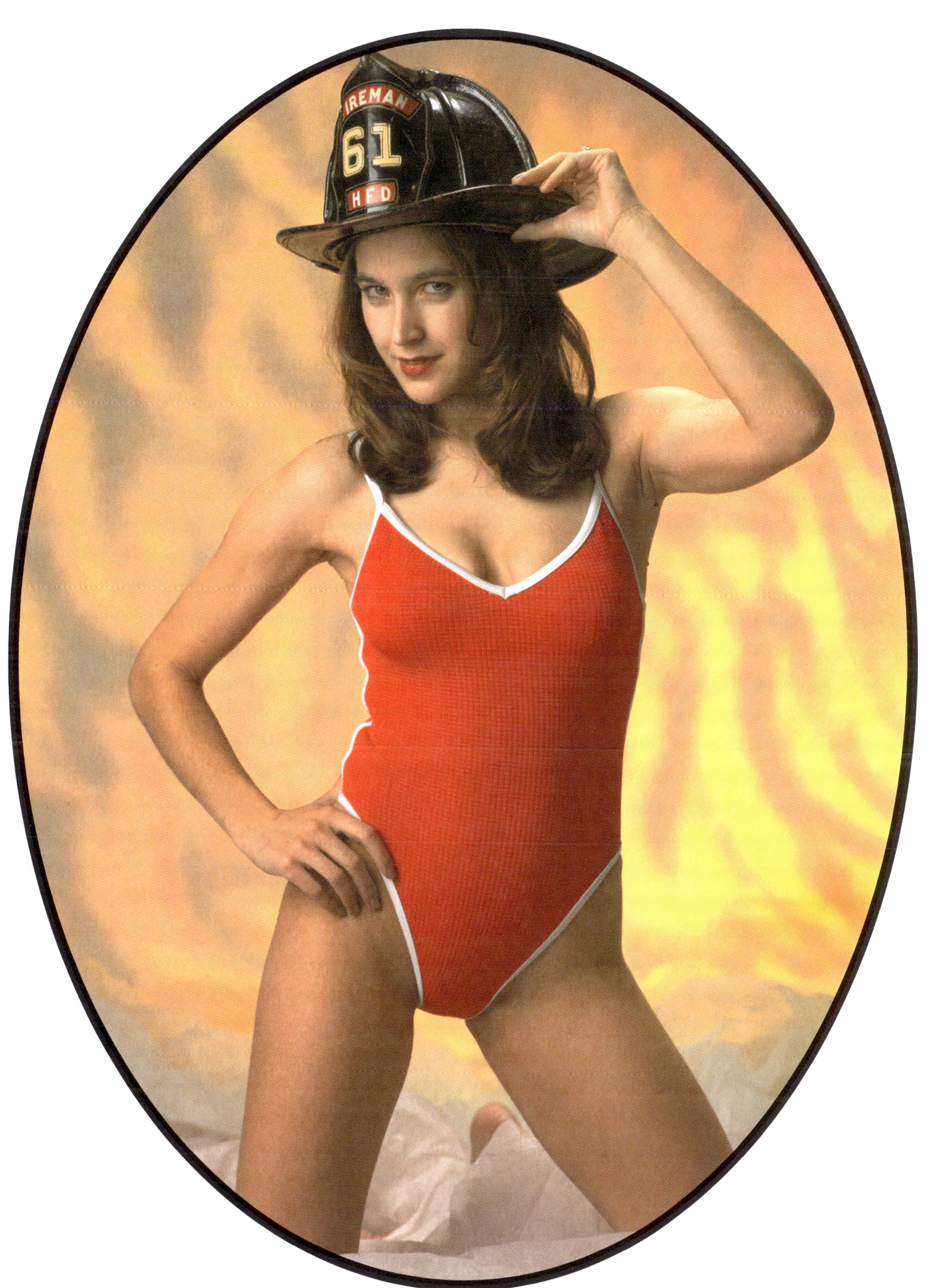
IREMAN
61
HFD

Reflections

Blake is an exceptional model. She is a talented dancer and model who I met while shooting a dance catalog. Blake needed some new images for her portfolio, so we decided to do a lingerie shot for her and for my book.

I wanted to include a newly purchased mirror in the shot. I set up the mirror in the background to reflect the rear side of Blake. I also used a fabric-covered screen with a few accessories. We had the ingredients for some spectacular images. I used a magenta gel over my background light to create the hot pink background and another magenta gel on a small light, lighting the fabric-screen.

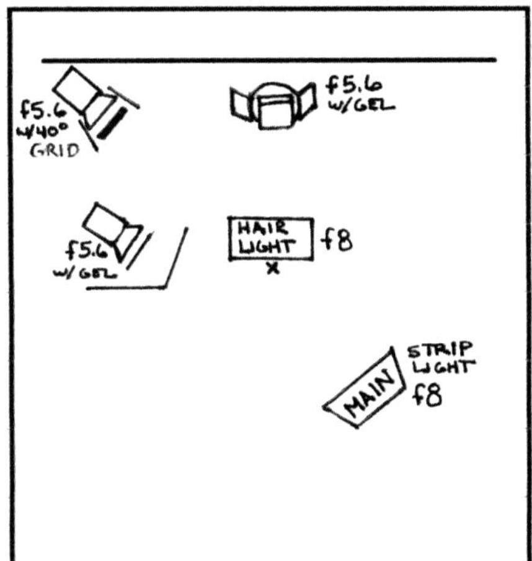

Five light set-up; Main light was a large plume wafer strip light soft box to the right of camera set for F:8. The white fabric screen next to the model created a fill light with the main bouncing light off the screen, creating a 2 to 1 lighting ratio on Blake. A rim light was set with a 7" reflector and 40 degree grid set for F:5.6 created the glow on the right side of Blake's body. A 7"reflector with magenta gel was aimed at the background and set for F:5.6. The fourth light was a small and inexpensive backlight combo light with a magenta gel to light the fabric screen to the right of the model. Set for F:5.6. The fifth light was my standard small softbox hairlight set for F:11. *Backlight combo light is available from Backdrop Outlet.*

Diffusion

Over the course of many years of instructing in my photographic workshops and seminars, I have noticed photographers have a reluctance to using diffusion filters on their lenses.

I mentioned elsewhere in this book that talented photographers always have a bag of tricks. Diffusion is part of my bag of tricks. When I want to create a mood or feeling, I ask myself if diffusion will help or hinder my image. In the case of lingerie or tight head shots, mild diffusion can put a polish on your finished image.

There are many useful filters like the Softars made by B&W, the Nikon Soft #1 or the Tiffen Warm-Soft filters in varying grades, along with many others that are equally good.

If you do not want to make the small investment in a diffusion filter, you can make your own by taking your UV or Skylight filter, placing a coin in the center and spraying the filter with a light layer of water soluble hair spray , on it (water based lacquer), and then shaking off the coin. Finally, add a little more hair spray to the filter without the coin. This gives you a little more diffusion to the edges than the center. If you do not like it, wash it under warm water and the hair spray washes off. Then you can try again.

Mild diffusion makes people look better! No one wants to play "connect the dots" with a close-up photo you took of them. When your subject is looking at your photo and makes the comment that your photos are really sharp, this may not be a compliment! It may be a statement that they see more than they feel comfortable seeing.

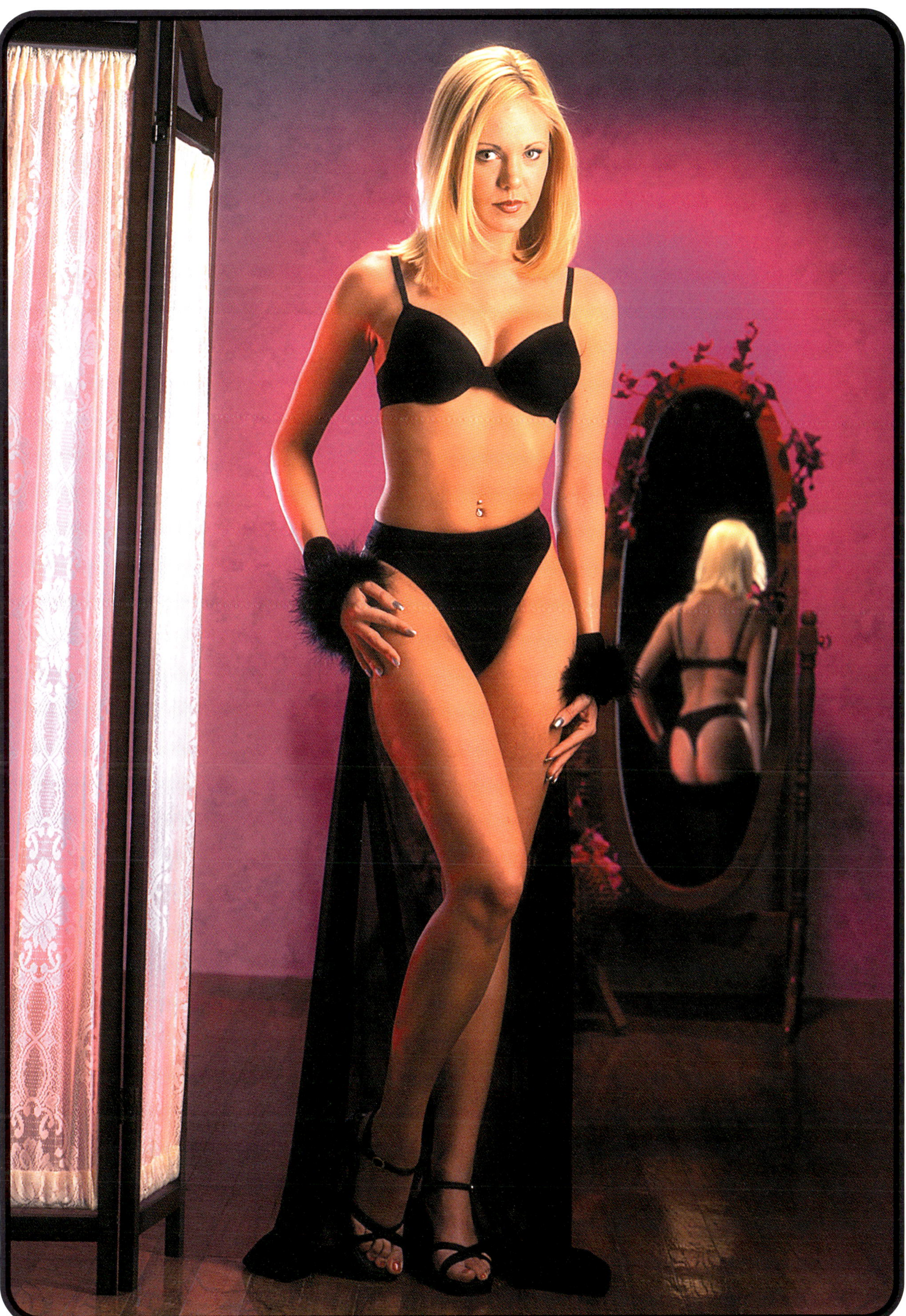

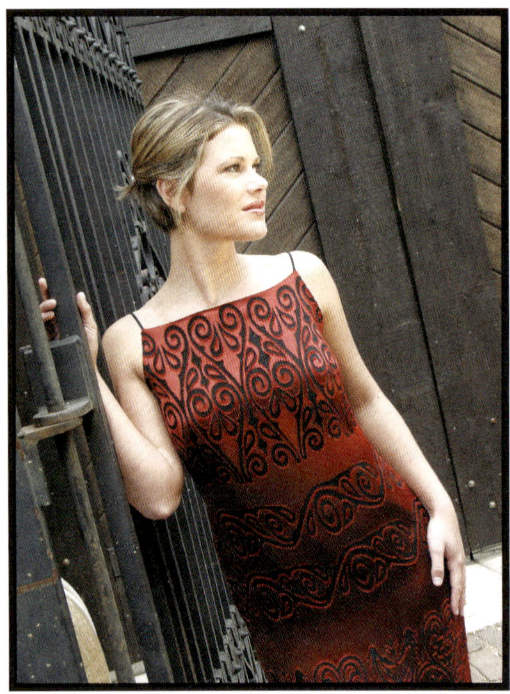

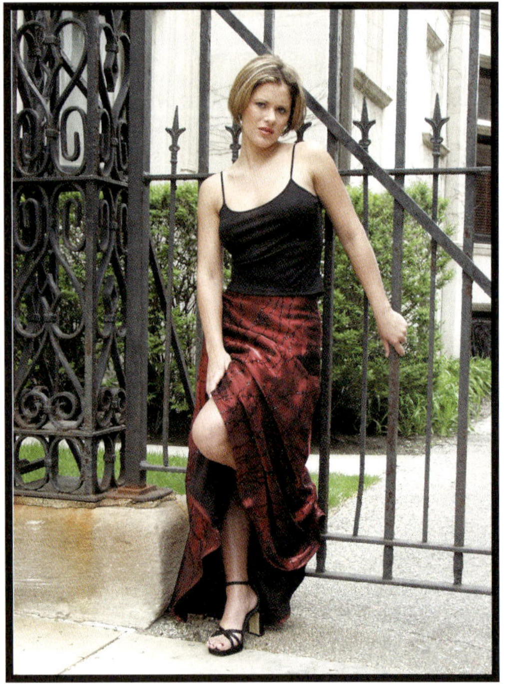

Iron Gates

I am always in search of interesting backgrounds. A few blocks from my studio is a small park with some interesting backgrounds for outdoor photography. The small park that I use in most of my outdoor shoots consists of a few huge turn-of-the-century homes with iron gates surrounding these homes. with stone staircases and fascinating architecture. With every turn, I can find a whole new shooting scenario.

Recently, I was shooting a model who came to me recommended by a good friend in Kalamazoo, Michigan. When Kelly arrived at my studio with the classy outfits she chose to model, I could not resist shooting at my favorite outdoor location. The images you see here were taken at this park. All photos were taken with natural light on an overcast day, and on a few occasions I used a mixed silver/gold reflector to add a small amount of warm light to the subject. All images were shot at 1/500th second at the most wide open F:stop for the individual shot. The shot was Metered with a Sekonic L-308 incident meter for accuracy and shot on an Olympus Camedia E-10 digital camera.

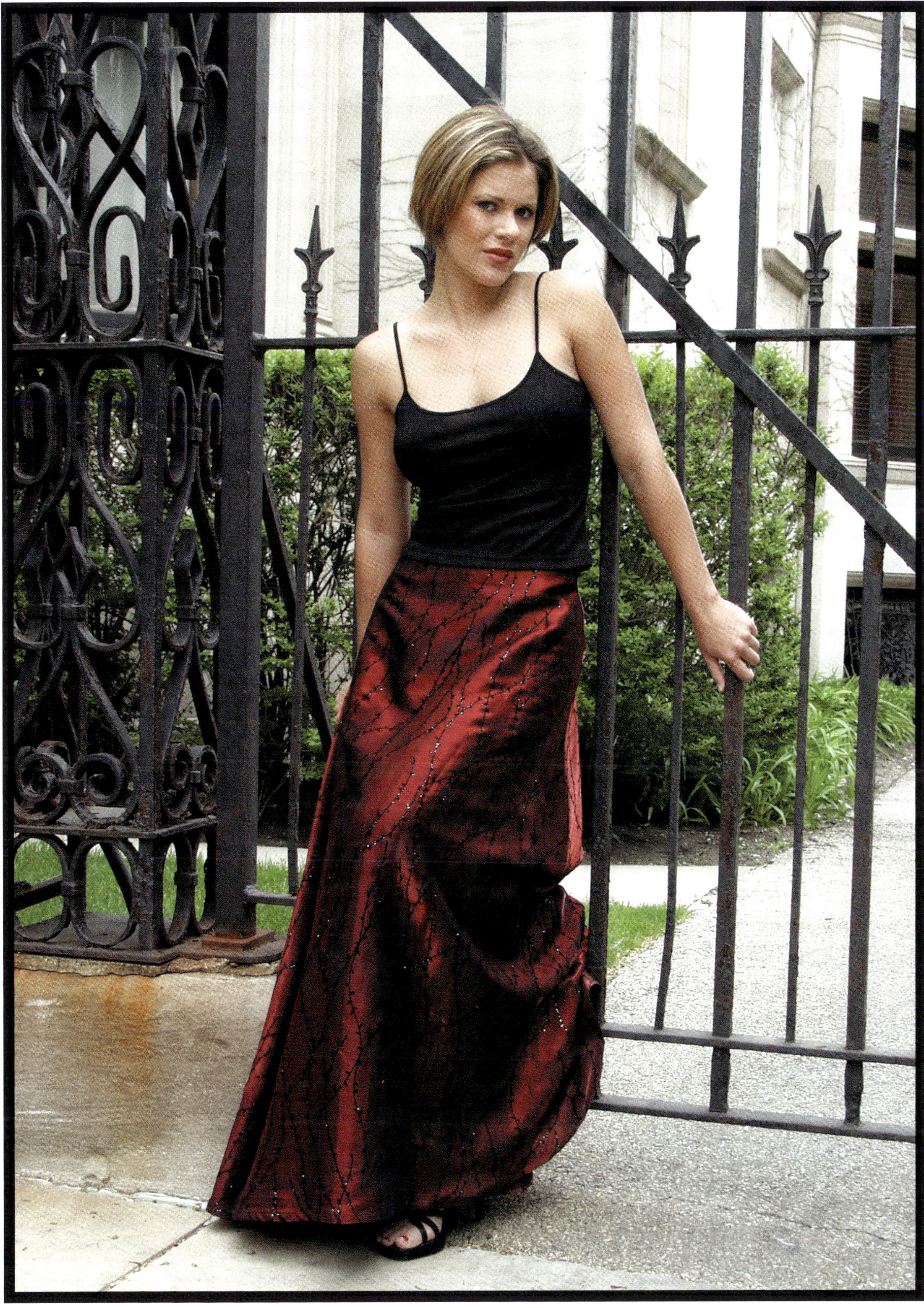

Attitude

Creating stunning photographic images takes more than understanding lighting and posing. One of the ingredients that turns a mediocre image into a fantastic one is when attitude is introduced into the scenario. The image of Sue was created when I saw the outfit she brought in and knew I had to shoot this in a natural environment (like the brick wall outside my studio). The light was bright sun in an afternoon sky. I shot this image with natural light; no reflectors or fill-flash.

The strength of this image is the tough, assertive attitude Sue exudes. Sue retains a sexy undertone, and the image is helped by the heart-shaped belt buckle.

Posing Tips

Some years back, just after publishing my second book "Profitable Model Photography" my publisher asked me to start working on a new book on posing. I started this book many times but could not find the way to make it work without showing images of bad poses along with good ones. I did not feel this was a way to instruct on posing.

Over the 20+ years I have been a professional photographer, I have learned how to pose by a number of different ways.

The hard way: make mistakes and then make improvements on my posing techniques.

The copy method: go through magazines, trade journals and books looking for posing ideas. This method is highly recommended, as you learn when you copy other photographers and many times improve on the original image. *Poses are not copyrighted or trademarked.* My advice to any photographer is to build an idea file of images and the poses you are impressed with. Go to your idea file when shooting a subject or model. Look for a pose that you think your subject will be able to do then go for it!

The third way: Angles and Curves. When I shoot any subject, I am always looking for angles and body curves. As you look through this book, you will see arms and legs bent to create diagonal lines. By creating angled shoulders, you create attitude. When you bend an arm it creates diagonal lines that add interest and makes for lines that pull the viewers eye to the face of the subject. Vertical and horizontal lines are boring. We live in a vertical and horizontal world. When you see a diagonal line in nature your eye is attracted to it. because, Diagonals are Dynamic. Diagonal lines also create the infamous S-curve we have all heard of. I feel the ugliest part of the human body are the knees. By bending the knee closest to the camera and having your model press the bent knee to the straight knee, you create beautiful legs. This was a pose you will see repeatedly in this book. It was a pose Marilyn Monroe did automatically every time a camera was pointed in her direction.Even she realized it made her legs look much better.

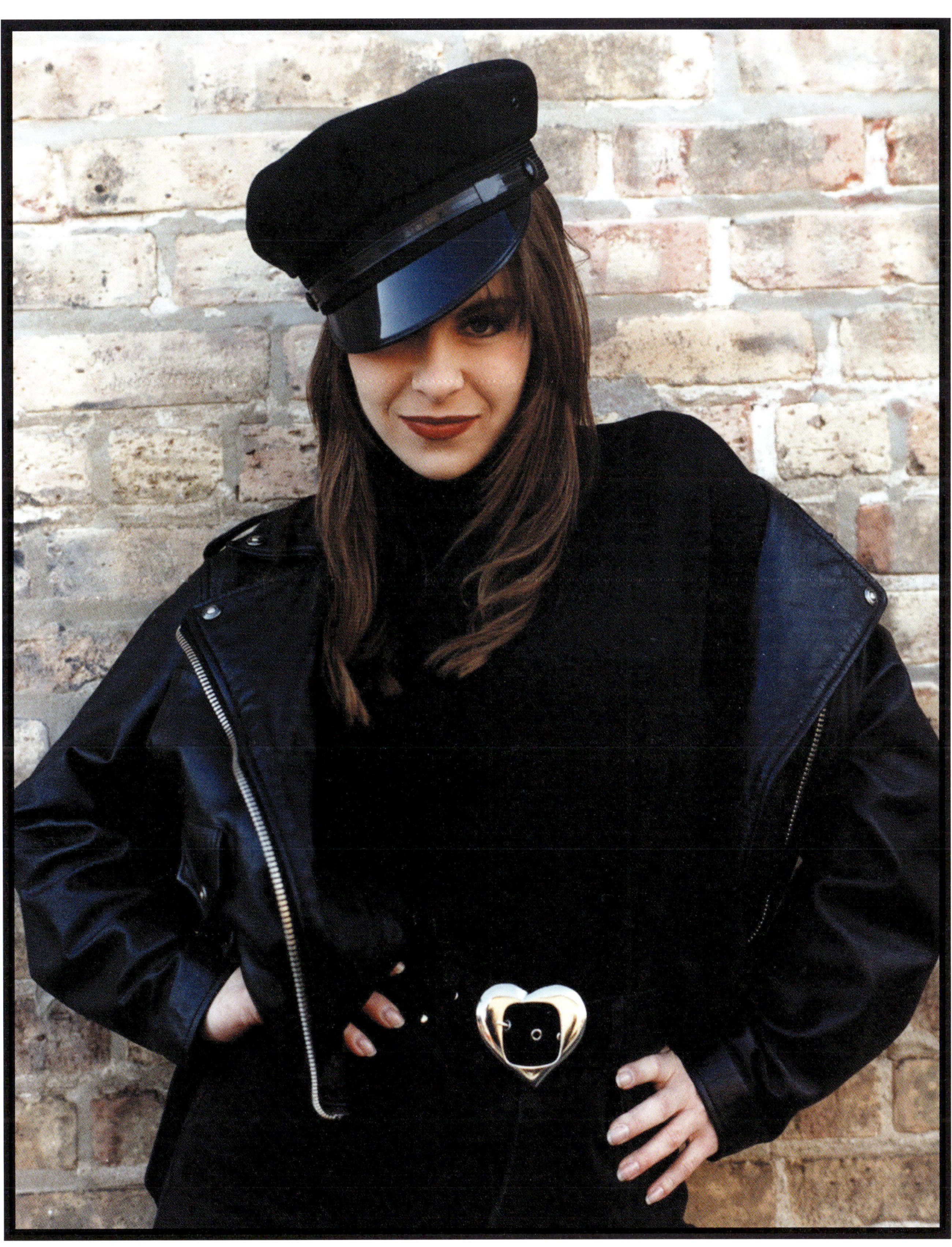

Infrared

It has been said that the most important ingredient of any successful business is location location location. I believe the same is true for profitable location photography.

I am fortunate to live close to a park and historic district a few blocks from my studio that contain some very old graystone-style homes. These 100+ year-old homes have been turned into small museums and make for superb shooting locations. There are two buildings next to each other. One is white stone, and the other is a dark brown stone. Depending on my model's outfit, I try to choose the building that will best show it off. When Hillary showed me the old fashioned white outfit she had purchased in a resale store, I knew the old homes would make a great backdrop. Backgrounds like these bring a drama and timeless beauty to the image.

The unique thing about the images of Hillary is that they were photographed on Konica Infrared black and white film with a red filter over the lens. With the Konica and Kodak Infrared film, whites tend to halite (glow) and turn super white. Skin tones look flawless and very bright. Infrared film creates a surrealistic look and works best in bright sunlight.

Shooting with Classic Cameras

Not being an afficiando of the newer and much heavier hi-tech 35mm cameras, I choose to do most of my photography with what I refer to as "Classic Cameras". You cannot imagine the enjoyment of creating an image that is truly spectacular and know YOU figured out the exposure, YOU composed the image, and that the entire creative and technological process was in YOUR hands.

Notice when a professional photographer shoots with a Hasselblad, Mamiya 6x7 or a 4x5 view camera, they do it without the luxury of Zoom lenses and built-in multi-matrix metering. They have to focus the camera by themselves. Yet they create some of the best images you will ever see. Maybe it's time to do the image-making yourself and not let the camera do the job.

Quite often I see photographers using sophisticated autofocus, built-in metered single lens reflex cameras. These cameras are utilized identically to a point and shoot camera. I doubt that you could guess as to which camera took the photo. The primary difference between the automation of the latest Canon EOS, the Nikon F-5 and some of the point and shoot cameras is the available selection of lenses. In a nutshell, both the point and shoot and the full feature system cameras take away the creative freedom to think, thus becoming point and shoot cameras.

Try using your camera as a manual camera with a hand held meter. You may find that you are more gratified because you are the brain behind the image. This is the way it is done with the professional cameras like the Hasselblad, Mamiya 6x7 and 4x5 cameras.

Discover the joy of shooting with classic cameras where you plan the focus, you meter the scene and you compose the image. Experience the thrill of shooting professional images with classic cameras (or your camera) in a manual mode.

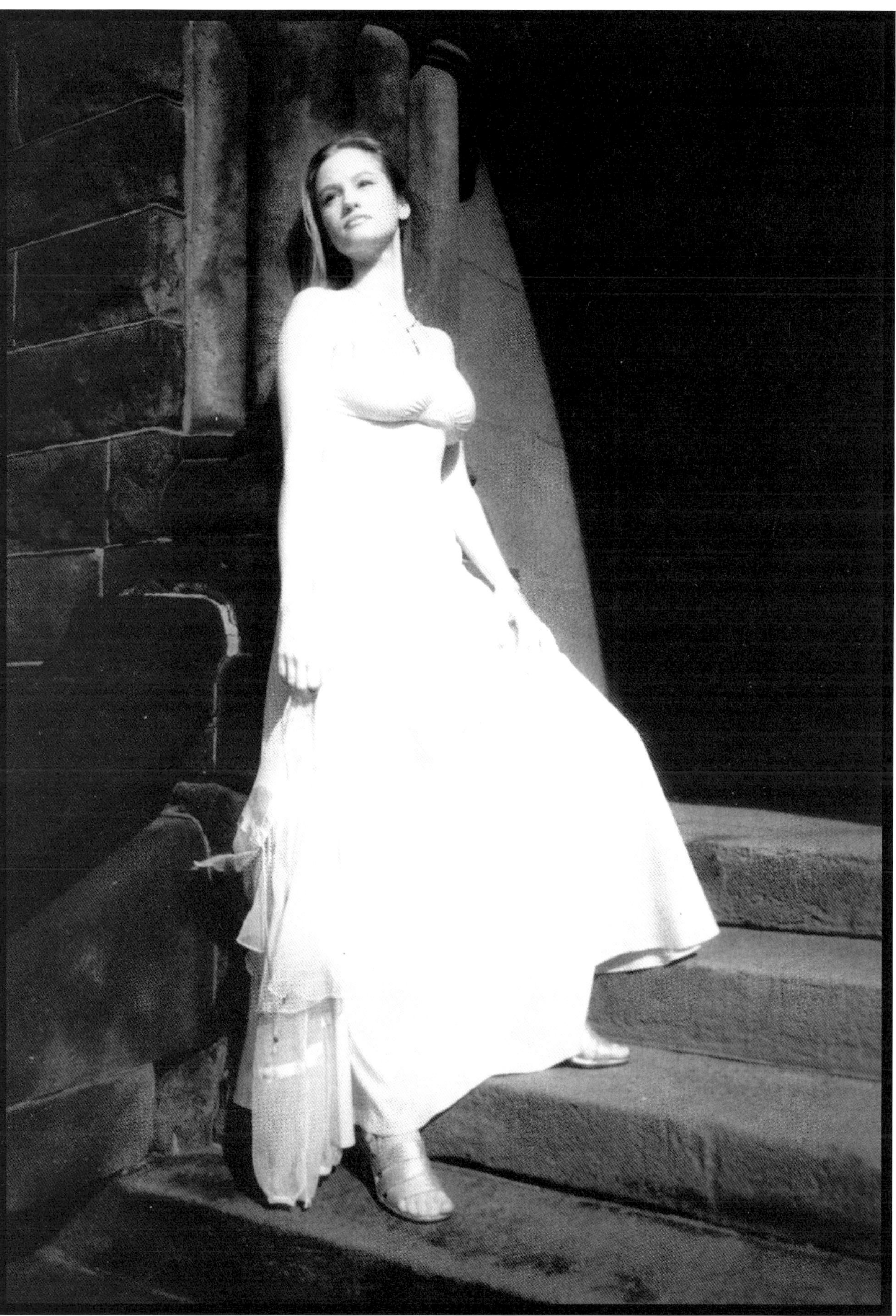

Gangsta

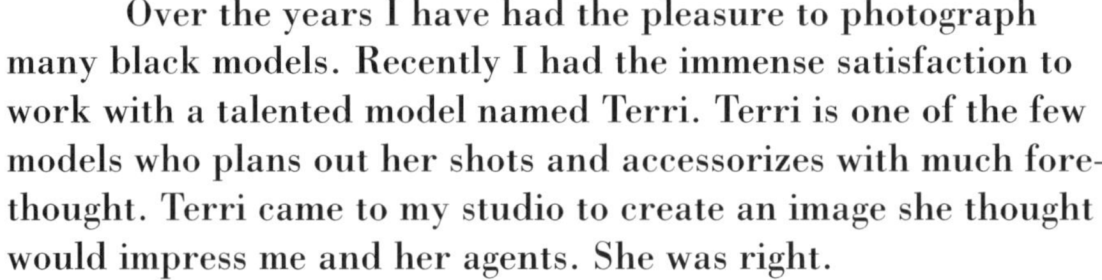

Over the years I have had the pleasure to photograph many black models. Recently I had the immense satisfaction to work with a talented model named Terri. Terri is one of the few models who plans out her shots and accessorizes with much forethought. Terri came to my studio to create an image she thought would impress me and her agents. She was right.

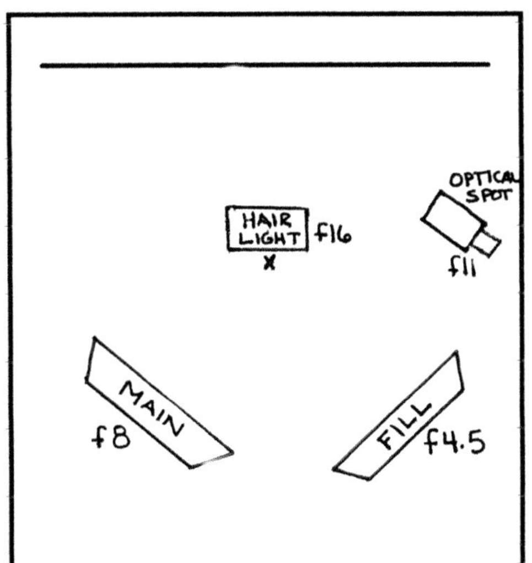

I set up the shot of Terri in a business suit with her 1920's hair style and dated accessories. I thought about how I would like to show Terri in this stylish outfit. I knew I had a cookie of my optical spot projector that gave the feeling of a skyline. I tried the optical spot, lighting the plain wall in my studio and proceeded to light Terri separate from the wall. I positioned the one large soft box as the main light and used my hair light or, in this case, a hat light 2 stops brighter creating the third dimension in this image. The photo was very successful with her agent and in her portfolio, and is one of my favorites.

Props to add Excitement

Looking for new ways to add excitement to your photography? Maybe you need some new props to add sparkle and pizazz to your images.

Props can add a new dimension to your portrait sitting. Adding something as simple as a new chair, a painted ladder, or graphic props such as cubes, circles or a column will give you many new opportunities in posing your subject.

If you are anything like me when you are trying to be creative with a new subject in front of your camera, you look for originality in shooting, lighting and posing. Nothing adds a new dimension more to your photography than a neat prop,especially when the prop blends with the subjects outfit.

Through the years I have become bored with the subject sitting at a posing table and doing conventional portraits. I am influenced by images in fashion magazines or portraits I see at the photo conventions with originality in pose and propping. I am constantly scanning the foreign photo and fashion magazines even though I can not read the copy. Photography is a universal language, and I can usually understand a super image in any language.

Look at the way other photographers create with innovative lighting, posing and the use of props. Build an idea file by cutting out images that impress you from magazines and start your own idea file. When you are called upon to create your own masterpiece of photography, you will produce a work of art if you have some innovative props and an idea file to draw new ideas from.

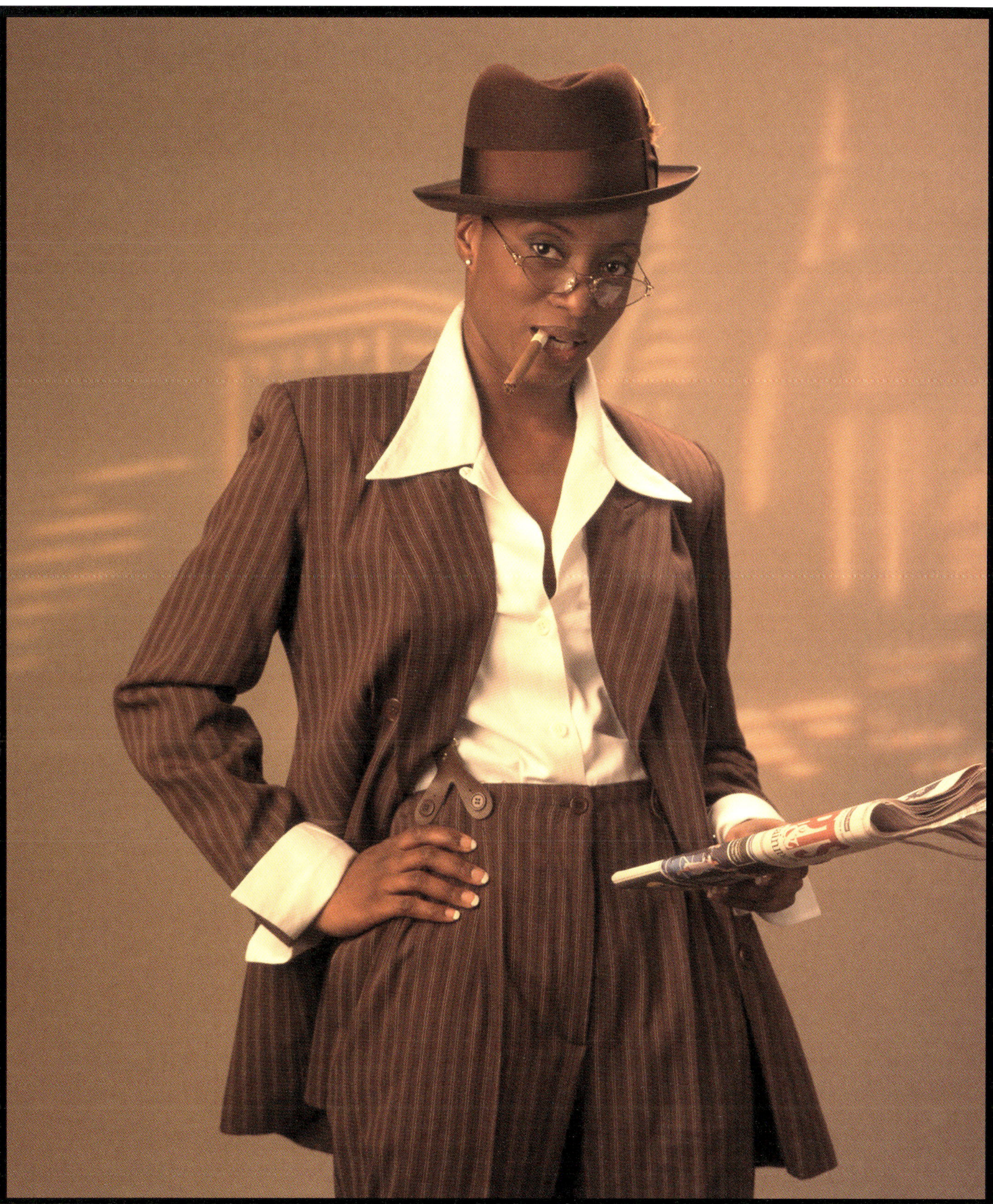

The Portal

Doing workshops across North America has allowed me to find many exotic locations and work with some talented models during my travels. I have developed many friendships, and one in particular is with one of my students , Spencer Calquhoun, and a west coast photographer named Bill Lemon. These men are fine photographers and terrific friends. We have had the opportunity to work together in a few workshops. One of these workshops took place in Bill Lemon's studio, just north of San Francisco. Bill knows many beautiful models and has written two books on the subject.

Bill found a location for us to shoot that was ideal. The location was a catholic boys school that resembled an old spanish mission. The image illustrated shows how photographs can be improved by the right location. While we were shooting, I noticed that other local photographers were bringing brides and engaged couples there for formal portraiture.

The image on the facing page was created in one of the portal ways and created a strong, natural frame for the beautiful model standing within it. Natural light with silver reflector intensified the model's face and body. Exposure was calculated by taking an incident meter reading from the model's perspective and aimed in the direction of the camera's position. Exposure was 1/500th at F:5.6 photo taken with a Leica M-6 35mm camera and 35mm lens.

Filters for Eye-Popping Black and White images

One of the ways to spice up your black and white photography is with the use of filters.

Yellow filters create increased contrast in landscape and portraiture.
Orange filters add a three dimensional quality and increase contrast in landscape and portraits.
Green filters add tonal value when shooting subjects with an abundance of green. Also for portraits.
Red filters increase contrast in landscape photography making clouds whiter, sky darker.
Dark red filters create surrealistic effects in landscape and architectural photography (Stormy clouds)
Blue filters are ideal for correction of available light shooting, darkens skin tones.

I highly recommend the medium -yellow or yellow-orange filters for enhancing portraits and landscape photography. Red is also highly effective in creating wonderful scenic, architectural and nature photography.

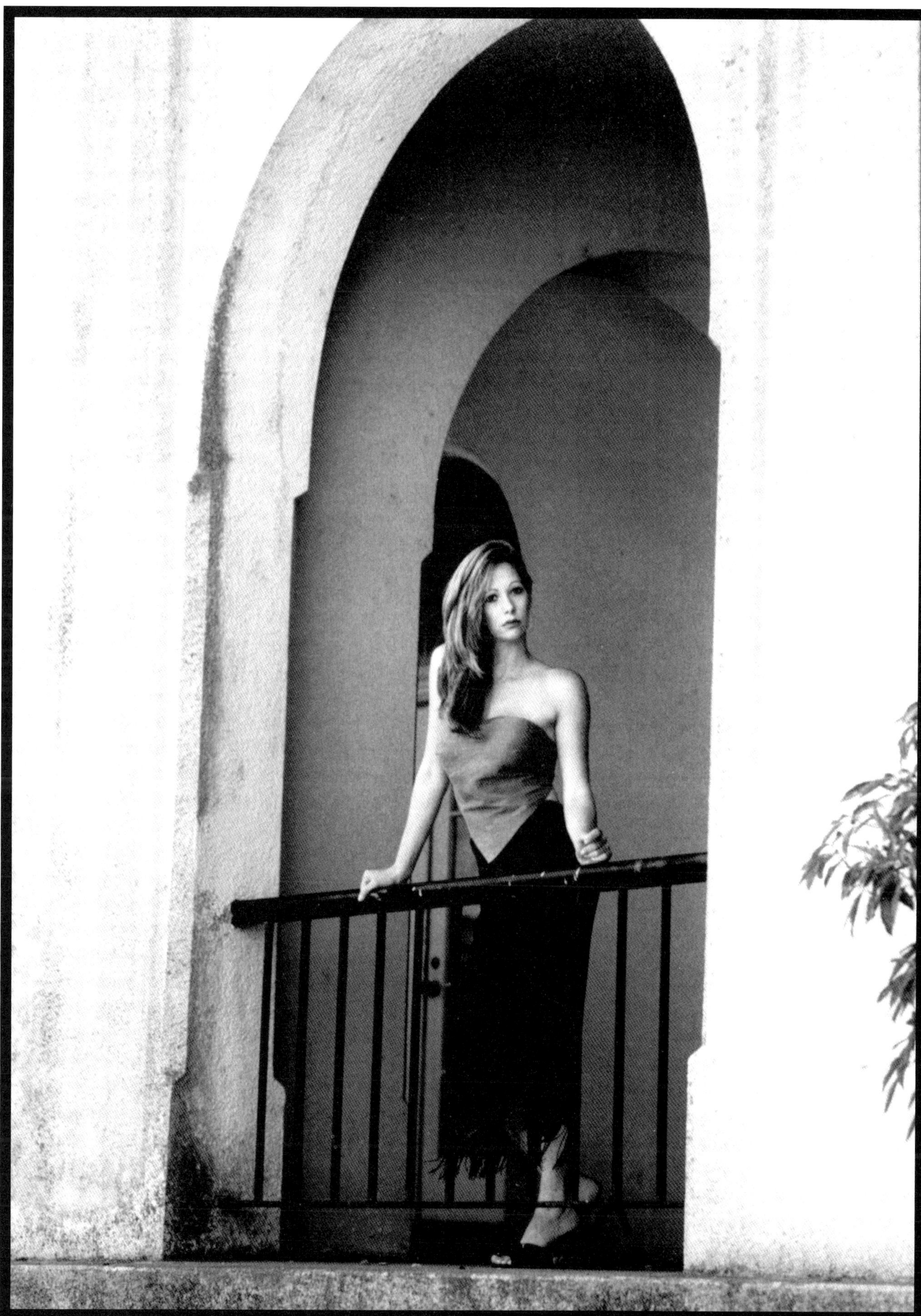

Antique Boudoir

Creating an antique or dated image is easy when you have the correct props to make your shot work. Heather is a collector of old fashioned clothing and with her mother's antique furniture, we had all the ingredients for an interesting photo shooting.

We arranged to meet at her home and, after going over some of the outfits, I chose this antique lingerie outfit for the image you see illustrated on the facing page. The light used was afternoon natural light coming in from a large window nearby. I used the window light as the main light with a floor lamp behind Heather creating a warm glow and the needed fill light.The floor lamp was a conventional bulb (3400K), so the light from the bulb would create a warm glow. After metering the light falling on Heather from the window with an incident meter, metered F:2.8 at 1/30th, I moved the floor lamp to get the same F:stop so the secondary warm fill light would not overpower the main light.

This image had to be taken on a tripod with my Hasselblad using a 110mm lens. I placed the phone and hung a piece of material on the mirror to help build the set and create a mood for this image. The one other important part of this image is the use of a Hasselblad Softar #2 filter to heighten the image's romantic nature. The softar filter makes the image spectacular. Without the filter, this shot would be too sharp and lose the romanticism. I purposely watched how the light was falling on the face, making sure the face was bright from the combination of the two different light sources.

Lighting with two different colors can be tricky. I recommend you try this combination, but be aware that incandescent light is of much lower intensity than daylight or electronic flash. The best way to combine different types of light is to use a tripod, metering carefully and shooting at slow shutter speeds to get the effect you desire.

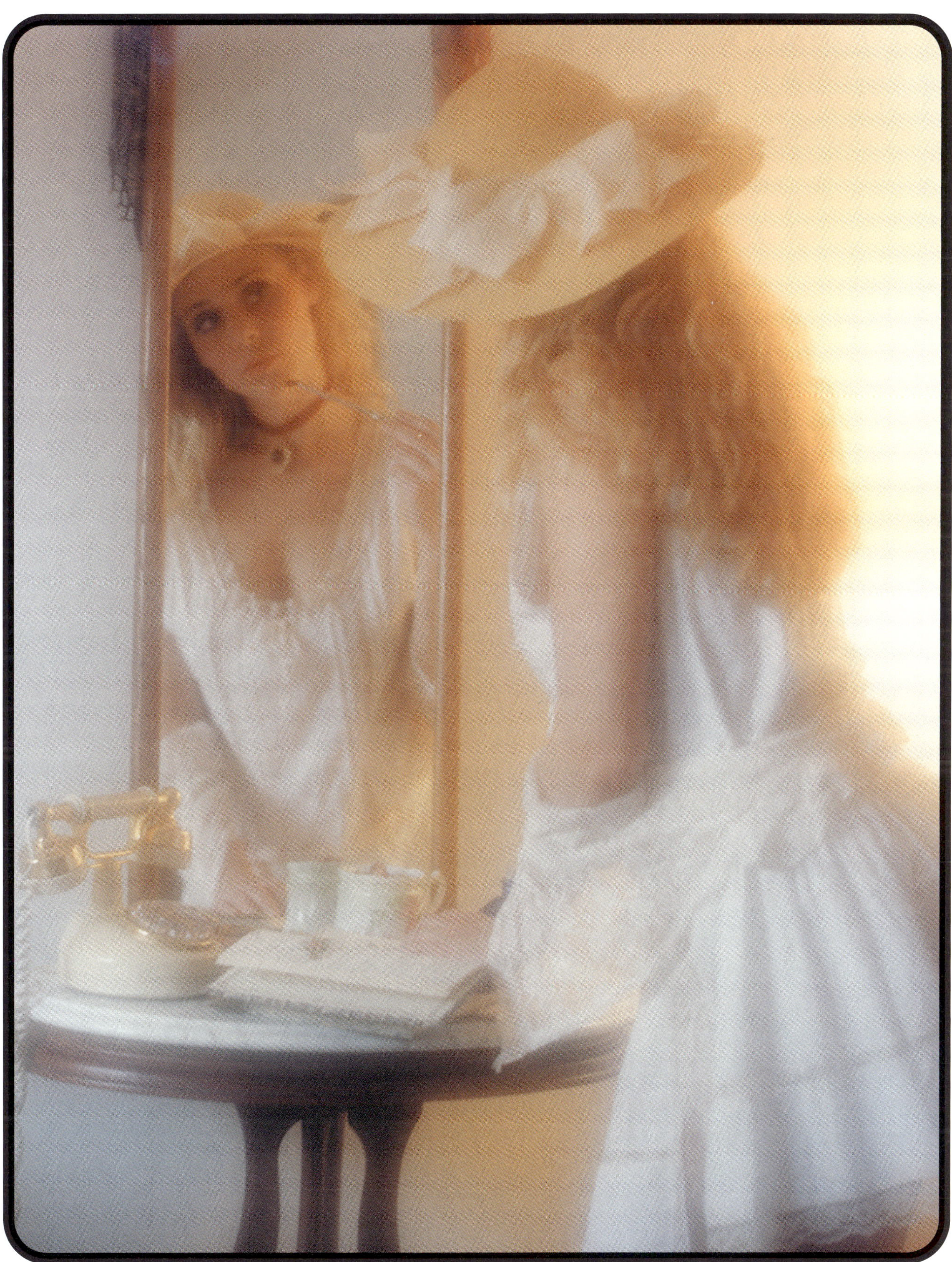

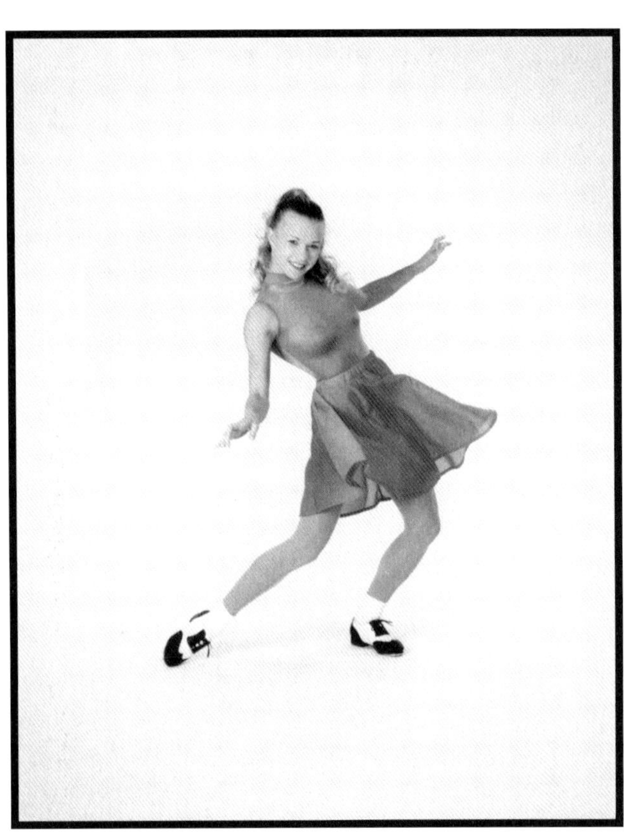

The black and white image was taken with my Leica M-6 and 50mm Summicron lens. This image was used in my black and white mini portfolio.

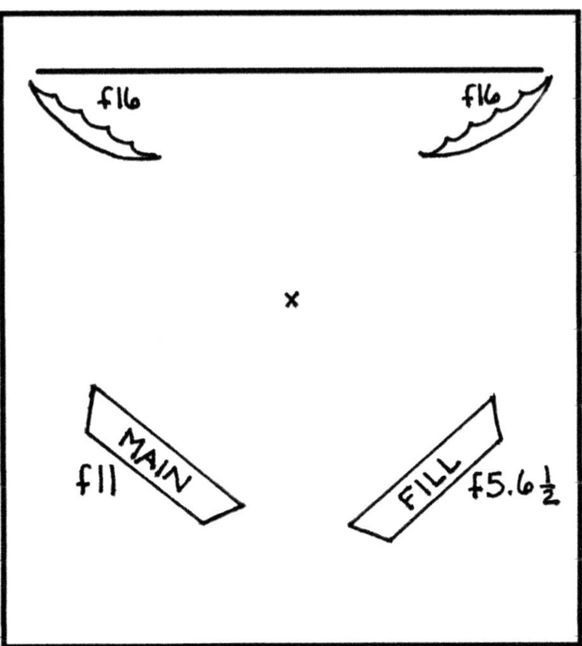

Swing

As time and fashions change, so do dance trends. It has been said that everything old is new again.

A short time ago, the Swing dance trend made a revival. When this happened, my dancewear account decided to make costume wear and shoes for the 40's era. As Jennifer is an excellent model and dancer, she was a natural for this high-key shot.While I did the shot in color, I decided I wanted to try this image in black and white for my portfolio. Jennifer makes the costume come alive in this creative pose caught at the end of her swing movement.

High-key lighting is one of the most misunderstood lighting techniques and one of the easiest to accomplish.I notice that many photographers make mistakes on high-key lighting. At the numerous workshops I do across North America, I am constantly asked how I do high-key lighting.

The theory behind high-key lighting is to create a continuous background where the floor is white and endless. In reality, the endless floor is a curved white surface that goes up the wall. When properly lit, you cannot tell where the wall ends and the floor begins.

Lighting for high-key: The use of two lights on the background in this case was two umbrellas set at equal power and designed to wash light down the background aimed toward the center from each side and tilted down to light the curve in the paper background. This is very important. If the curve is not lit correctly, you will create a horizon line and the curve will become darker than the wall or the floor of the paper.

Two background lights set for F:16, one stop brighter than the main light is the key to a clean white background but not to make the background so bright as to halite the subject. In this case I chose 3 to 1 ratio lighting on Jennifer with the main to the left of camera in a large plume wafer light box set for F:11, the fill light was a plume wafer strip light, set to the right of camera for F:5.6and a half.

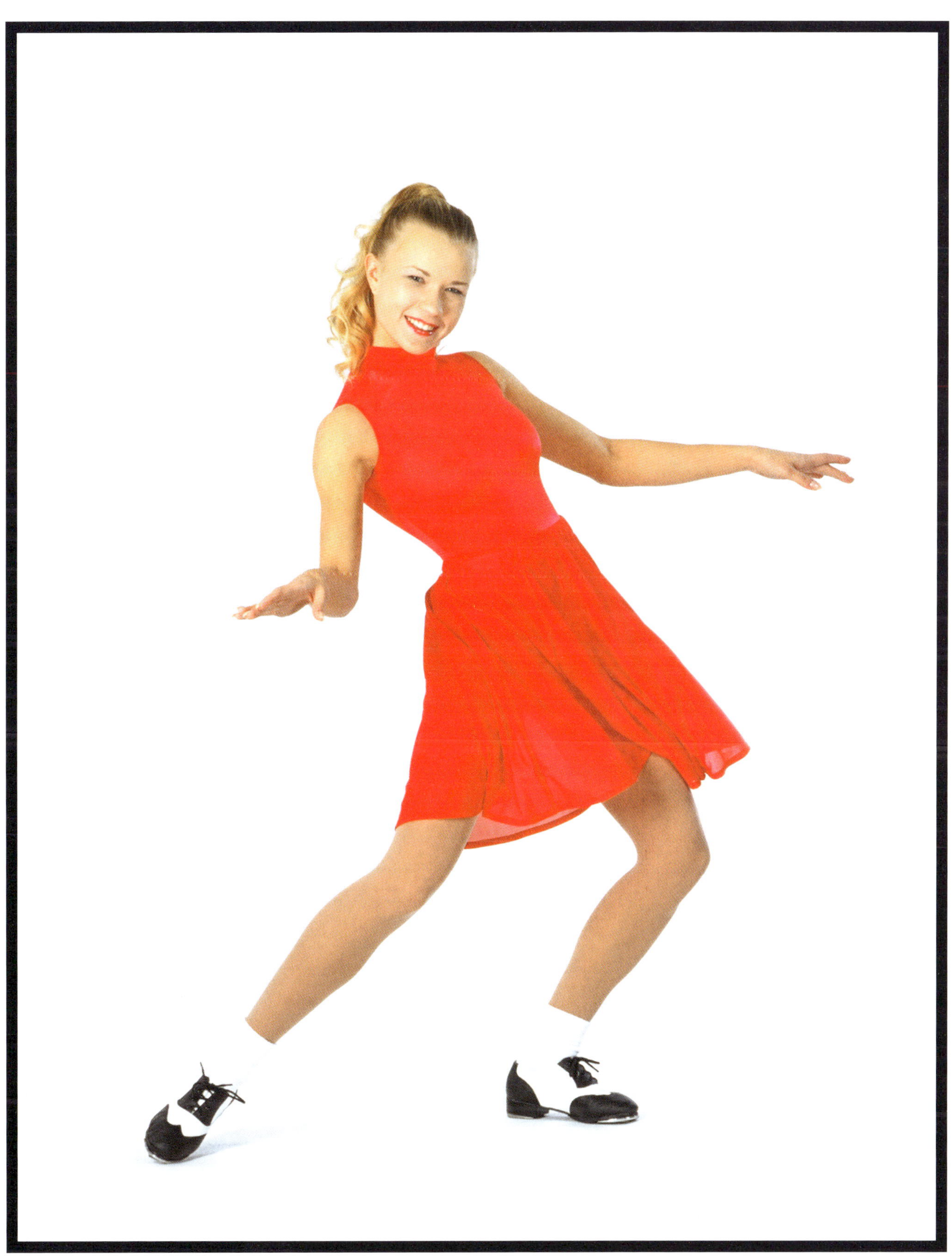

Chain Link Projections

The use of an optical spot projector as the main light source provides many opportunities for creative lighting. The optical spot is generally an attachment for many of the lights being made today. I have two optical spot lights and use them extensively. One of unique things about an optical spot is that it allows the use of patterns, or cookies, (cut-out designs) to create a mood in your photographs.

I chose to use this pattern out of the thousands available. In the example on the facing page, I purposely kept the pattern slightly sharp.behind Katie. The image of Maggie on this page showing the pattern more out of focus.

Lighting: Simple lighting with the optical spot set for F:8 on the subject and a second fill light aimed at the subject set for F:4, two stops lower to lighten the shadow created by the optical spot light. In the case of the Maggie shot on this page I also used a Bowens wind machine aimed at her hair to create a more life-like image.

Maggie with the optical spot set slightly out of focus with the Bowens wind machine.

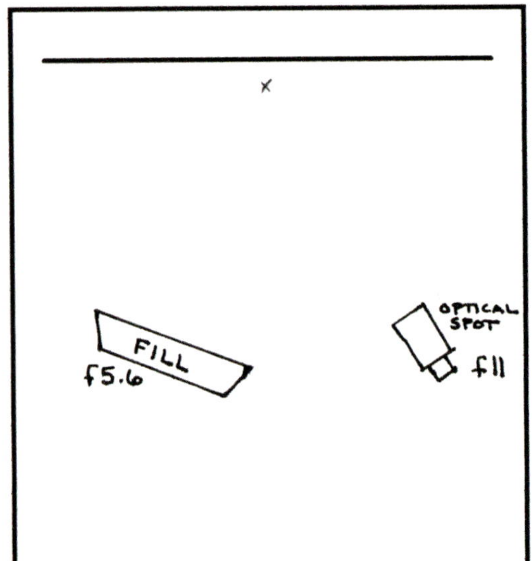

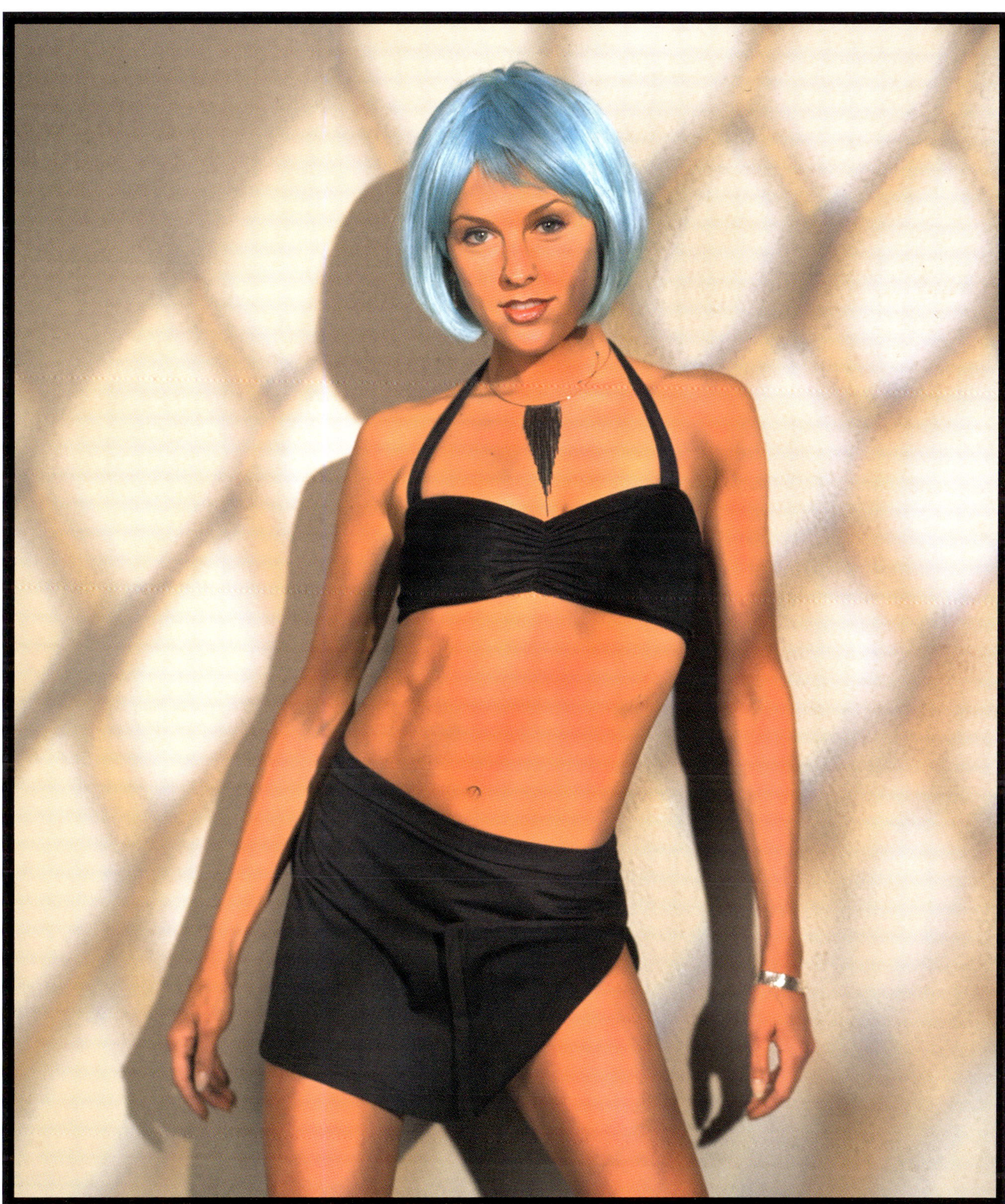

Hollow Man

Hollow man was created when this model came to me for some new images for his portfolio. When he saw some of the special effects images I do, he asked if we could produce something more exciting than the normal fashion images.

As I love a challenge, I chose to do a location shot.and suggested we try a double exposure. My thought was to create a feeling of moving through the set.

I positioned the camera on a tripod and took a reading of the scene with the incident dome on my light meter. Once I established the correct setting, I closed the aperture down one stop. I was going to shoot the scene twice and did not want an overexposed negative. The correct reading was 1/250th at F:5.6. I closed the lens down to F:8 and shot the first frame with my model in position. After the first exposure, I had the model leave the scene and took another shot without advancing the film. Therefore, I created two images on one piece of film. As the subject was only in the scene for the first exposure, he becomes semi-transparent in the final image.

The Tripod

One of the most valuable tools you will own as a photographer is a good tripod. If you are like me, you hate using a tripod as it is clumsy and slows you down. But no accessory will improve your photography more than a tripod. As photographers, we tend to think we can hand-hold a camera outdoors and get steady pictures. Well, it's not true....... I have proven to myself many times that a tripod will give me better results in any format and at any shutter speed I choose to shoot with. The image on the facing page could only be done with a tripod. There is no way to do a double exposure while hand holding the camera.

I personally recommend a well built tripod such as a Gitzo or Bogen with a ball head. If you choose a sturdy and simple tripod, you will be more likely to use it. Watch your photography improve when you start shooting on a tripod.

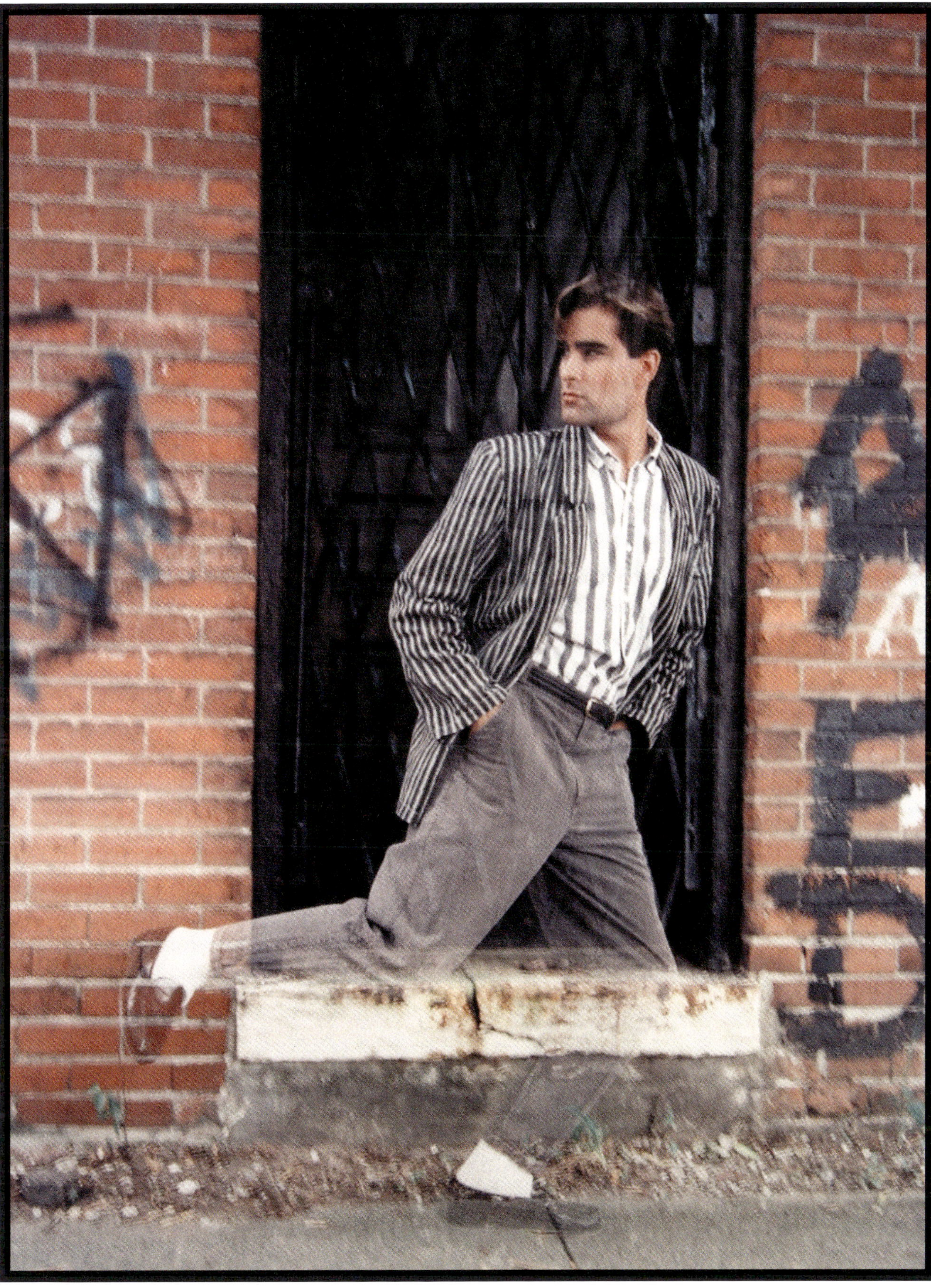

The Gloves

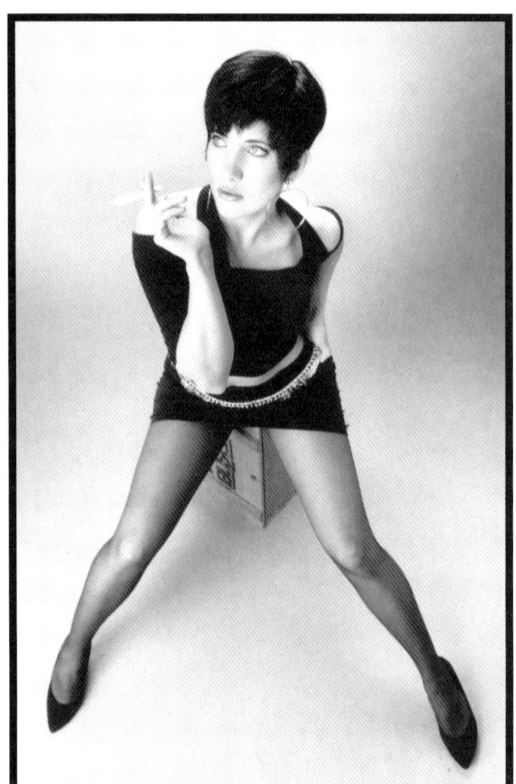

The image of Kim on the box was photographed with a Leica and 35mm wide angle lens to add distortion for special effects.

When Kim came into my studio, I could not help but notice her fantastic eyes. Kim came to me to build her portfolio images. I set up this shot of Kim with gloves because the gloves forces the eye to the face. The dramatic pose, the dress, her gloves and the dynamic earring make this shot a fantastic face shot.

Both of these images were shot on light gray paper. Lighting; Two umbrella lights from the front set for equal power (flat light) creating an F:11 aperture combined, background light mounted to the ceiling lighting the area behind the models shoulders, set-up with 7" reflector with a 40 degree grid metered at F:8, the background light creates a glow behind the models upper body and therefore draws your eye to the main part of the subject. The final light is a hair light, using my small 12"x18" balcar prisma-light soft box with a white lightning Ultra 600 mounted on a bowens adjustable boom, I was able to set this light about 12" over the models head and create the glowing hair and slightly brighter shoulders for a more three dimensional image. *I consider this as my trademark light. I use it in as many images as I can because of it's unique quality.*

The image of Kim on the box with cigarette was created with a 35mm wide angle lens on a Leica M-6. I wanted to create something totally different and knew I would add a new perspective to this dynamic shot by using a wide angle lens.

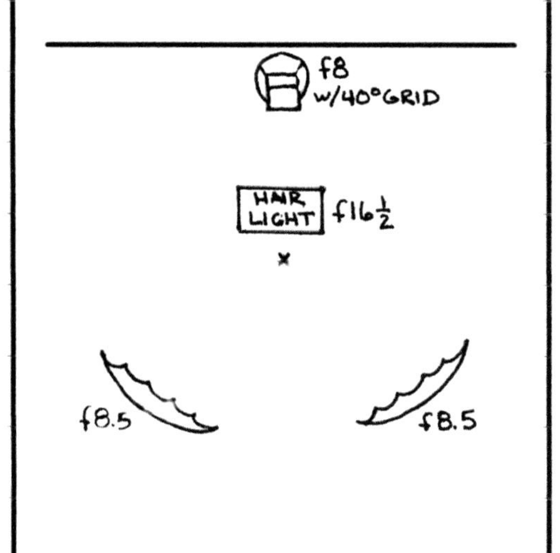

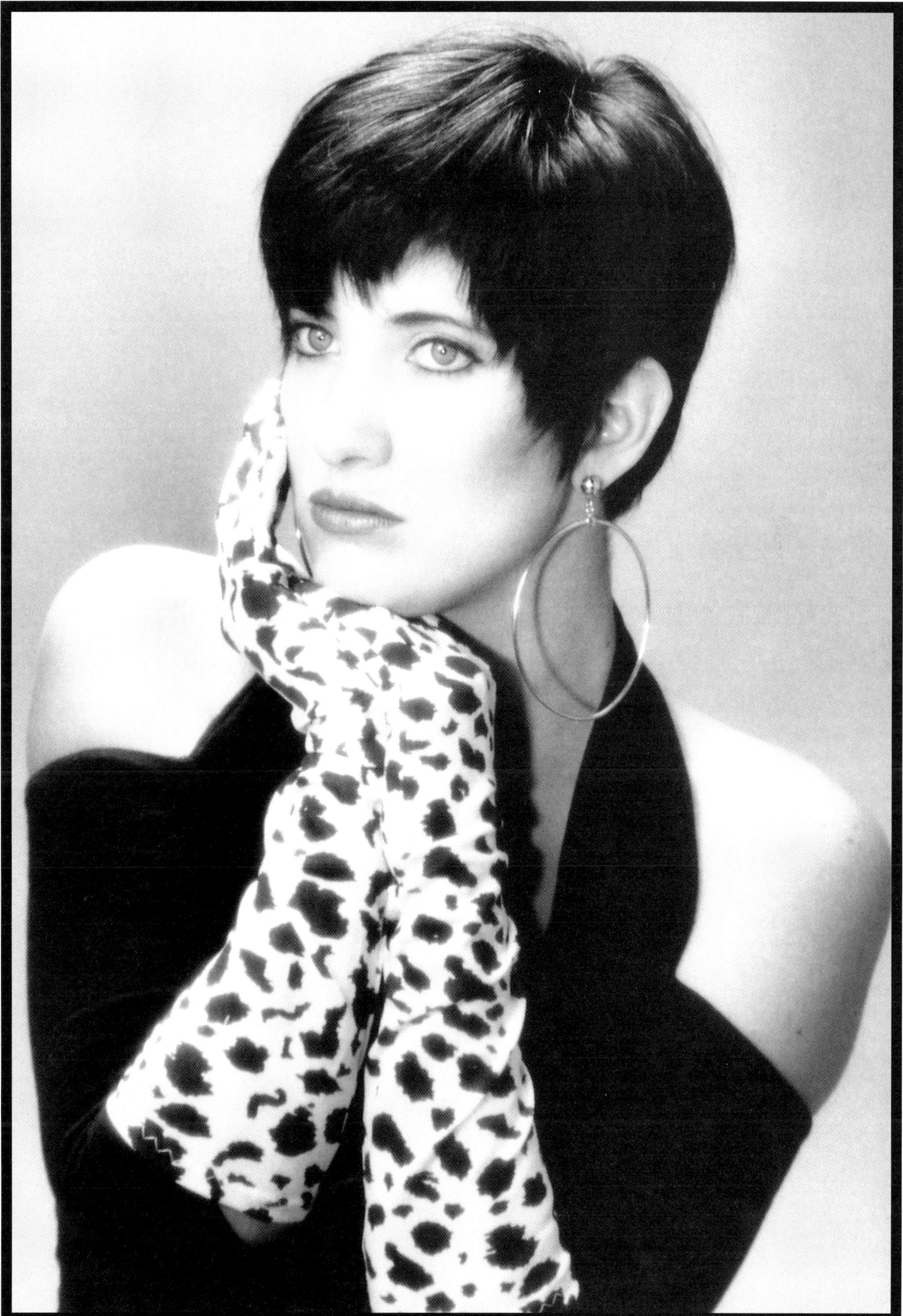

Liquid Light

If there ever was an oxymoron, the term 'liquid light' would be it. Obviously, the light used in creating these images was not liquid, but the images take on a liquid quality.

I was contacted by an excellent Chicago advertising agency for this campaign. The owner and creative director, Nick, asked me to do some experimental photography and show him what I could do.

I contacted a dancer/model I had worked with previously and we did some testing of theories that I thought would work for my client.When I showed the test images to Nick, he finalized his decision based on the type of images you see on these pages. Nick suggested we do a shoot with 5 models. When the day of the shoot arrived, we produced over 500 images by noon. It was necessary to shoot many images because there would be many rejects caused by too much blur or not enough blur. As each dancer we photographed would move through a routine, we shot at least 12 to 24 images.

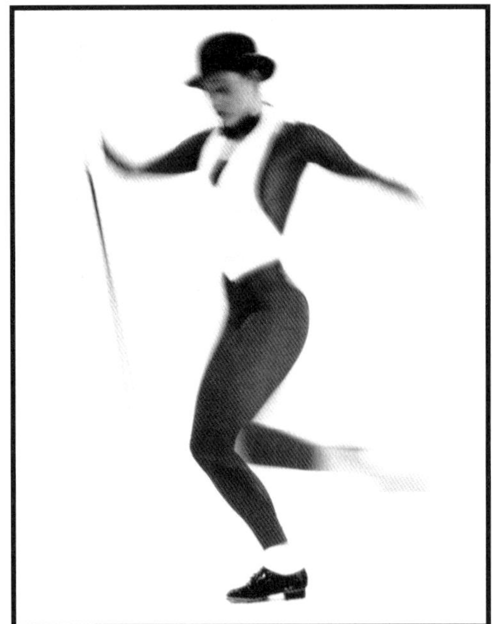

We decided on high-key photography using a white paper seamless. We bracketed the images not for exposure, but for blur. All the images were shot on 125 ISO Ilford FP-4 black and white film. Only the modeling lights of the White Lightning flash units were used. The exposure on the subject ranged from 1/4 sec. to 1 second at the correct respective F:stop. The background was one stop brighter than the exposure on the subject.

This image was to promote the client's dance shoes. A number of different brochures were created with dozens of the blurred dance images. The campaign was very successful. Nick also submitted the final brochures in contests and both the ad-agency and I were presented with awards for the design and photography. By some of the most respected Art award committees in the United States. We were voted into the top 100 new photography and design awards.

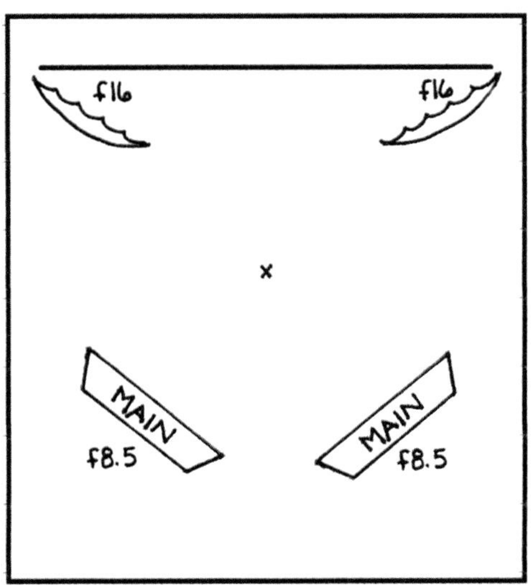

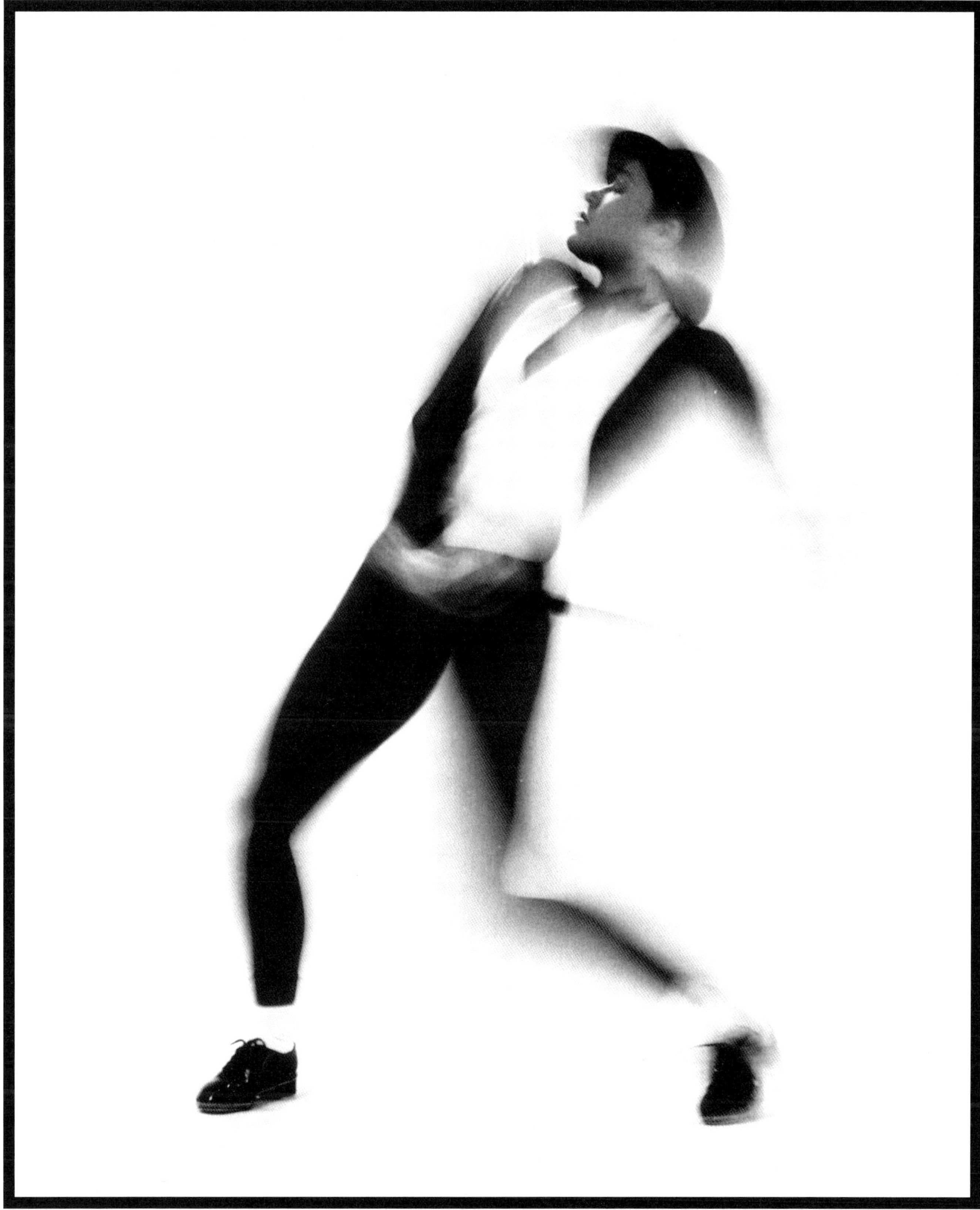

Golden Girl

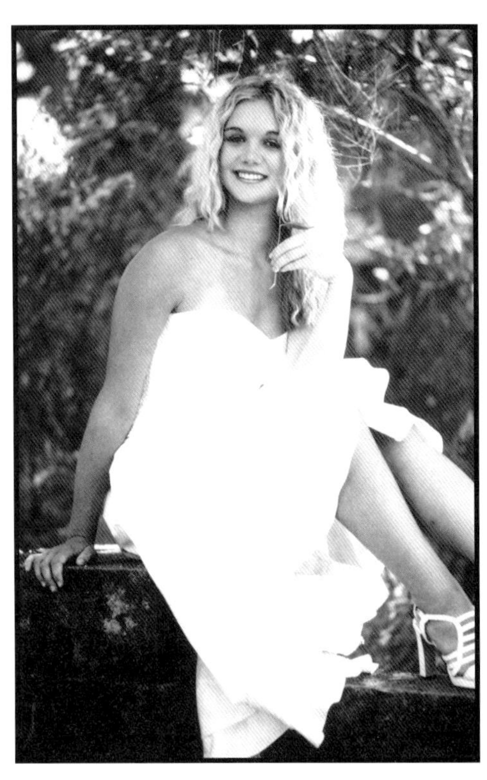

I recently held a workshop with my friends, Bill Lemon and Spencer Calquhoun, in Bill's studio in California. We did an outdoor shoot at a nearby catholic boys school because of the phenomenal backgrounds in this mission-style school. Crystal was one of the models at this workshop.

When I saw all of the wonderful wrought iron gates and window grills, I knew this was going to be some awesome shooting. One of the unique properties of this building is the white walls, which acts as a natural reflector when shooting people.

When Crystal showed me her outfits, I chose this dress because I knew it would work perfectly. The dress was white, and its style could be from a past era. The image becomes timeless. Using the iron gates as a frame for Crystal created a dynamic image and pulls the eye to the subject.

The only thing necessary to making Crystal's shots better was a silver reflector to pump some fill light into Crystal's face. I used my Sekonic L-308 meter and did an incident reading from the model's vantage point. This gave me an accurate light reading. If I had used an in-camera meter, the meter would be fooled by the white dress. The in-camera meter would have underexposed the scene because of the brightness of the dress.

Advice for the Model Photographer

A few years ago I brought my portfolio to some of the local talent agents in Chicago. One of the agents was kind enough to tell me what needed improvement. Trying not to hurt my feelings, she told me she liked my creativity and style but that I needed better models. I did not understand. I thought the people in my book were fantastic. She explained that they were pretty but were not professional models. She arranged for me to shoot with a professional model to show me the difference.

My advice to any photographer showing his or her work is to show only those images with very attractive people. This does not mean you turn people away who are unattractive. It means that if you show extremely attractive people, the viewer of your images will consider you a talented photographer. People relate to beautiful people. My case is proven by picking up any fashion magazine. Billboards, TV commercials, and magazines all use good looking people to sell their product and create an image. They do not use unattractive, overweight models.

We, as photographers, also need to create an image. Then why not do what the professionals do? Mimic the successful people in the image industry. Does this sound shallow to you? It may be to some degree, but it works. We are all in the image industry. When I create photographs for a client, I am going to make the best possible images I can regardless of their look. I know they will like what I do for them. But this does not mean the image will end up on my studio wall or in my portfolio.

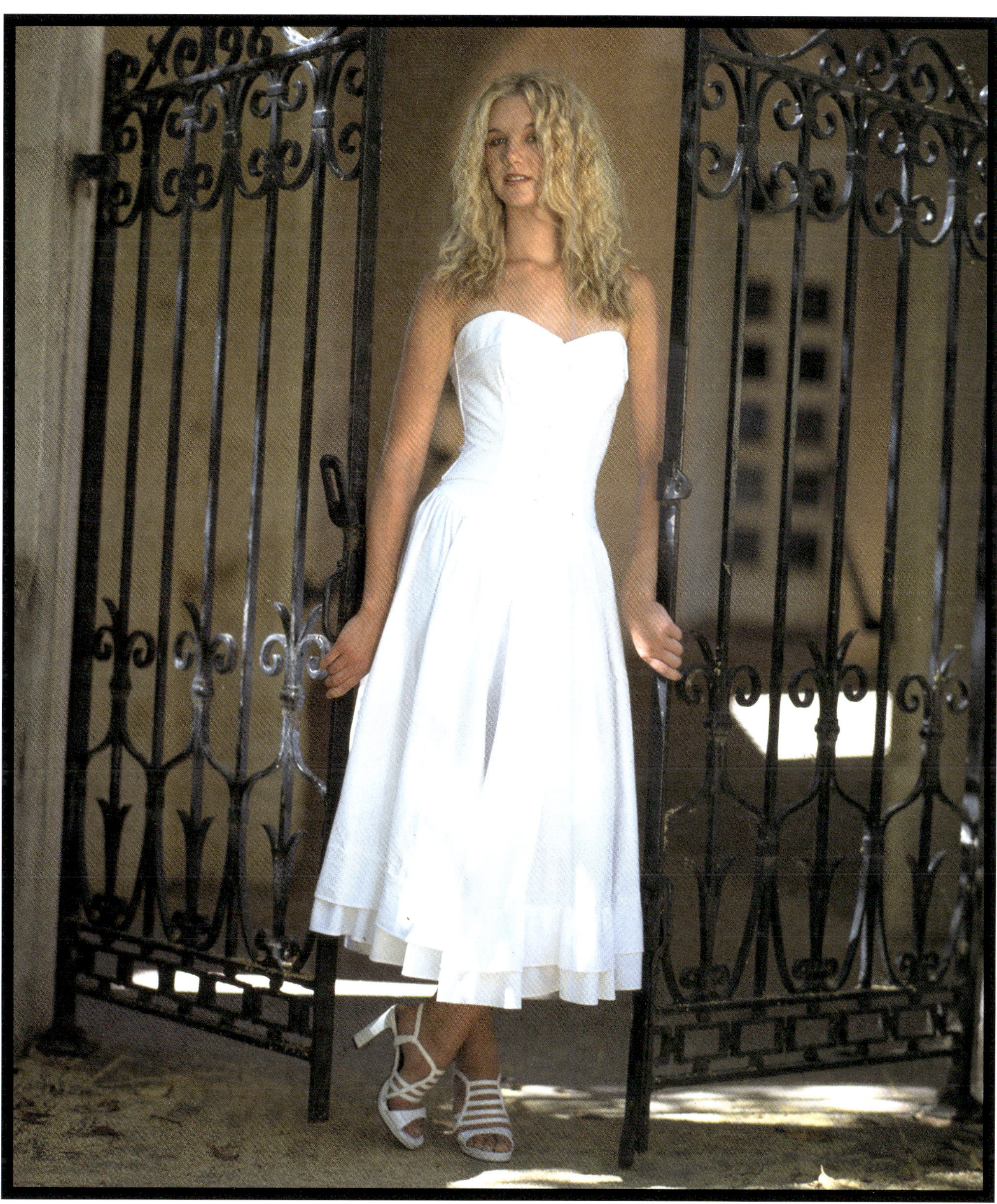

Western Woman

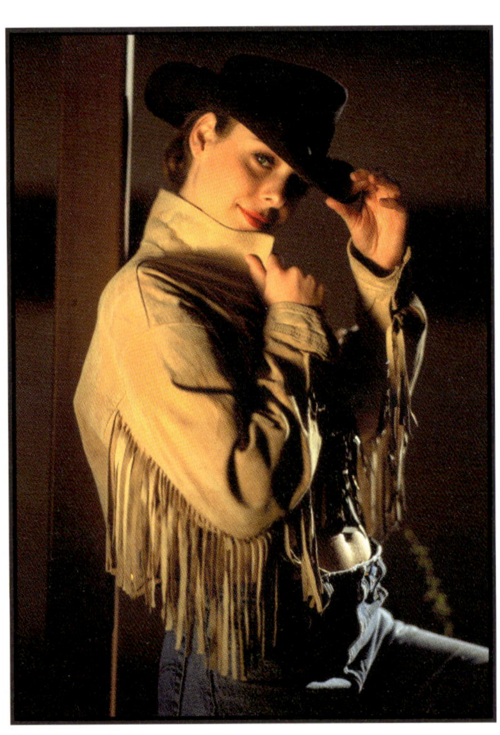

One of my first traveling workshops was to Taos, New Mexico. I made arrangements with a talent agency in Santa Fe to provide models for the on the road 4 day workshop.

When doing workshops, one of the unknown variables is the quality of models you may have to work with. I have found that if one or two of the models are experienced talented professionals, the workshop will be successful.

I knew Heather, the model illustrated here, from a previous workshop. She had done a fantastic job of modeling, so I was happy to cover her hotel and air travel costs to ensure a success in Santa Fe. Heather brought clothing that enhanced the western influence of Santa Fe that we were trying to capture in our images.

These images illustrated here were taken at a bunkhouse on the porch in the late afternoon. I used a gold reflector to direct light onto Heather's face and body. It was metered with a Sekonic incident meter and shot on a Hasselblad 201F with a 110mm lens, exposure 1/125th F:4.

Reflectors

If you photograph people outdoors, the most useful accessory are reflectors. As a part of my bag of tricks, I carry reflectors with me in my car at all times. When I go outdoors to photograph a model or portrait, I rely on my Photoflex reflectors. I use the larger 54" in silver, white, gold and soft gold along with an even larger translucent for blocking direct sun from the subject.

Silver is best for low contrast days, and when you have to use the reflector at a great distance from the subject.

Soft Gold is my favorite, and is used to slightly warm the subject and create a warm, glowing fill light.

White works best close to the subject and fills in light naturally to create a more natural light ratio.

Gold has limited use because of the warming effect it creates. Gold creates the same glow as late afternoon sun. Be careful because the gold reflector can give a false look if not used correctly.

Translucent is very effective for shooting in direct sunlight but requires the use of an assistant to hold the translucent. Creates the same effect as shooting with a large soft box but in an outdoor situation.

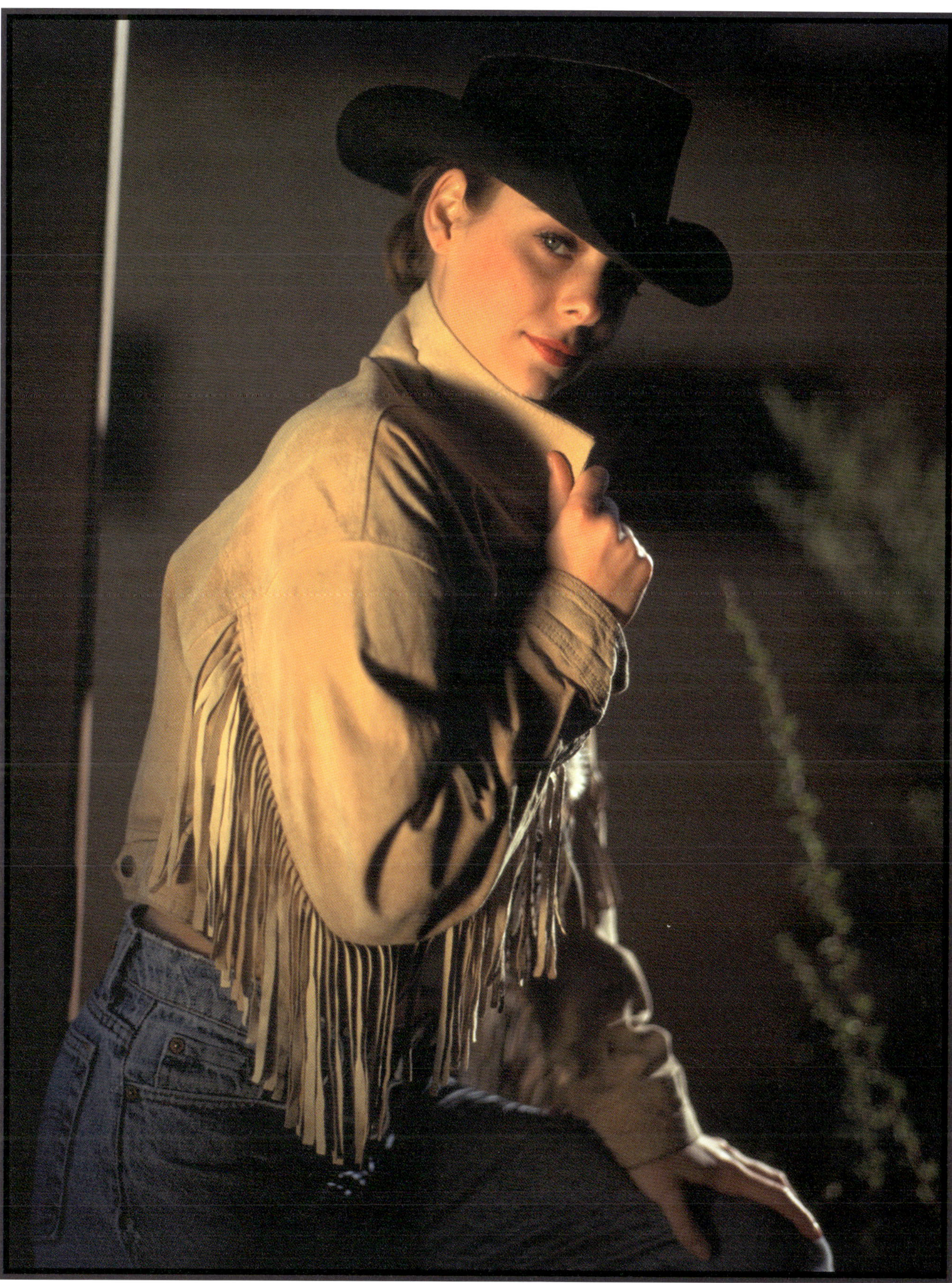

Denim Dreams

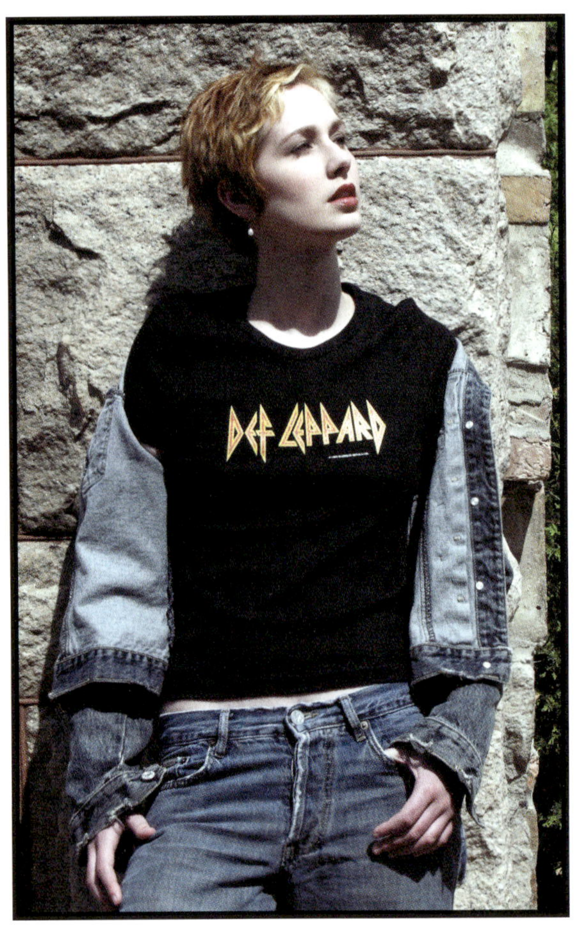

Kat is an aspiring Chicago model with tremendous potential. She was referred to me by my friend, Matt, in Kalamazoo, Michigan.

Many people enter the modeling field in Chicago, but only a few will make the grade and become professional models. Kat is one who will be successful in the modeling profession. She is 5' 8", the right size, and has exceptional features, including a great complexion.

The images you see illustrated were taken at my favorite outdoor location, a few blocks from my studio. The texture of the stone steps and the cut stone wall background was a good choice for placing someone with beautiful soft features.

I look for contrasts in backgrounds, when photographing beautiful women. I find using exteriors that are rough and textured make wonderful backgrounds, as they force the viewers eye to notice the fine detail in skin against a rough surface. The backgrounds in this shooting add to the models natural beauty.

It was an overcast day, but suddenly the sun broke out for a short time. I had the model face the sun in the shot on the brick wall, as I liked the way the face was illuminated by the direct sunlight. The image was exposed with an incident meter measuring the light falling on the models face.

Kat on the steps was shot a short time later using a white reflector to add fill light to the shot. It was metered with an incident meter for the light on the face. Exposure was 1/500th at F:4.5 using a film rating of ISO 80.

Both images were taken with the Olympus Camedia E-10 digital camera.

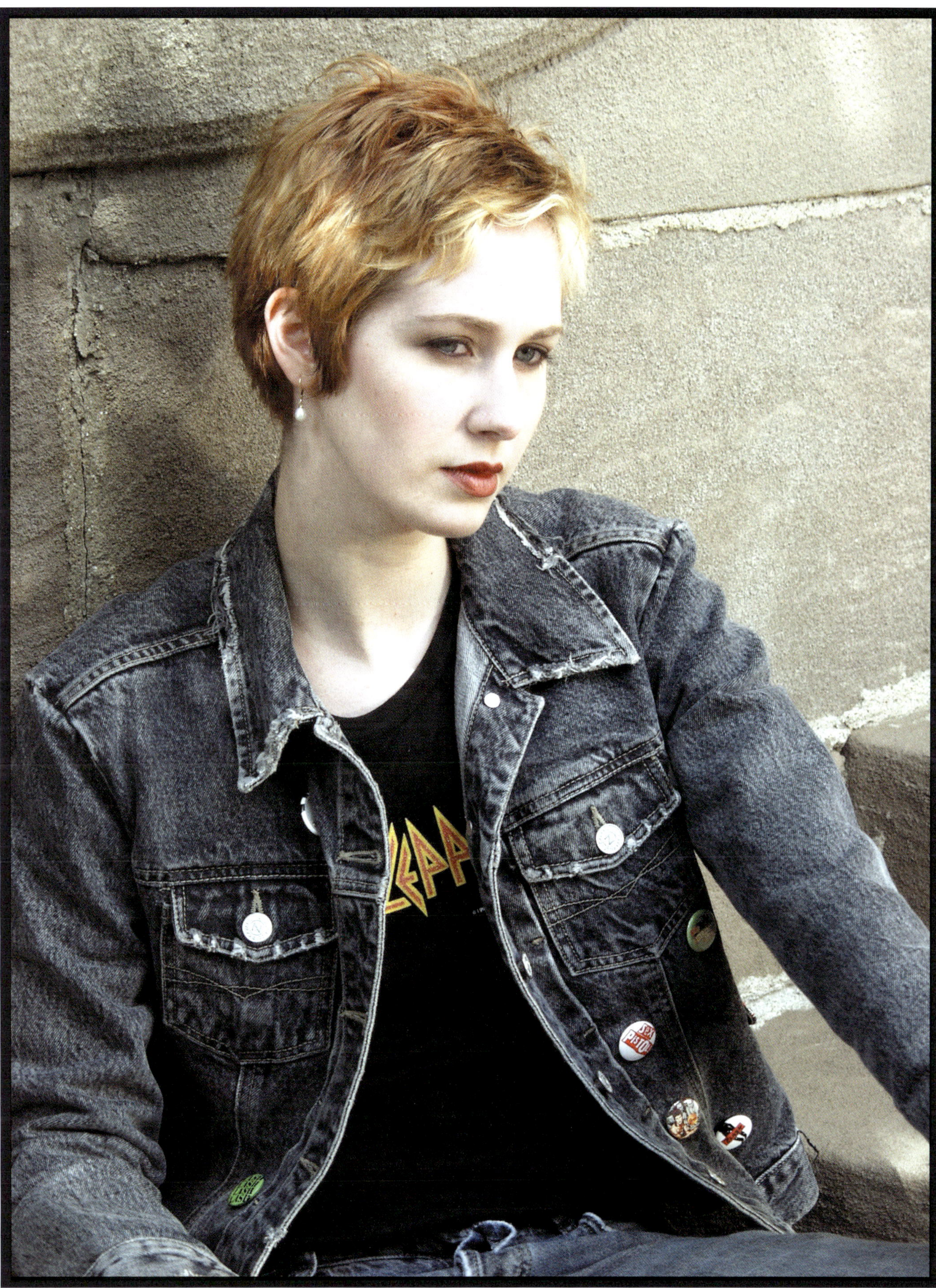

The Gangster and the Moll

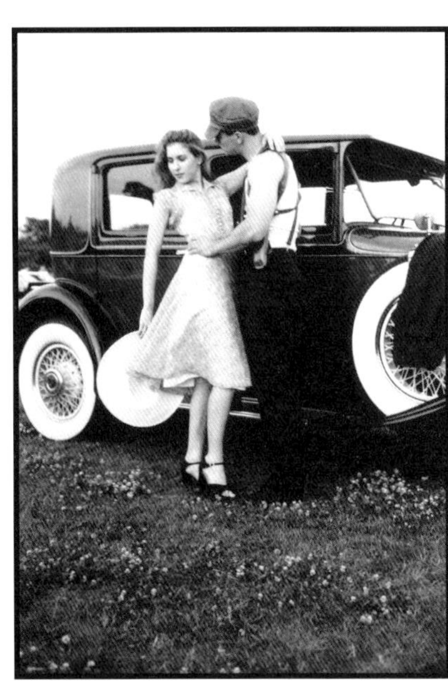

In the course of giving photo workshops, I have had the opportunity to meet some fantastic people across America. When I did a workshop for the Professional Photographers of New England, I met many photographers from the various state PP of A organizations.

As I mentioned earlier in this book, my association with one excellent photographer named Walt Steinmetz led to my meeting Dan Rodrique who became the president of the Maine P P of A. Dan invited Walt and me to assist him in a teaching program at his studio in downtown Portland, Maine. Walt, Dan and I gave an exciting program on our individual style of photography to over 100 professional photographers.

In the afternoon, Dan had made arrangements for the group to shoot at a location on the beach in a nearby state park. Dan had also arranged for models and the antique car illustrated in these images. As the sun set, we had some awesome light with a warm glow. There were no reflectors necessary, and we could shoot with the models being illuminated totally by the sun. No reflectors or fill-flash were necessary. Walt initially set up the pose with the models, then we created many variations of the pose.

What makes these images spectacular are the props. The old car, the models outfits and the details such as the gangster's hat and gun provides for some great images.

Outdoor Shooting Tips

Planning an outdoor shoot is very different from the typical indoor shooting. As photographers, you have the opportunity to choose from a number of different lighting styles to make the most of the image you want to achieve when shooting in a studio.

When you plan an outdoor shoot we are limited to the type of day that nature provides. While it is true we can create images any time of the day. Some of the superlative outdoor images are created when the sun is about to set. This last hour of daylight is called sweet light. There is no sweeter time of day for shooting outdoor images than this last hour of sunlight. The light becomes very warm, with the color temperature rising to give a warm glow to your images. At this time of day, there is no need to use a warming filter like the 81A or 81B. The 81 series of warming filters are designed to create the illusion that you shot your outdoor images during the sweet light of the day.

If you examine all the reflectors that are available for outdoor shooting, you will notice they come in different surface varieties. Gold is used for creating the warm glow of sweet light. Sunlight (mixed gold and silver) is for warming but not to the extreme of the all-gold reflector. White reflectors are used for the most natural fill light but are less reflective than the metallic reflectors. The Translucent reflector is utilized for blocking the direct sun from the subject and works extremely well in creating wonderful outdoor images, But it usually requires a larger translucent and an able-body to hold it in the correct position. Black is used to scrim light and not allow direct sun to light the model. I personally recommend the mixed silver/gold, silver and the white for maximum versatility.

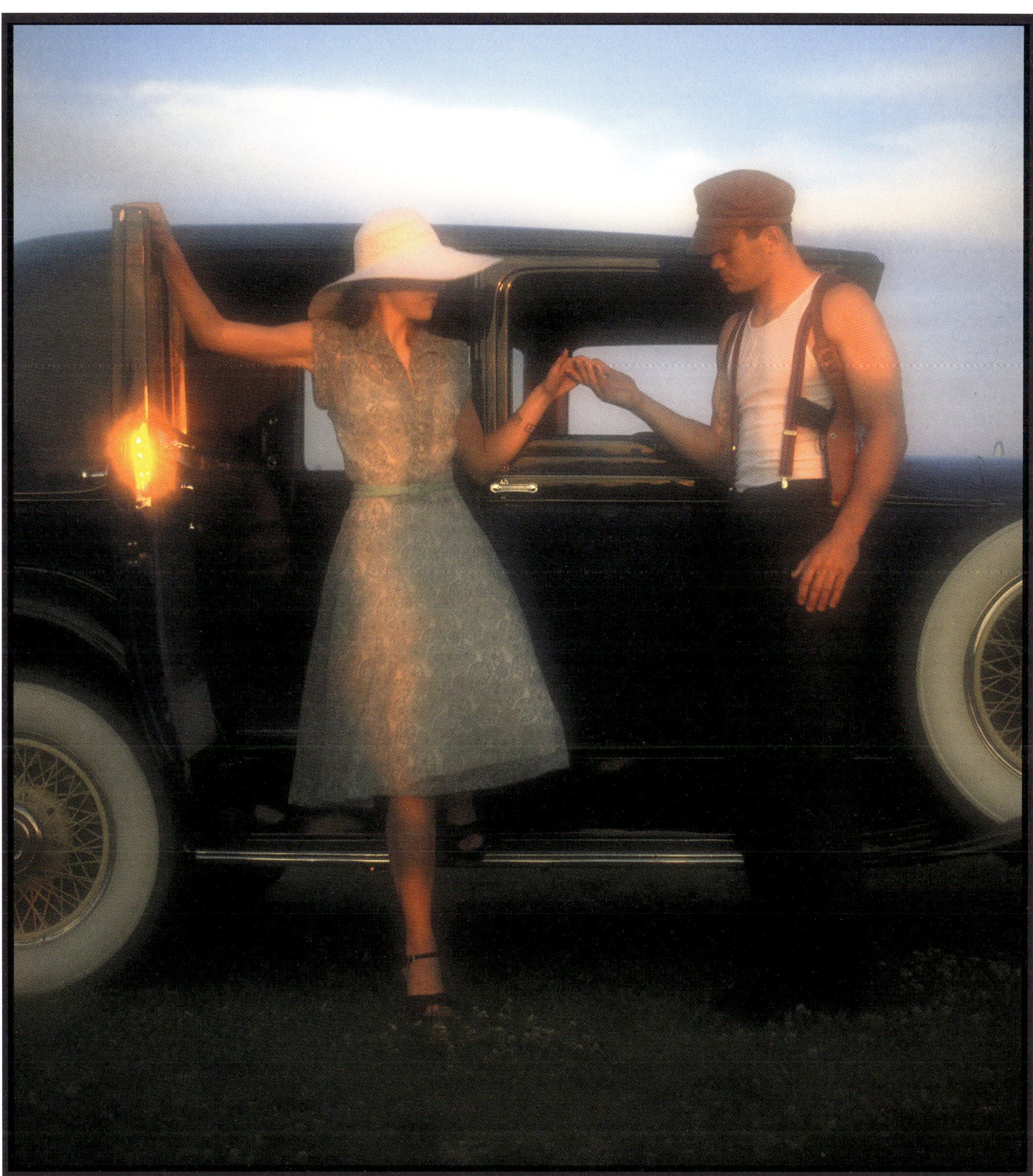

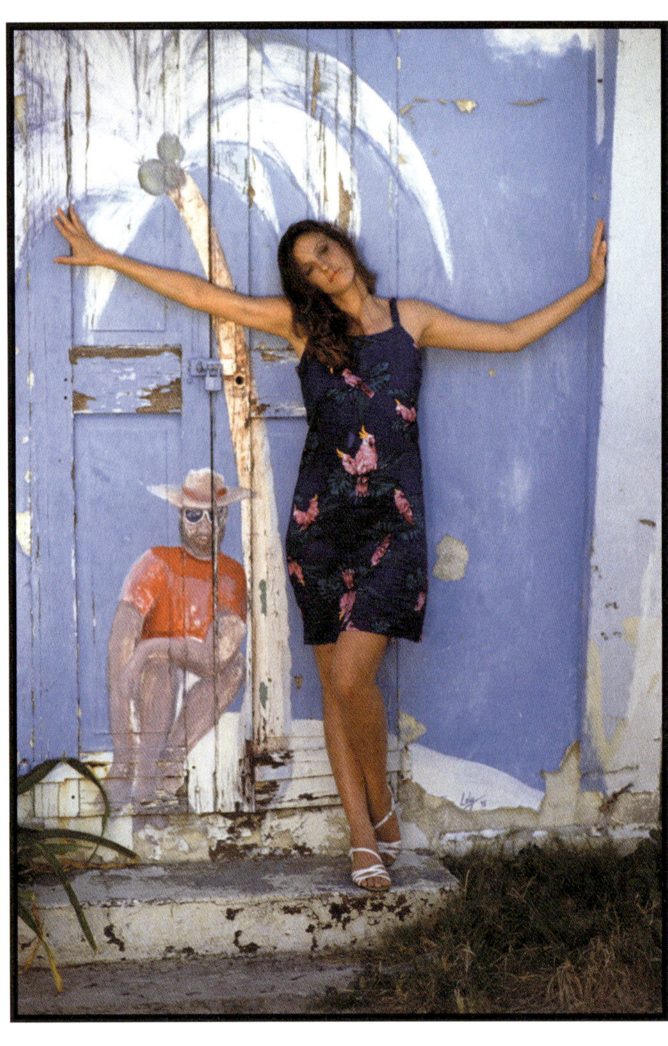

Surf

Pam was photographed on the island of St Martin in the Carribean. For shooting water shots, I can not think of a more exciting location than the waters of the Carribean. These image were taken in the late afternoon using a mixed gold/silver reflector to direct the warm light onto Pam's face and body. Without the use of a reflector, the ratio of sun on Pam's shoulder and back side would have been too extreme for the film.

One of the tips I have learned about how light works was that the human eye can see about 11 stops of light from black to white. So we see far more than film can, as color film only has the ability to see about 2 1/2 F:stops. So it becomes necessary not to allow the bright or highlight area of a photo to be more than 2 1/2 stop difference from the darkest shadow area. This translates to using fill-flash or reflectors in bright sun to give you the best images.

Since switching to digital, I have found there is more latitude with digital imaging than with film. However, while there may be more latitude, it still does not equal the 11 F:stops we see with our eyes.

When this shot was taken, Pam did not have a bathing suit with her. But when she saw the beautiful light, she quickly decided to wear her sundress in the water, and we created some fantastic images.

The image of Pam against the painted building was another example of the exotic backgrounds just begging for a beautiful model to create some amazing images.

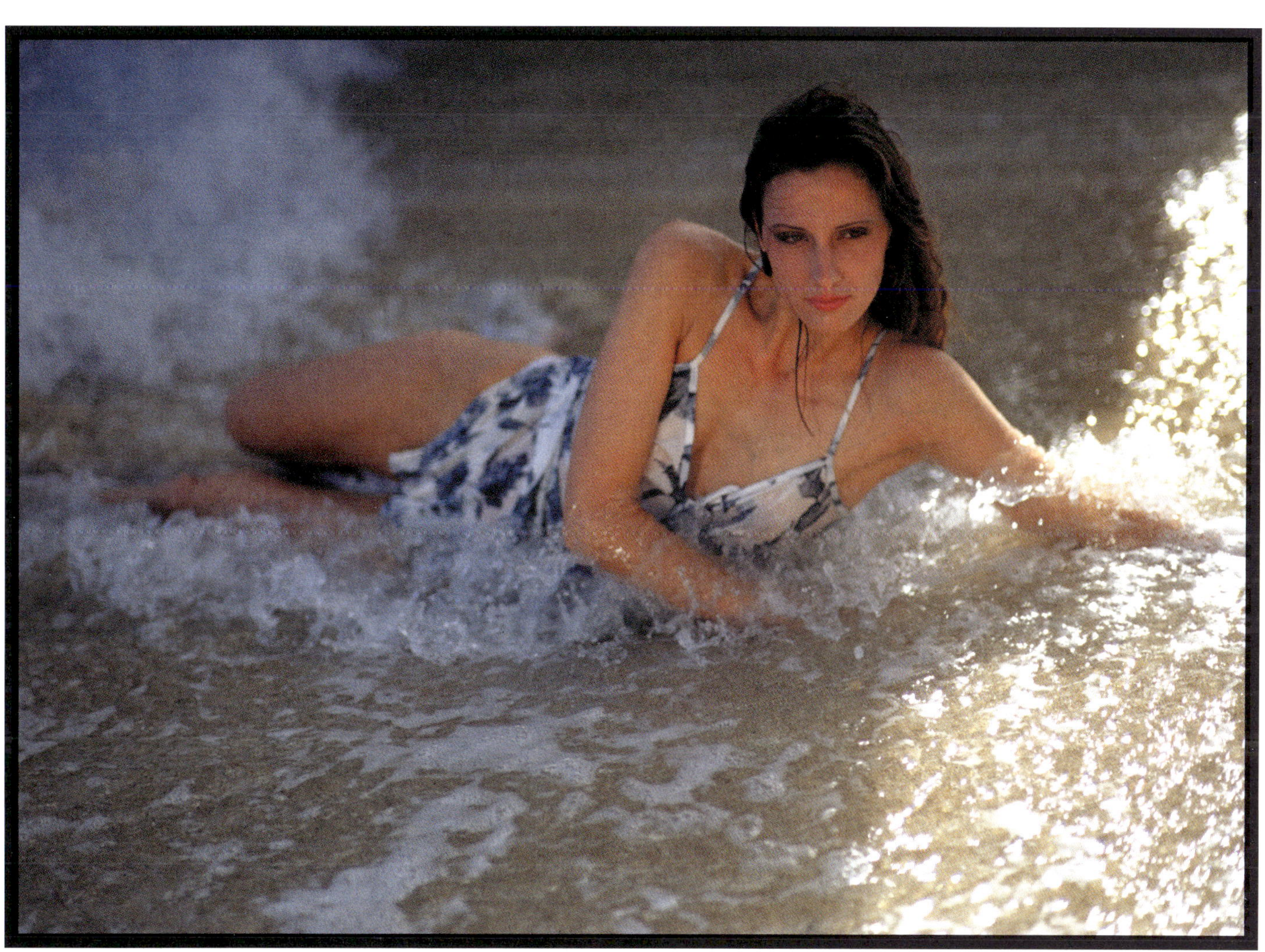

Mellow Yellow

Another shooting situation I set up in my workshop in St Martin was this image of Sabrina against a yellow wall.

In the course of shooting on this beautiful island, I looked for locations that would give the feeling of the island experience. When we were in the town area, I noticed the yellow wall with the purple stripe. I knew this had to be a choice location as I had never seen anything like it in the United States.

Sabrina is a of those model who takes suggestions easily and poses naturally. She made this image look like she was born near this wall, and stands like she was part of the wall.

Natural light was coming into the vestibule, and with the white walls nearby creating beautiful fill light, the result was spectacular. No additional reflectors or fill-flash were necessary.

Developing a Photographic Style

Creating a photographic style is one of the most difficult things to define and create in all aspects of photography. For many years, I knew I wanted to create a unique photographic style like many of the famous photographers I read about in books and magazines.

People like Ansel Adams, Bert Stern, Avedon, Robert Farber, Diane Arbus, Jeanloup Sieff, Art Kane, Helmut Newton, and other talented photographers have developed unique photographic styles. How did they do it? It took a long time for me to figure out how to develop a style. But after many years of photographing people, I have finally figured out my style.

Through all the many years I have been in photography, I have discovered that a style emerges after you create thousands and thousands of images. You begin to do many of the same things over and over again. You apply your personality to your photography. Deborah Turbeville has created a style that is unique to her using elaborate room settings with high fashion models and exotic lighting. Helmut Newton's style is to use high-fashion models in bizarre poses and usually adds an erotic element to his images. Each of those people have created their own unique style.

Most styles are created by seeing other people's photography and emulating the images you see. In my case, I have always been fascinated by poster art and poster photography. I want the image I create to be strong enough to be considered for a cover shot or poster. Creating a dynamic image usually requires some planning. It requires the right model, a pose that is dramatic, Lighting that is well balanced and designed to create separation between subject and background. This separation provides a three dimensional feeling to the image.

There are hundreds of things that define style. My use of hair lights, rim lighting and colored gels combined with strong posing are all elements that design my style. Try to define your style......

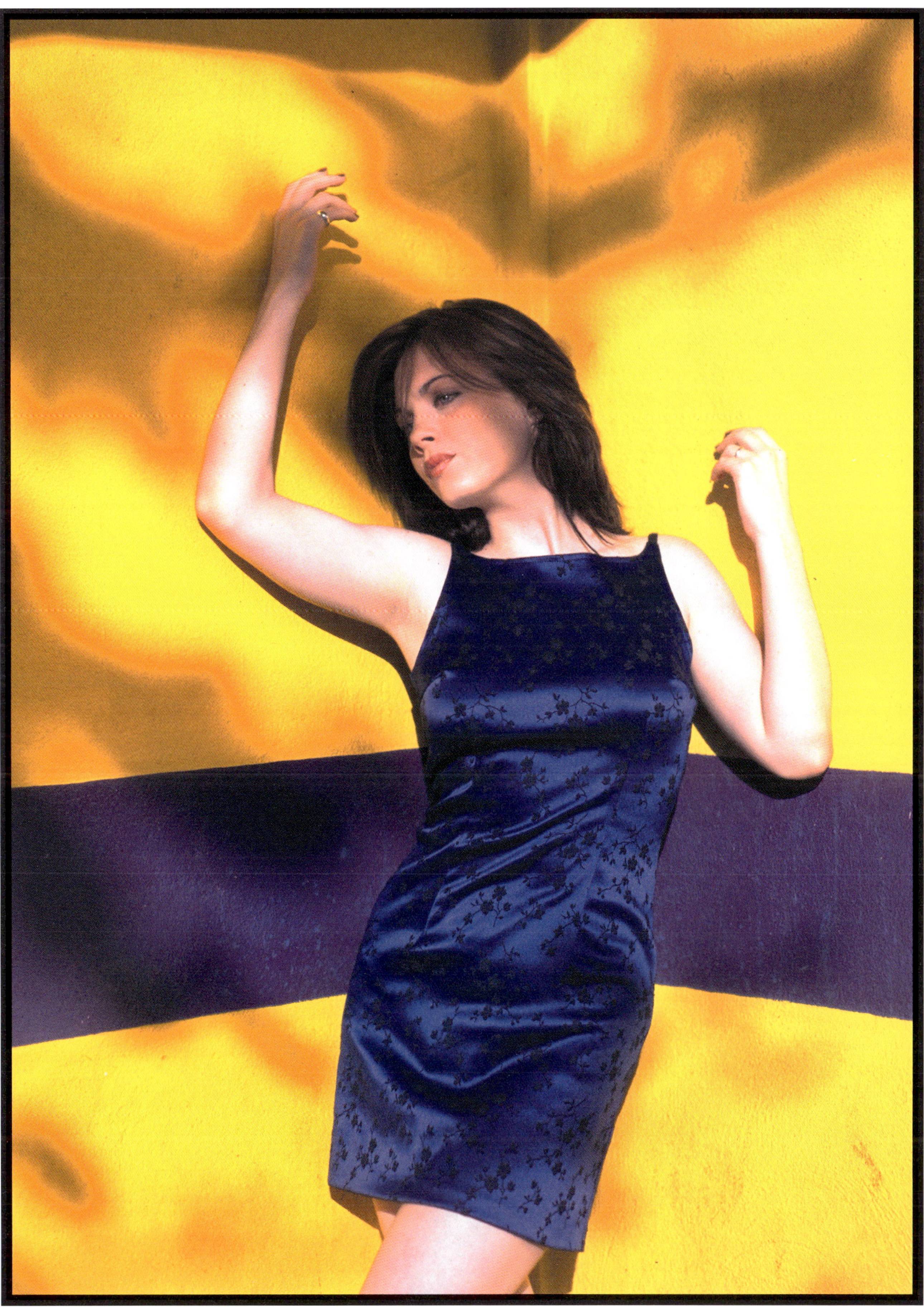

Pensive

A few years ago I had the opportunity to photograph an excellent model named Mary-Alyce.We produced many images for her portfolio and for the Backdrop Outlet catalog. On one occasion Mary-Alyce brought her two daughters with her, and I decided to photograph her daughter, Rachel. The image illustrated is Rachel in a pensive mood. When Rachel put on the gown, I felt the image had an old fashioned quality. I set up the set using a product called fantasy cloth to give the image a mystical, glowing quality.

To further enhance this quality, I decided to use a #1 softar filter on my Hasselblad, along with my homemade edge diffusion filter. This filter has been used in many images in this book and is extremely effective in creating a moody old-fashioned quality and a dreamy feeling.

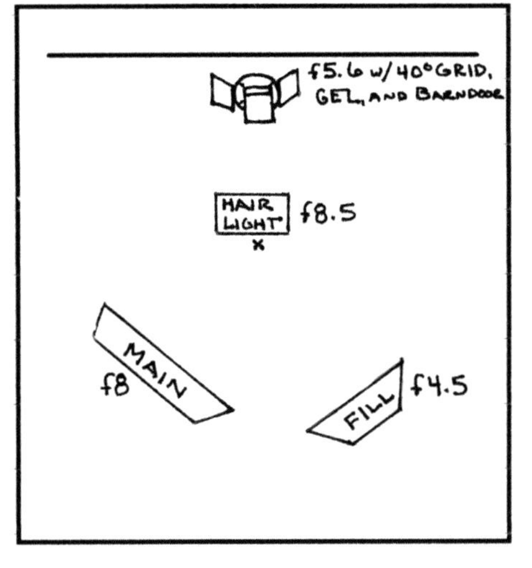

Because of Rachel's bare arms, ratio lighting was the best option in keeping arms and legs looking trim and not creating unwanted broadening of the image. Also ratio lighting gave this image the dimensional lighting that only ratio lighting can achieve. I set up the main light to the left of camera with a large plume wafer soft box set for F:8, the fill light to the right of camera was another soft box set for F:4 & 1/2 creating a 3 to 1 light ratio. I added a hair light (balcar prisma-light soft box with honeycomb grid) set one half stop brighter than the main light at F:8.5. I also added a background light with 7" reflector and 40 degree grid with a magenta gel to give the romantic pink color to the cream and white fantasy cloth background.

Making your own Edge Diffusion Filter

Start by choosing a UV or Skylight filter that you most likely bought with your camera. I understand that most photographers feel it is necessary to keep this filter on your camera to protect the lens. It has been proven the skylight or UV filter actually degrades image quality. A lens shade not only improves image quality visibly but protects the lens better than a filter. I now ask you a question; *How come the manufacturers of point and shoot cameras do not provide for filters to protect the lens?* Answer: <u>It is Not Necessary.</u>

Try doing something positive with this filter. Purchase a bottle of Sally Hansen Hard as Nails nail polish. This brand of polish is totally clear, no color. Apply a layer to the inside edge of the filter and try your new tool with a slightly longer focal length lens (ie. with 35mm camera an 85 to 105mm lens) on medium format (100 to 150mm lens). Leave a clear opening, about the size of the 50 cent piece, on filters that are 62mm or larger. You can always go back and increase the effect by applying more polish for additional diffusion.You can also make the circle smaller to increase the effect. This is a mandatory filter for my photography and becomes useful in creating mood. I also find this filter useful in photographing old buildings to create the feeling of age and texture.

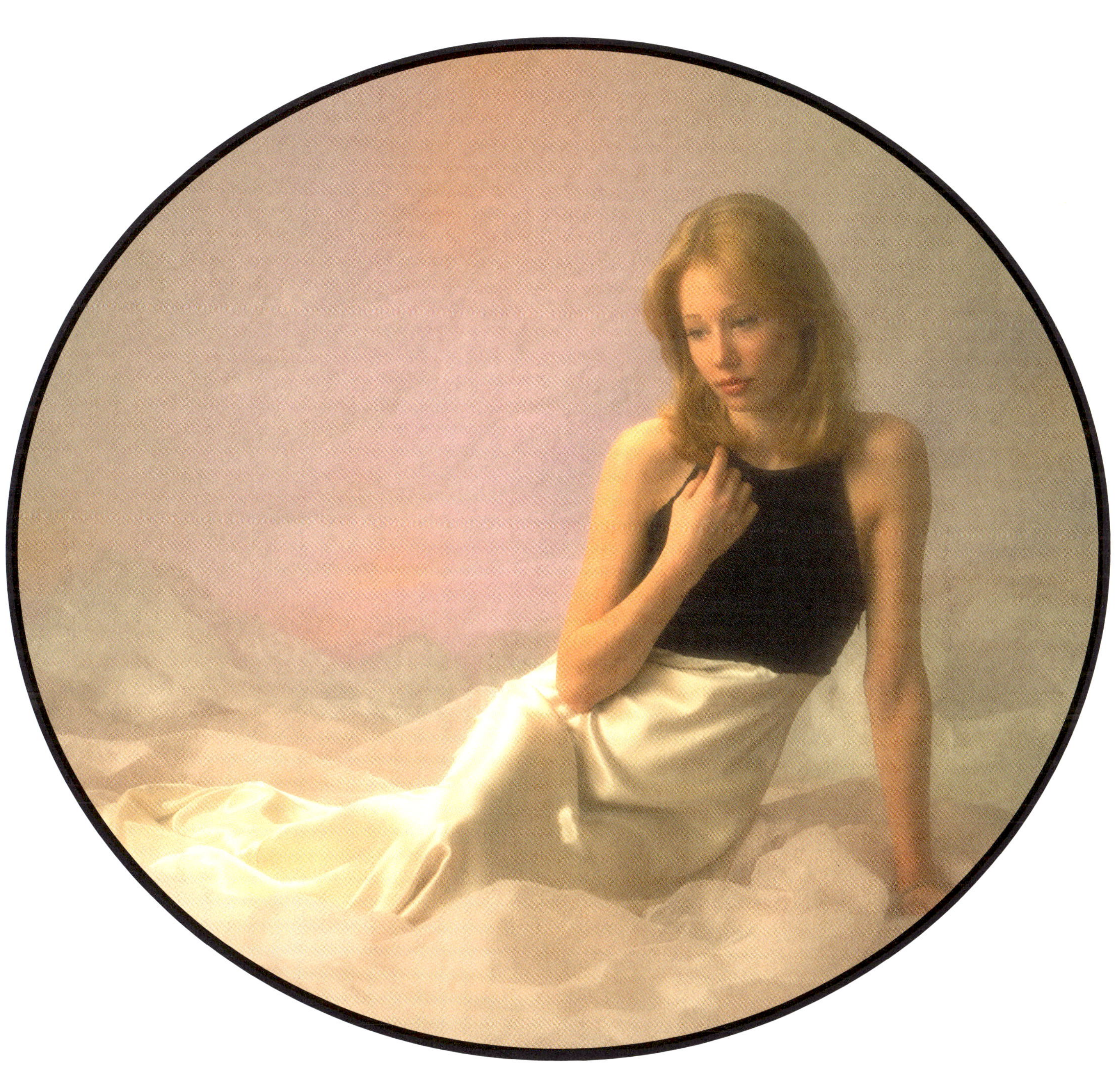

Mylar Reflections

Karen on the gold reflector material was created while my assistant, Clay, and I were giving a two-day workshop in Las Vegas. Karen, one of the local models, decided to model lingerie. Lingerie modeling jobs pay double rate over most normal clothes modeling jobs. So it is advantageous for a model to have some lingerie images in her portfolio.

I arranged for Backdrop Outlet to ship a few different backgrounds and assorted props to the workshop. One of the items that we requested was the gold mylar you see under Karen. I crumpled the gold mylar into a ball. When laid flat, the material had thousands of wrinkles in it. I wanted that effect for a background.

The gold mylar acts as both a reflector and a background, I instructed Karen to bend her arms creating the diagonal lines I was looking for. The luminescence in the hair was created by my small soft box hair light. The brilliant hair along with the models shapely figure and face make this shot pull together.

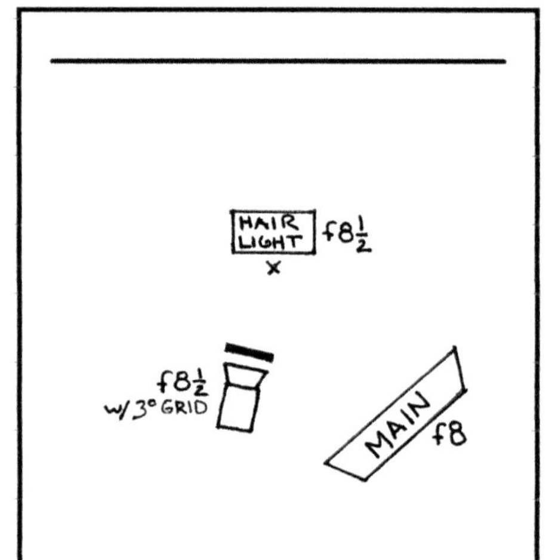

I used a Hasselblad softar #1 diffusion filter to create more mood in my image. This is something I do in most of my boudoir or lingerie images.

Lighting on this image was created with a soft spot on the face 1/2 stop brighter than the main light, creating a glowing face that is slightly overexposed to wash out detail. A soft-spot is created with a 7" reflector mounted on a monolight. (ie. White Lightning) and a 3 degree grid spot attached to the front of the reflector. The 3 degree grid is the smallest of the grids creating a very small circle of light

I started by setting up the main light with a large soft box set for F:8, adding the hair light set for F:8 1/2 (only slightly higher because of Karen's light blonde hair). The soft spot was set for F:8 1/2, The camera was set for F:8. By shooting at F:8, I am overexposing the face by 1/2 stop.This is a three light set-up, easy to accomplish and dramatic when you want to create a beautiful glowing face.

<u>A word of warning:</u> Do not shoot the older, overweight real estate agent with this type of lighting. This style of lighting works best with an attractive face.

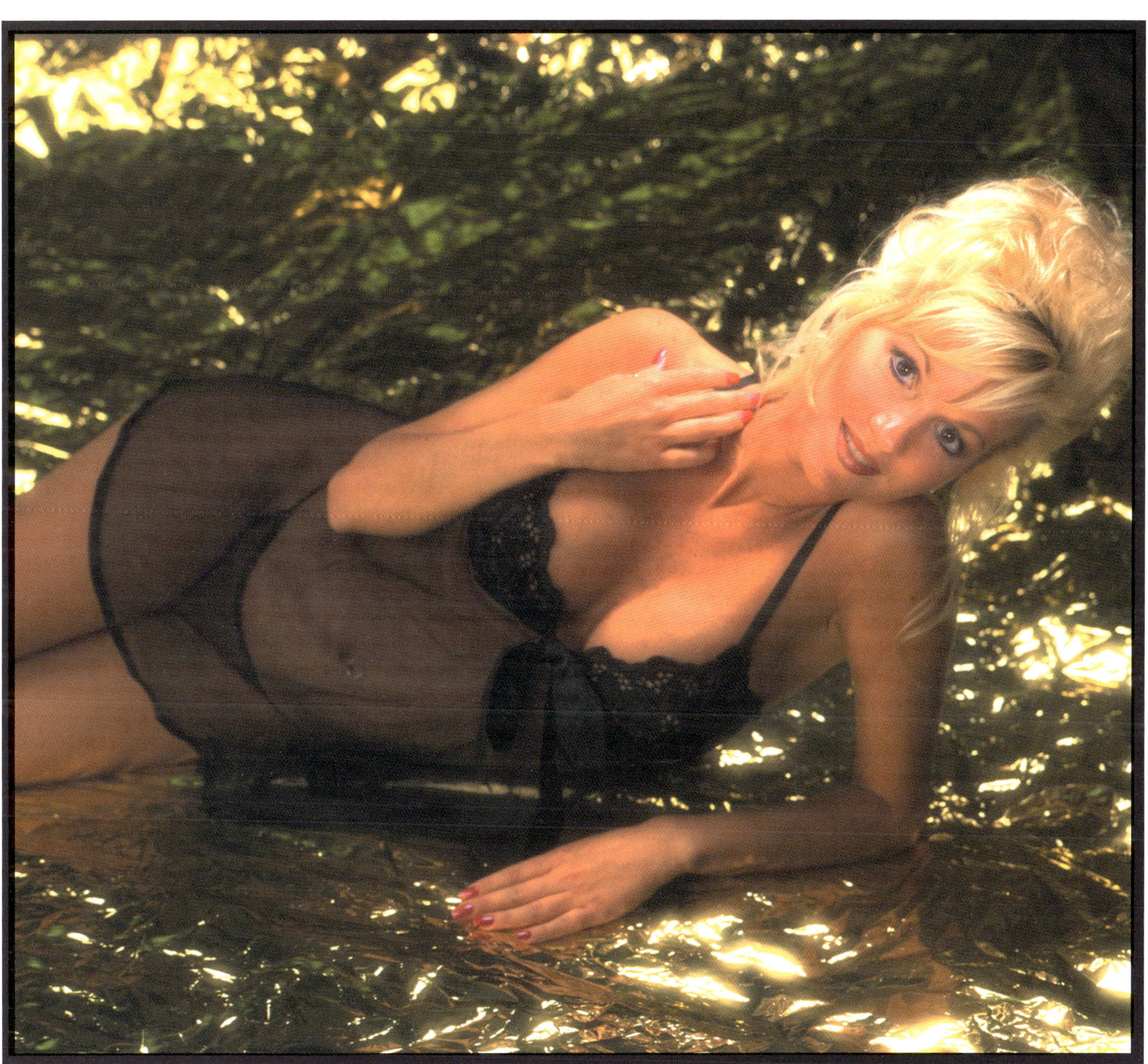

City Girl

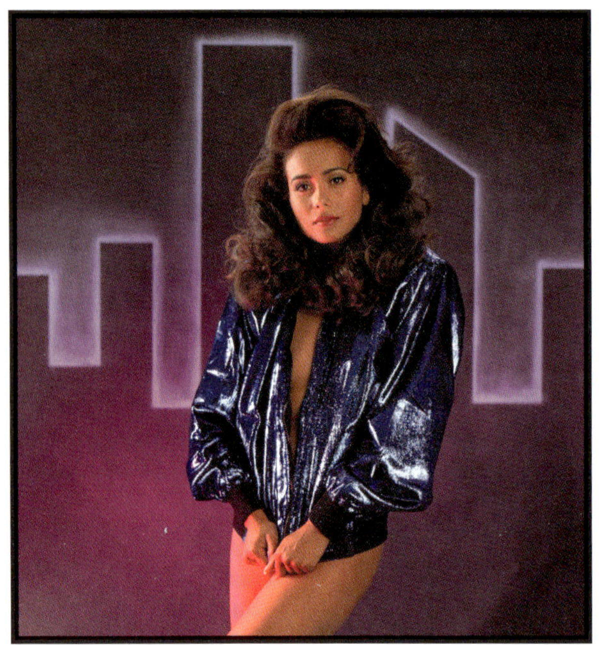

When I opened my first studio in 1978 I met a model named Ruth Vasecky who became a friend of mine. Ruth now owns a talent agency in the Chicago area. Ruth referred Alex to me for some test shooting and during this test shooting we had some jackets for a client to photograph. I suggested to Alex we try the jackets in a shot.

Alex is a beautiful model and was willing to help in this project with her excellent modeling talents. I wanted to create a classy but sexy look for the jackets, and Alex pulled it off with ease.

Lighting: I decided to use the optical spot with skyline cookie creates the city scape behind Alex for effect. I used a purple gel over the optical spot to give the cityscape more symmetry with the blue jacket. I set-up a softbox left of camera, as the model's body was facing in that direction. I wanted ratio lighting to best emphasize her great legs. The main light was set for F:8, with a fill light to the right of camera set for F:4 & 1/2. I also used a hair light two stops brighter than the main in a balcar prisma-light soft box with grid set for F:16. The hair light needed to be two stops brighter because of Alex's dark hair. The hairlight gave her hair a highlight and glow.

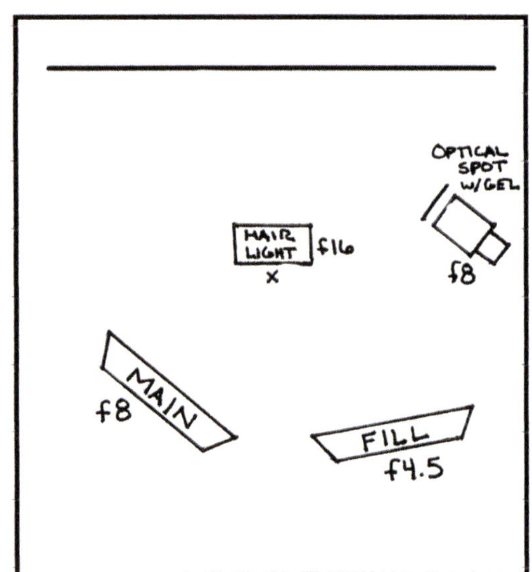

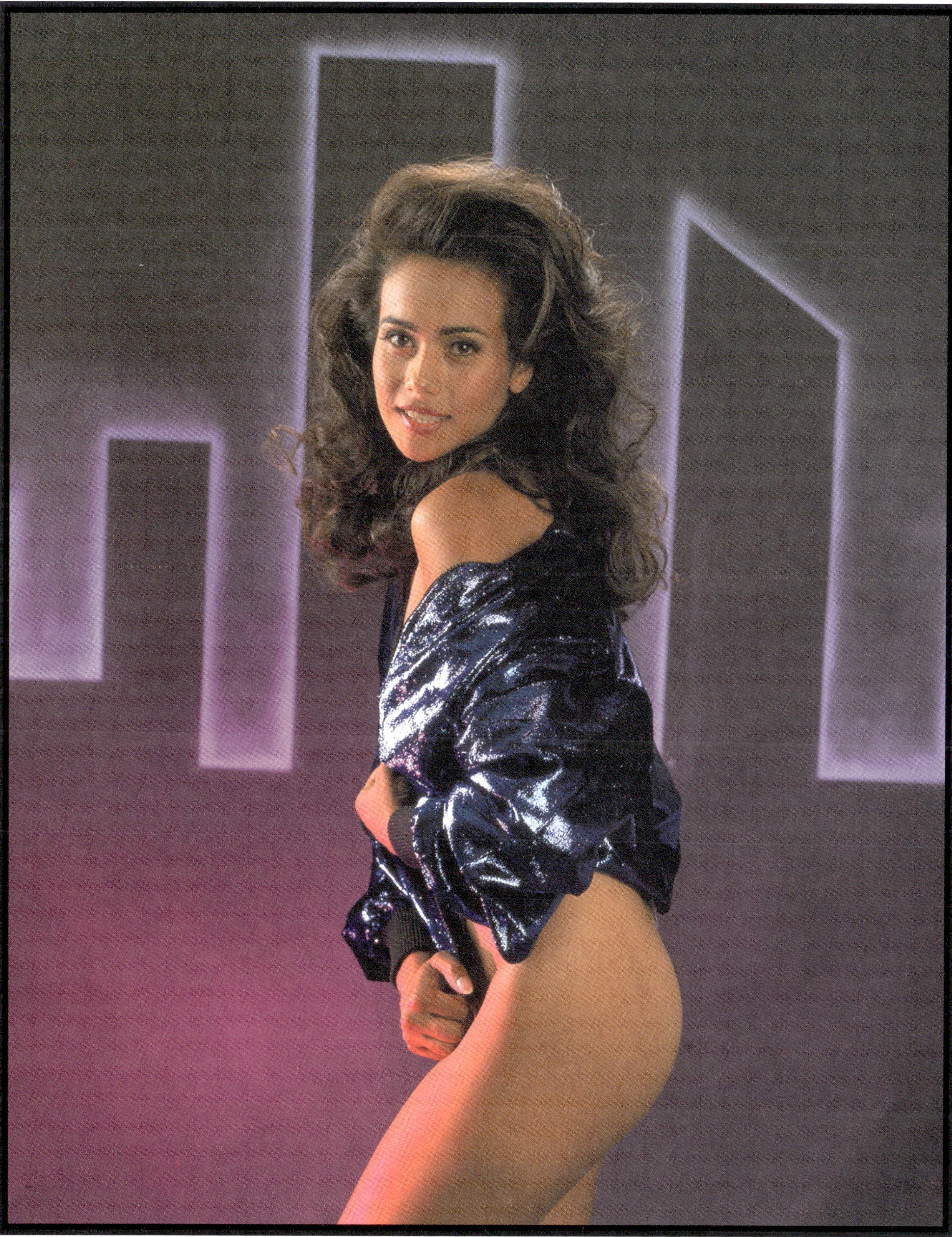

Barn Beauty

I am always looking for new exciting outdoor locations to shoot. My assistant, Clay, suggested we plan a shoot at his farm. He told me about the buildings and the machinery. I felt this would be an ideal setting in which to conjure up some new image material.

Upon arrival at the farm we planned out our shots based on the direction of the sun and which time of day each location would work best. I knew that the late afternoon sun would provide fantastic light, but we would have limited time to shoot. Generally, there is only about one hour of this perfect sweet-light, and you can shoot only a limited amount of film in this last hour of day-light.

I arranged for two models to meet us at the farm. The models arrived in the early afternoon, and we started shooting some interior shots with the sunlight coming through open doors and windows. While these shots were good, none were of the quality that we would get at the end of the day.

This image was done for the model's portfolio and ended up in my portfolio also. Clay and I set up a bale of hay near the entrance door to give the models a place to sit or stand. When I suggested our model stand on the hay bale with her fashion style outfit, I knew we had a winner.

I wanted to create a leggy look as the model was 5'10". I raised the model's height up two feet by having her stand on the hay bale. This image was photographed using my Hasselblad with the 110mm lens, Note; I positioned the camera at the same height as the model's ankles to over exaggerate the look. By doing this, I was able to create an extremely leggy photograph of a beautiful model.

What helped make this image dynamic is the drama of the model's body language. She struck a pose that makes you wonder what the story is behind the image, creating an air of mystery.

This photo was metered with the Sekonic incident light meter reading the light falling on the subject with no additional fill light or reflectors.

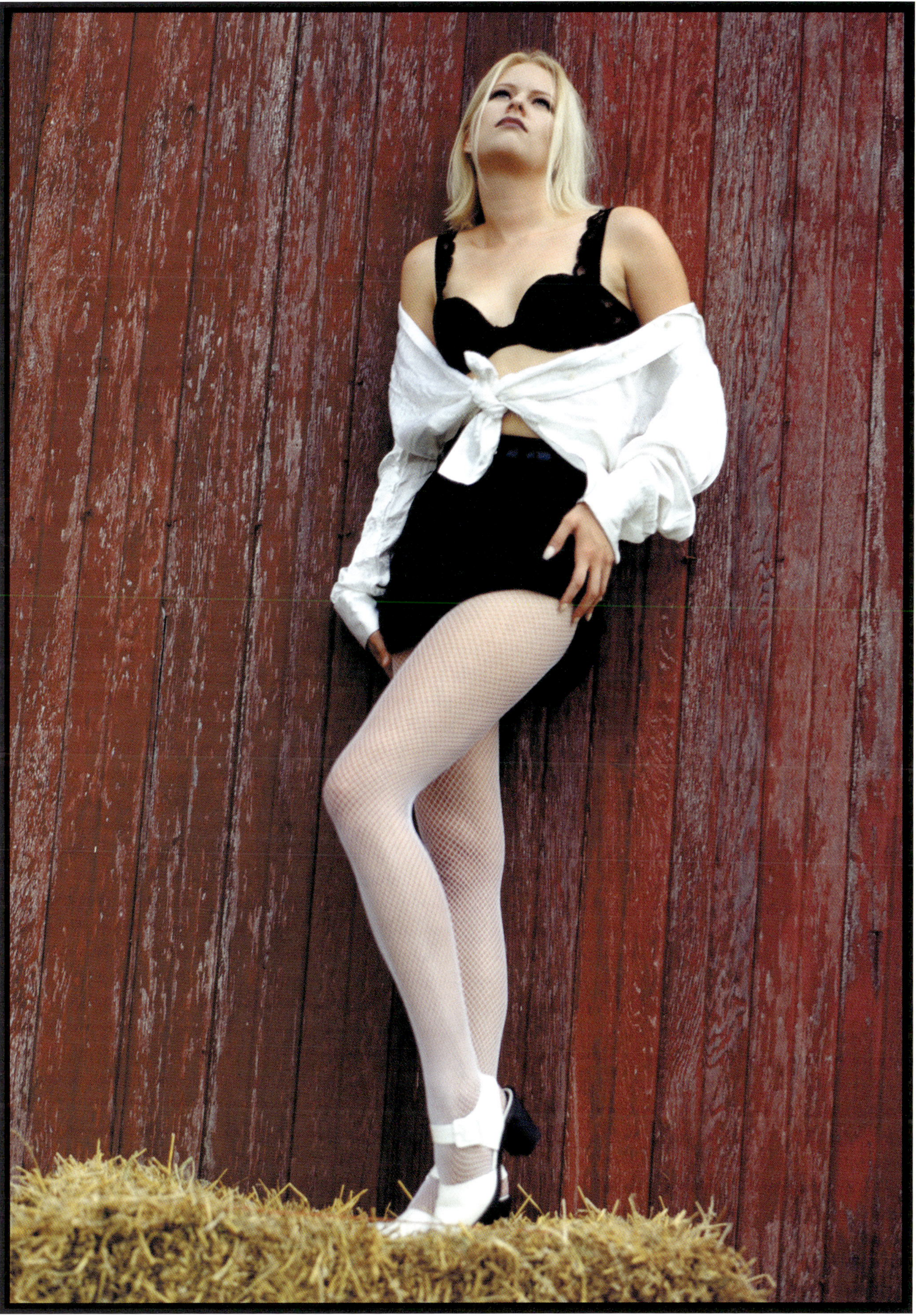

Shadow Dancing

When working with commercial accounts it is necessary to always look for new and innovative ideas when producing images for these clients.

This image was created with the models about 1 to 1 1/2 feet from the background to intentionally create a strong shadow. The ad-agency proposed this idea to the client and asked me to test it to see if it would work the way the art director envisioned. Our tests proved successful.

Models were chosen on their ability to perform the high fashion look the client wanted in his catalog.

This look is high key with shadows. The models are so close to the background there was no need to light the background separately. Normally in high-key, you set the background lights one stop brighter than the main or key light. In this case because we needed the shadows, it was not possible to light the background. If separate lights were used on the background, there would be multiple shadows.

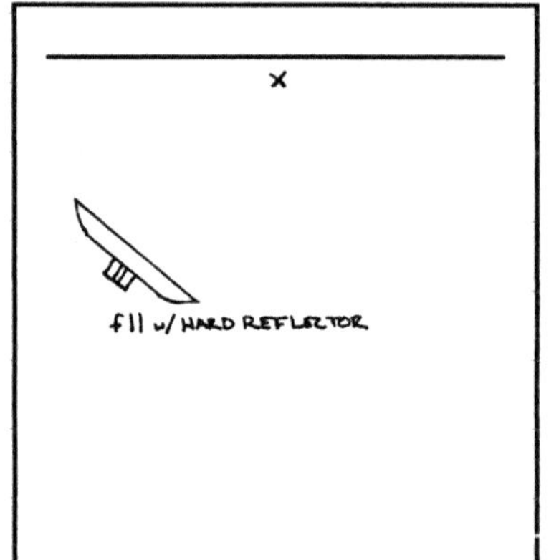

This is the simplest lighting set-up in the entire book. One light with a 16" polished reflector placed about 12 feet from the subjects created a strong shadow and provided the same F:stop on the subject and the background.

We used a dance choreographer for the poses since all of them had to look like dance poses. The campaign was very successful and continued for three consecutive years.

All images were photographed with Hasselblad 150mm lens, F:11 at 1/125th. and metered with Sekonic L-308 incident meter usingFuji Astia film.

Building your own Creative Team

A few years ago, I wrote an article for Rangefinder magazine about building a creative team. The article covered the use of other talented people in creating spectacular photography.

As photographers, we all have talents that many people do not have. This is why models want us to do photos for them. If they could shoot pictures, they would not need us. Make-up artists need photos for their portfolios to show the type of make-up they apply. Photo stylists need photos to show their artistic talents.

If you offer your photographic services to a make-up artist, model, photo stylist or others in this industry, you can trade services and have these creative people contribute to your photo shoot for no cost Provide an 8x10 to your back-up people and you will be surprised how many are willing to help you create your photo shooting idea.

I use this technique whenever I have an idea for a fantastic image and have found no shortage of talented professional people who want to help in the creation. Don't forget to ask them if they have ideas for photos. Many of the cutting edge photos I have produced were <u>their</u> ideas!

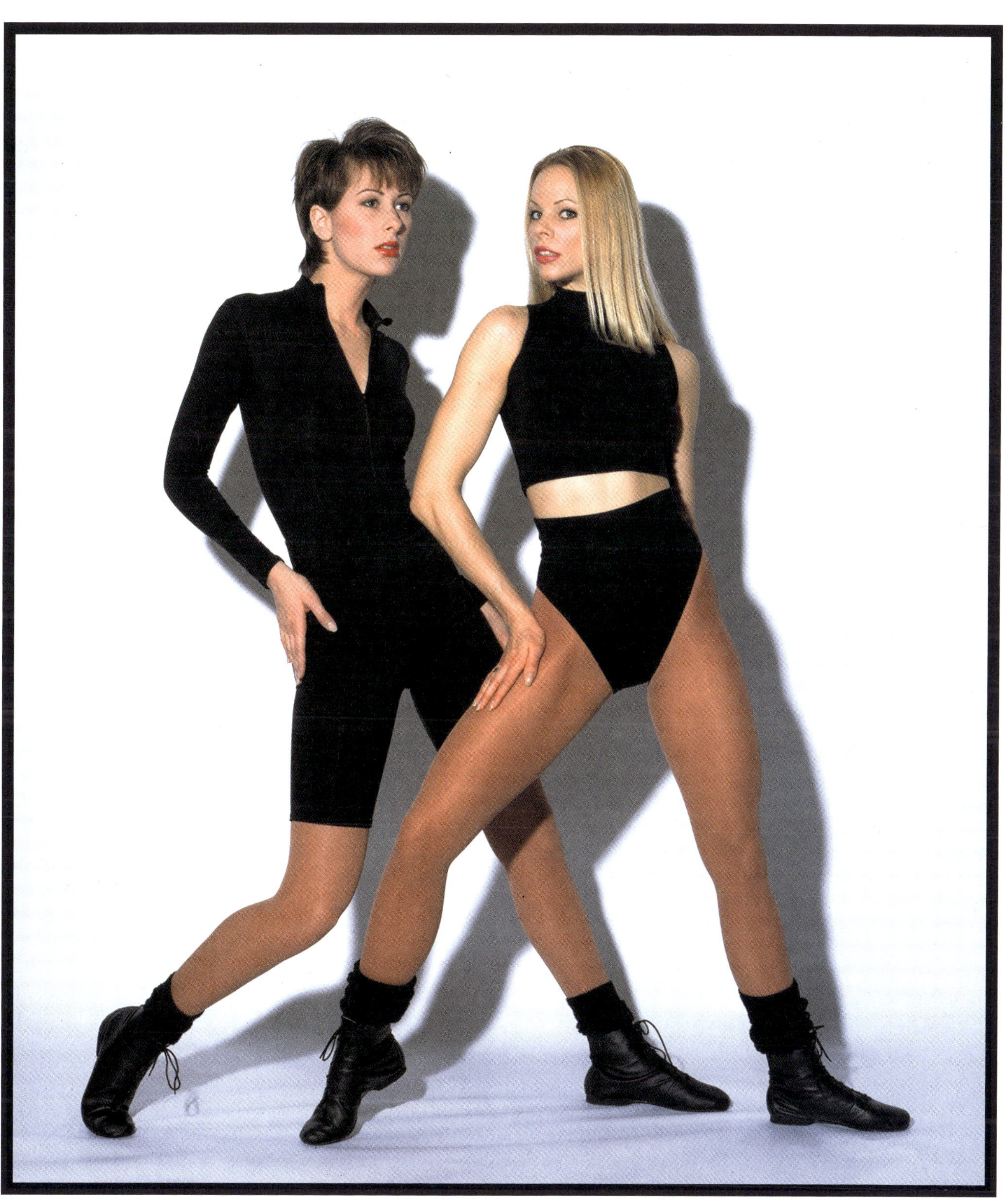

Black Magic

Shooting a model dressed in black on a black background is one of the more difficult lighting situations you may encounter. This is what separates those photographers in the know from those who do not know lighting basics.

This type of lighting is also known as low-key. I used a black muslin background, positioning Laura in a horizontal pose leaning on one elbow to show her face and hair. The black boa was chosen to add more elegance to the image.

Lighting: I started with a main light to the right of camera, as Laura's hair hung on that side of her face. I chose a large plume wafer soft box as the main light set for F:11. The fill light was an umbrella set to the left of camera with an umbrella set for F:5.6 & 1/2 creating a 3 to 1 light ratio. The most important light is the hair light directly over the model's head in a small balcar prisma light soft box with a grid attached to keep light from striking the model's face or contaminating the background. The hair light was set 1 stop brighter than the main for F:16. The hair light creates the highlight in Laura's hair and illuminates the shoulders to add the necessary round and create a three dimensional feeling to the image. Without the hair light, this shot would be flat and dimensionless. This effect can also be accomplished with a rim light.

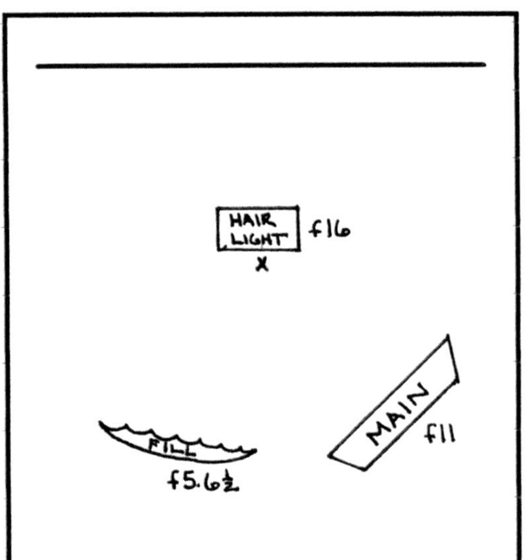

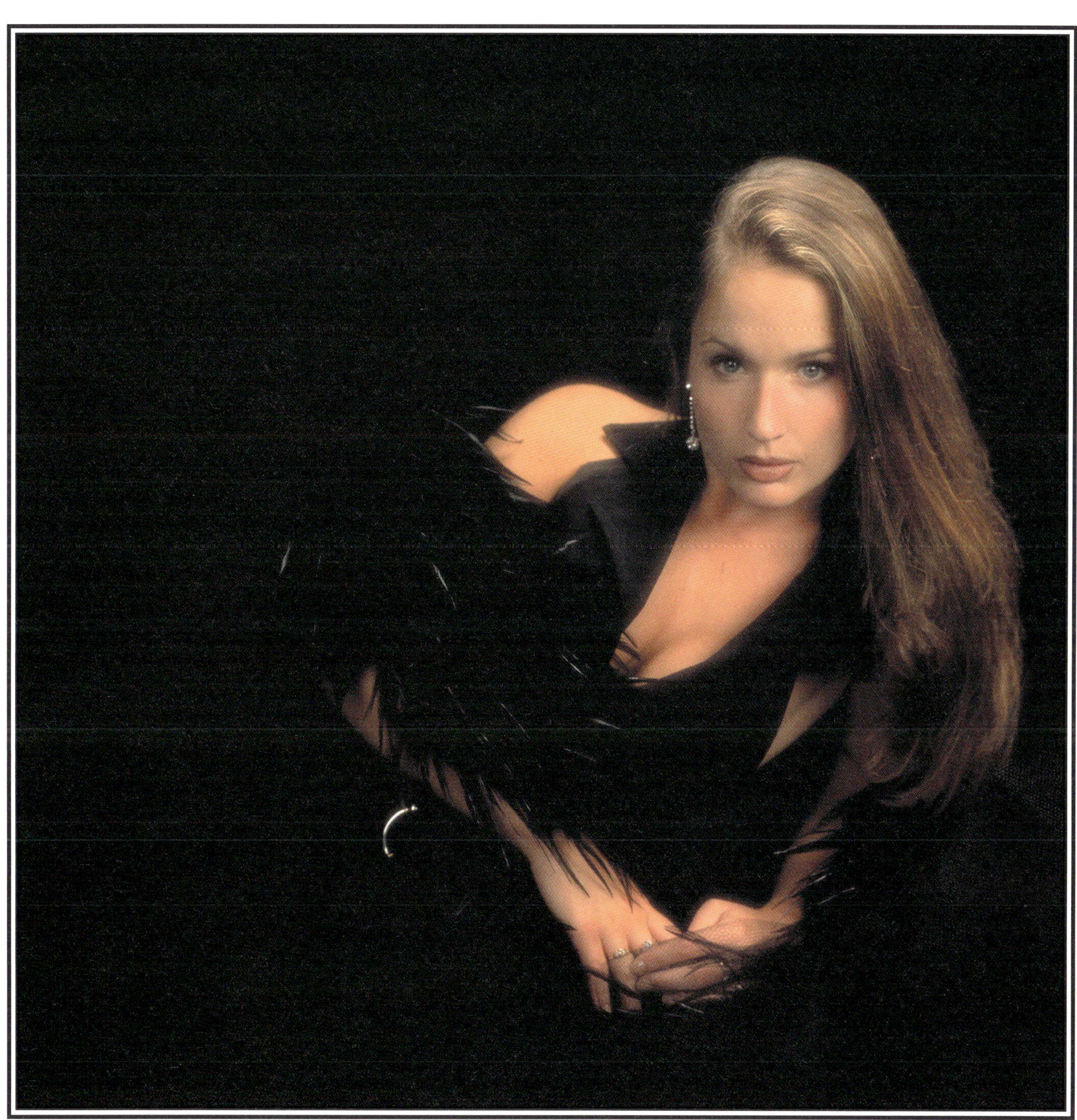

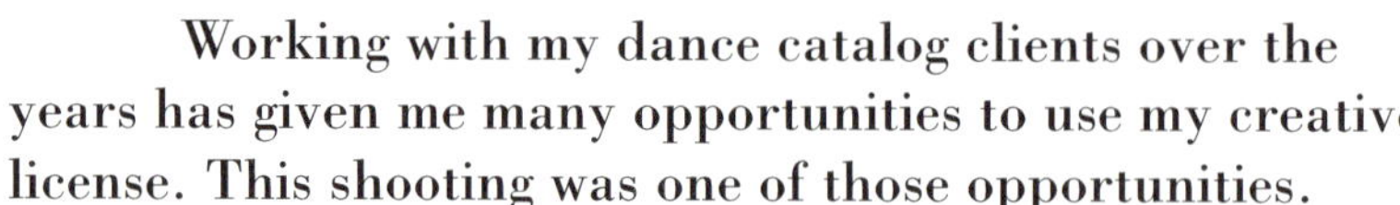

Red Dancer

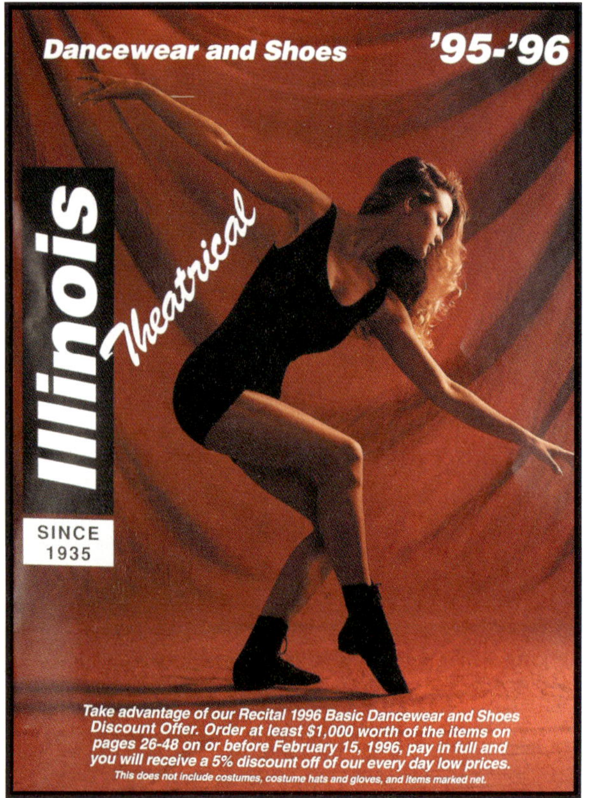

Working with my dance catalog clients over the years has given me many opportunities to use my creative license. This shooting was one of those opportunities.

Paul, the owner of my client company, came up with the idea you see illustrated. With the help of a talented dancer, an excellent make-up artist, and a great choreographer we came up with this creative dance image.

I knew from the dramatic red muslin background we hung and the draping we created, I had to come up with lighting on the subject that would be artistic enough to accomplish the silhouette look we were trying to achieve.

I set up one main light to the right of camera in a large plume wafer strip light set for F:11. I wanted a rim light to highlight the face and front of the models body. I used a 7" reflector with a 40 degree grid set at 45 degrees behind the subject. The rim light created the hair,face and body light with the strong highlight set for F:8 1/2.

It is important to remember that when a rim light is used, it will appear 2 stops brighter than a light originating from the front of the subject when set 45 degrees behind the subject. Therefore, the rim light set 1/2 stop less than the main light will still appear to the eye as 1 1/2 stops brighter, as in this example.Note how the rim light in this case highlights both arms, the hair the face, and the forward leg.

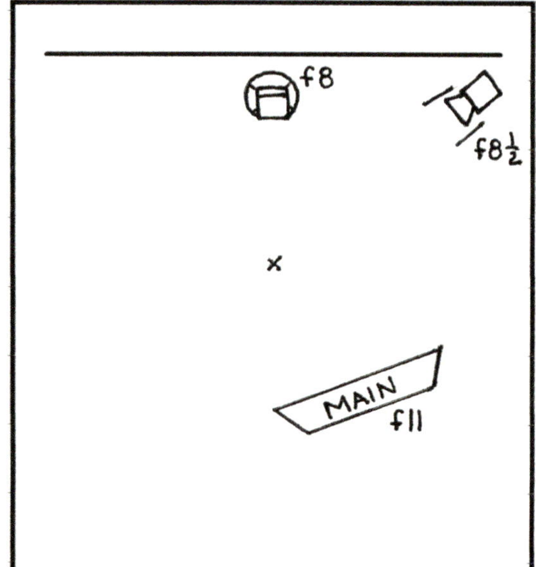

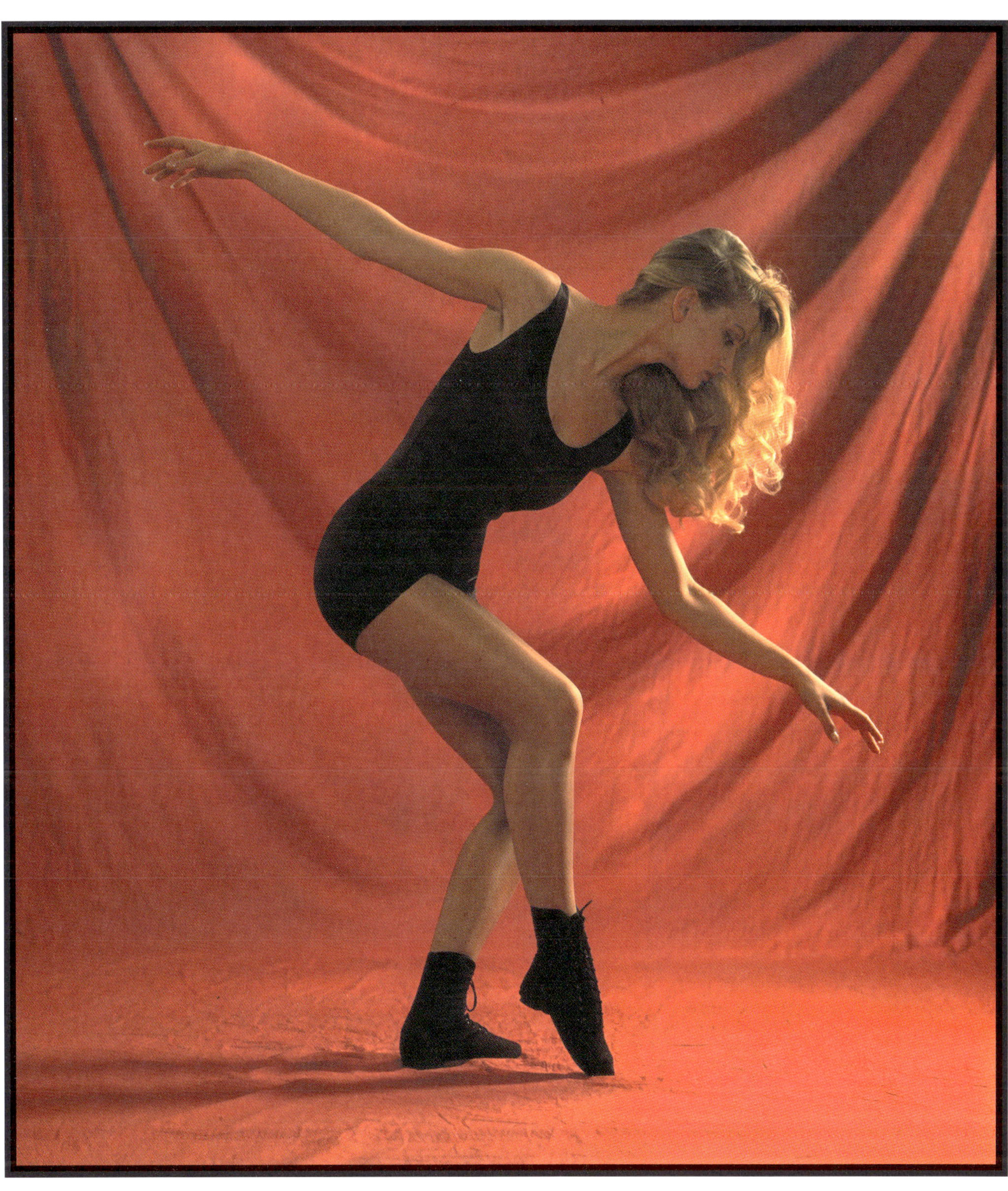

Lingerie Fantasy

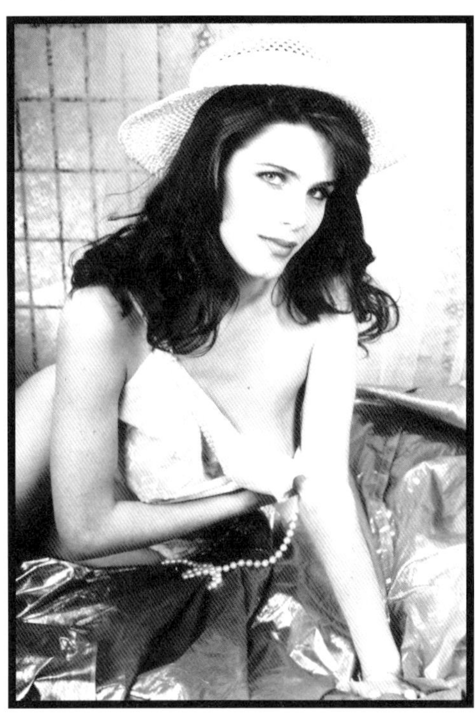

Shooting lingerie photos requires a change in conventional thinking. Lingerie makes a statement. Lingerie is packaging and gift wrapping a beautiful product. When you see a pretty woman in a bathing suit,you probably see more of the woman than you would in lingerie, but the seductive effect is different. A bathing suit can say sexy, but lingerie can mean far more and yet may show less.

Lingerie has a unique effect on the psyche. It is the forbidden fruit. We, as the viewer, are not supposed to be seeing a woman's undergarments. So the tittilation factor comes into play, and we fantasize about this person. Without showing as much as a bathing suit would show, the image can be far more sexual. Just pick up a Victoria Secret or Frederick's catalog and see if the images portrayed are not extremely exciting.

The point I am making is that shooting lingerie requires the photographer to help create the boudoir fantasy. I can not emphasize the importance of using materials and settings that help create the mood. I am a strong believer in using diffusion on your camera to help with lingerie fantasy.

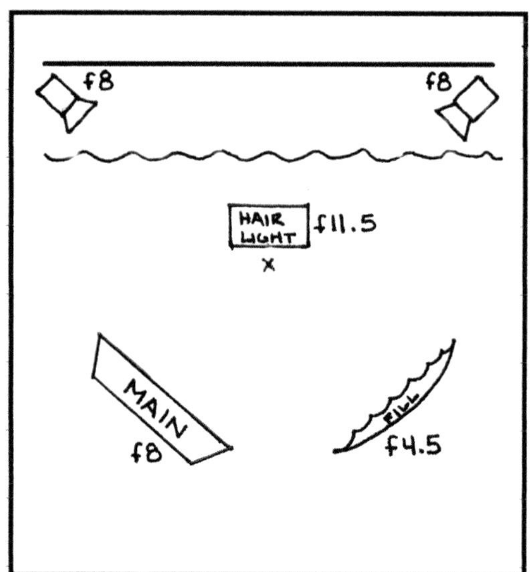

Lighting is just as important in boudoir images. When this photo was set up, I wanted to infuse a light, airy feeling. I built a temporary bedroom set using a mattress on a wood platform. By placing a folding screen behind the bed and draping some sheer fabric over the screen, I created a light wispy wall. I also used a sheer tent canopy hung from the ceiling. The tent surrounds the bed on three sides providing a frame of sheer fabric. These tents are usually shown in movies as a night mosquito netting over a bed. They work extremely well in boudoir photography and are simple to set up.

By lighting the fabric from behind, a high key effect is created. I used two small backlight combos to light the sheer fabrics. Both lights were set for F:8. The main light was a large plume wafer soft box to the left of camera at F:8. Fill light was an umbrella to the right of camera set at F:4 1/2, creating a 3 to 1 ratio. Hair light was set at F:11 1/2, one and a half stops brighter than the main light. *Sheer fabric,tent canopy and backlight combo lights are available from Backdrop Outlet.*

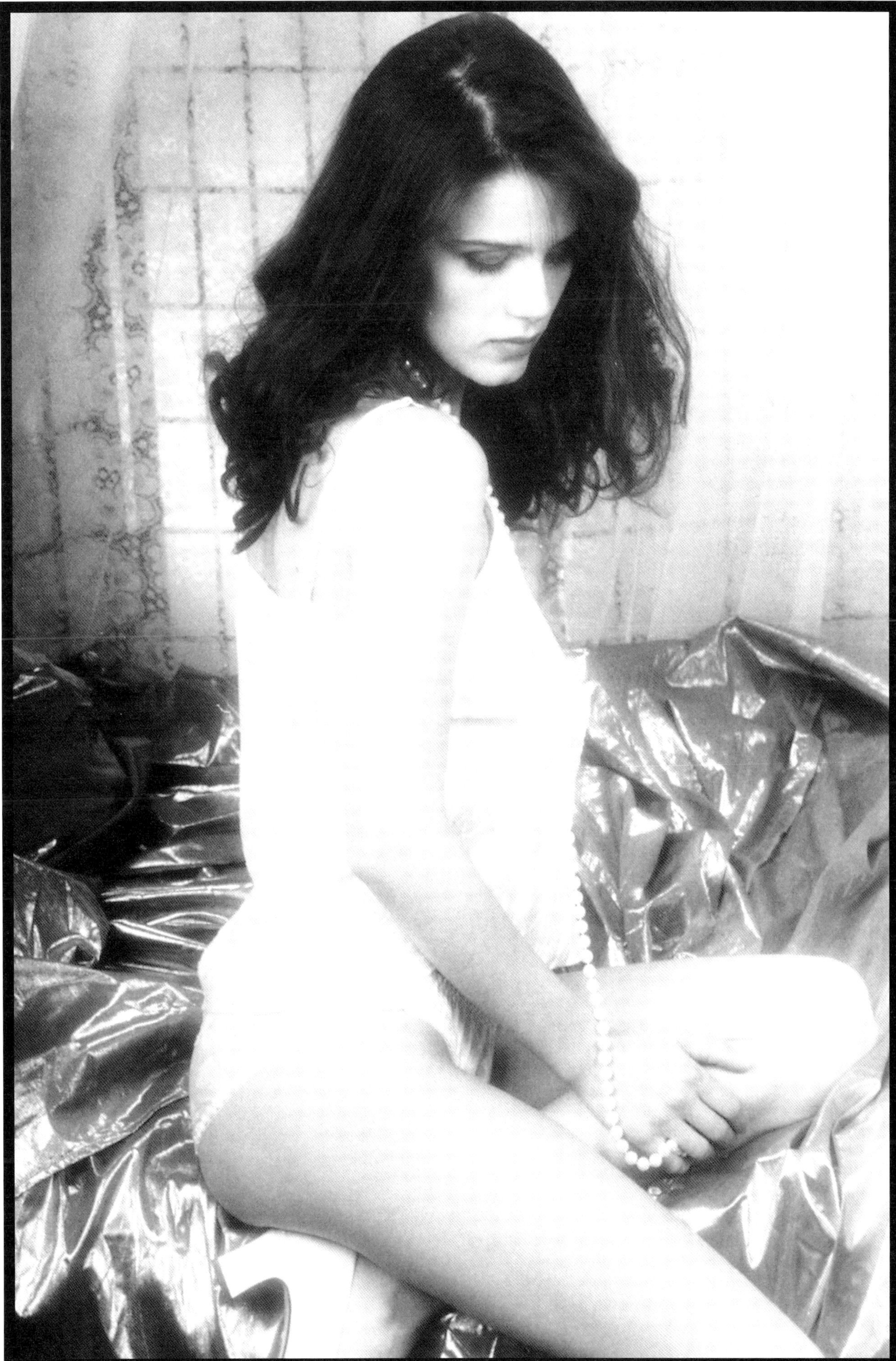

The Fort

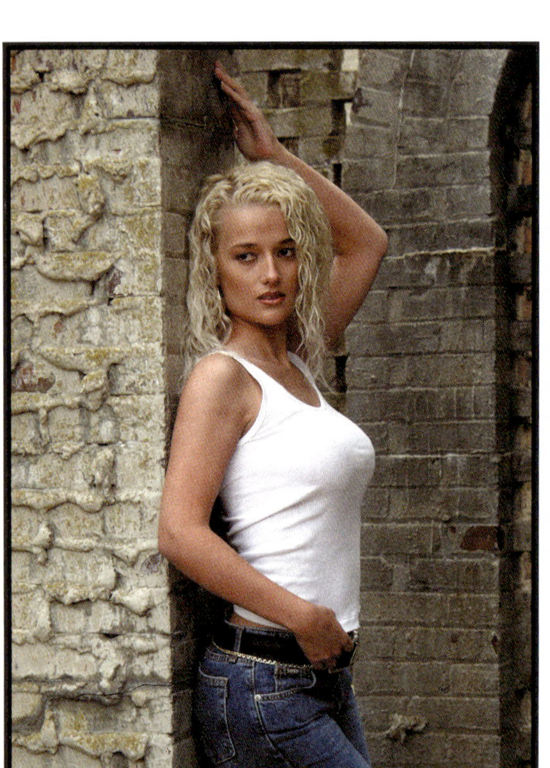

Traveling to different cities to give my workshops creates many unknowns and variables. But one of the benefits is seeing so many gorgeous locations and meeting some of the most fantastic people in North America.

Lisa and Clay Purifoy are two of these people Lisa emailed me about performing a workshop in her studio in Myrtle Beach, South Carolina. I thought the idea was a good one.

This was a workshop I gave with my friends, Bill Lemon and Spencer Calquhoun and with Lisa and Clay's help, it was a phenomenal workshop. On one afternoon Lisa brought us to a location on the beach that had been a civil war fort. It was an unbelievably interesting shooting location.

Our model, Tanya, was contacted by Bill Lemon to model in the workshop and was terrific. In this image the rough texture and arches provided some exotic images. Tanya creates an attitude with her smoldering demeanor and expression.

Lighting; Natural light was used, adding Photoflex reflectors to create some fill light on the subject. Metering was with a Sekonic L-308 meter using the incident dome and reading the light falling on the brightest part of the face.My Olympus Camedia E-10 camera was utilized for the shot.

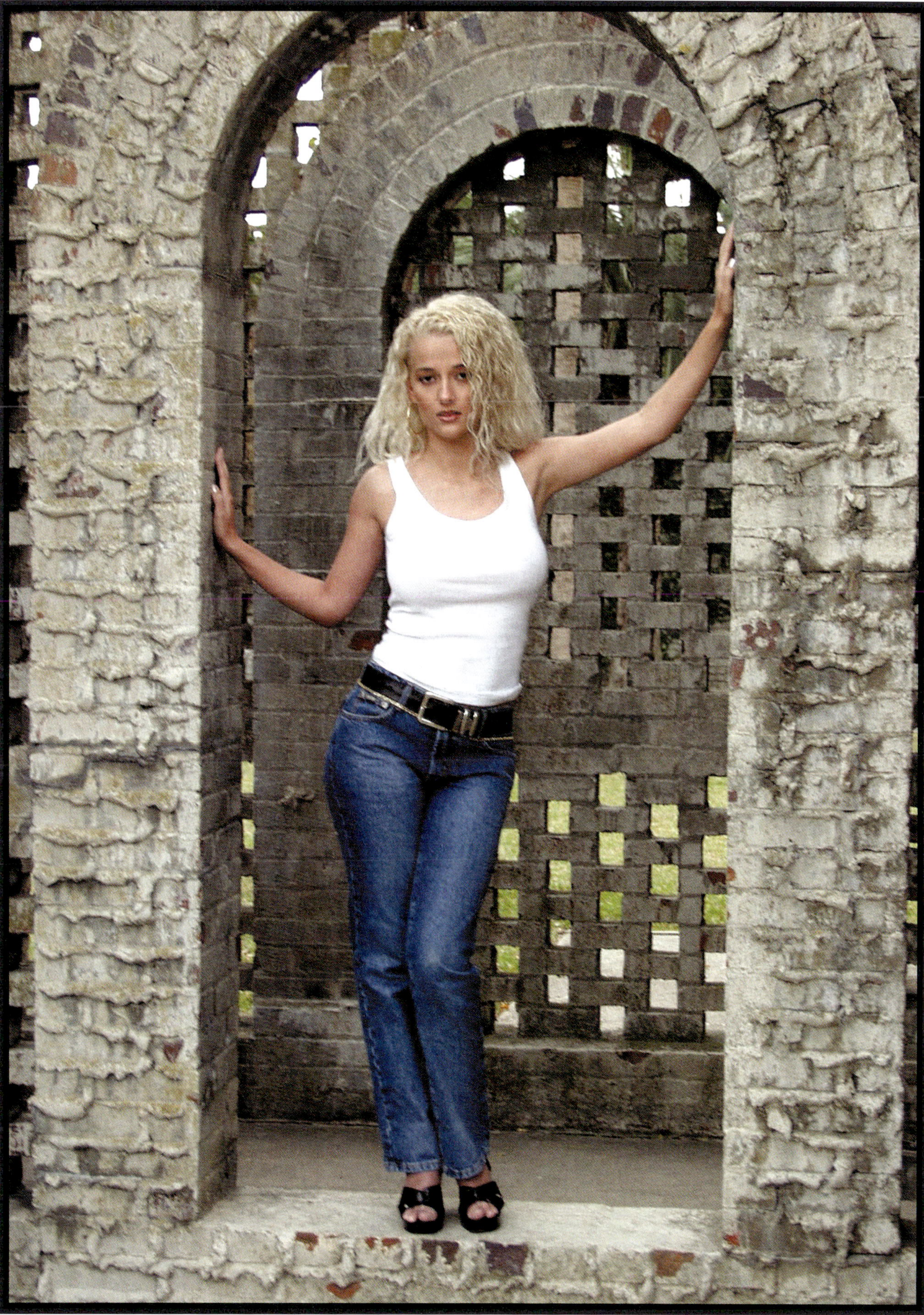

Legs

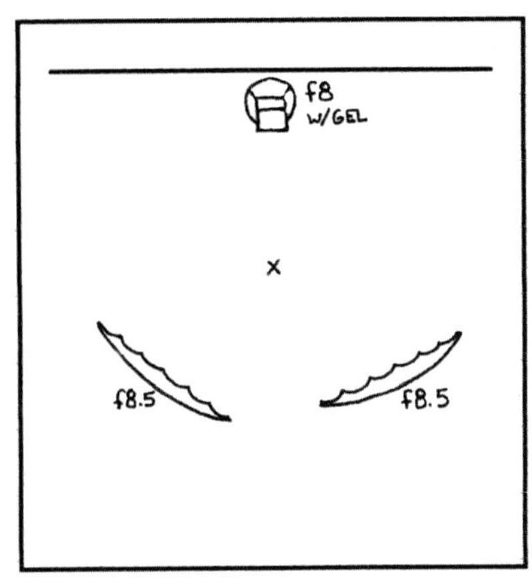

This whimsical image entitled "Legs" is a creation of mine out of necessity. A few years ago I had a shooting scheduled with a model for her portfolio. When she came in, her face looked a bit strange. She informed me that she just had two wisdom teeth removed an hour earlier. Her face was swollen, so, at first, I thought we had to cancel the shoot.

She was disappointed, that we could not shoot her face.However, considering that she had brought clothing for a lingerie shot, I had a brainstorm. In the corner of my studio were dozens of wrapped packages from a wrapping paper client of mine.

I told the model to put her outfit on and lay on her back with her legs up, then I started placing boxes all around her. I added the streamers of confetti, and an amazing idea was turned into a super image. Her choice of gold shoes and stockings instead of pantyhose made the shot dynamic. This image was shot with two large umbrellas set near camera position and at the same F:stop. A background light was set with a magenta gel to add some dimension to the background.

Later, I showed my image of LEGS to my wrapping paper client. He loved it and asked that I produce 75 8x10 prints for their upcoming sales meeting. He intended to attach my photo to every sales report for impact. The report was a resounding success and received more positive comments than any previous year!

See how, by using your creativity and quick thinking, you can turn a potential disaster into a spectacular accomplishment.

I felt this shot was the perfect END to my book.

I hope you enjoyed my book and learned from my photography, Now, go out and try my ideas and some of your <u>own</u>.

Art Ketchum